The Professional Paralegal

The Professional Paralegal
A Guide to Finding a Job and Career Success

Charlsye Smith Diaz, Ph.D.
University of Maine

Vicki Voisin, ACP
The Paralegal Mentor, Vicki Voisin, Inc.

PEARSON

Boston   Columbus   Indianapolis   New York   San Francisco   Upper Saddle River
Amsterdam   Cape Town   Dubai   London   Madrid   Milan   Munich   Paris   Montreal   Toronto
Delhi   Mexico City   São Paulo   Sydney   Hong Kong   Seoul   Singapore   Taipei   Tokyo

Editorial Director: Vernon Anthony
Executive Editor: Gary Bauer
Editorial Project Manager: Linda Cupp
Editorial Assistant: Tanika Henderson
Director of Marketing: David Gesell
Marketing Manager: Stacey Martinez
Senior Marketing Coordinator: Alicia Wozniak
Senior Marketing Assistant: Les Roberts
Production Manager: Holly Shufeldt
Senior Art Director: Jayne Conte
Cover Designer: Bruce Kenselaar
Manager, Rights and Permissions: Mike Lackey
Full-Service Project Management and Composition: Chitra Sundarajan/PreMediaGlobal
Text Printer/Bindery: Bind-Rite Graphics
Cover Printer: Lehigh-Phoenix Color

Credits and acknowledgments borrowed from other sources and reproduced, with permission, in this textbook appear on the appropriate page within the text.

Many of the designations by manufacturers and seller to distinguish their products are claimed as trademarks. Where those designations appear in this book, and the publisher was aware of a trademark claim, the designations have been printed in initial caps or all caps.

Library of Congress Cataloging-in-Publication Data

Diaz, Charlsye Smith.
  The professional paralegal : a guide to finding a job and career success / Charlsye Smith Diaz, Vicki Voisin.
      p. cm.
  Includes index.
  ISBN-13: 978-0-13-510578-8 (alk. paper)
  ISBN-10: 0-13-510578-1 (alk. paper)
1. Legal assistants–United States.   2. Legal assistants–Vocational guidance–United States.
I. Voisin, Vicki.   II. Title.
  KF320.L4D53 2013
  340.023'73–dc23

                                                                    2011045713

10 9 8 7 6 5 4 3 2 1

PEARSON

ISBN 10:   0-13-510578-1
ISBN 13: 978-0-13-510578-8

To Virginia Koerselman Newman, J.D.,
mentor extraordinaire to paralegals worldwide

BRIEF CONTENTS

CONTENTS

When you begin your paralegal career, you may feel overwhelmed, especially if you find yourself surrounded by seasoned paralegals with solid resumes. These paralegals manage, mentor, teach, write, speak, and lead. Finding your place among them is humbling and gratifying.

The Professional Paralegal: A Guide to Finding a Job and Career Success grew out of our interactions with experienced and excellent paralegals. As writers, speakers, and educators, we share what we have learned working alongside these paralegals, and on our own, to help you build your successful paralegal career.

If we have learned one thing about the paralegal profession and paralegal careers, it is that they are predictable and unpredictable at the same time. While your education and your job search may be somewhat predictable, the remainder is different for every paralegal: You may begin with one goal in mind, and as you grow and expand your skills, you may veer in a new direction.

We expect our audience to be high-achievers who are ready to launch their careers and/or are seeking avenues for creating successful careers. We are fortunate to have been involved with many paralegals who hold themselves to the highest standards and create excellence around them. After observing their career goals and success, we wanted to provide others with as much advice as we could about creating a career that is personally satisfying and professionally ambitious.

This book is for you if:

- You are nearing completion of a paralegal education program and are ready to search for an internship or professional position.
- You have started your first job, but want advice for building your professional reputation, for developing good workplace habits, and for creating a fulfilling career.
- You want to restructure a career that isn't as satisfying as you dreamed.
- You want a guide that will be useful throughout your career.

We want you to find a job and to build a career you love.

As a bonus, we address two areas that we both strive to do well, but always look for new ways to achieve: time management and office organization. Paralegals must be organized and efficient—and we are—but only because we work at this skill every day. We want you to have some strategies in your pocket to use when the paper starts flying, the files start piling up, and you suddenly have a desk stacked with projects and no idea where to begin.

We hope that you find this text helpful in landing the job you want and starting your career. We believe it will also guide you throughout your career. We appreciate feedback and suggestions regarding this textbook and encourage you to contact us.

Charlsye Smith Diaz
Vicki Voisin
TheProfessionalParalegal@gmail.com

PREFACE

PREPARING FOR CAREER SUCCESS

The Professional Paralegal: A Guide to Finding a Job and Career Success provides advice about how to have a successful internship experience, how to find and apply for work in the legal profession, how to start a job successfully, and once there, how to get organized and enjoy a successful paralegal career.

We believe paralegal careers follow a pattern that begins with education and is followed by getting a job in the legal profession. As time goes by, a paralegal will find a niche or develop an interest in a specific area of law and begin to specialize. Professional development and opportunities to participate in the profession follow, leading to new opportunities for career growth. This book focuses on the first part of your career: your internship, job search, and professional habits that will lead to a successful, satisfying career.

The first three chapters provide an overview of the skills and traits that paralegals need to be successful on the job, starting with an internship. Chapter 1 provides an overview of the paralegal profession and offers practical advice for identifying the paralegal career you can have where you live. Chapter 2 focuses on the internship experience itself. Chapter 3 examines the traits that many paralegals adopt in order to be successful.

The next chapters focus on networking, finding job opportunities, preparing your resume, and writing the perfect cover letter. Chapter 4 helps you strategize your job search. Chapter 5 offers information and advice about organizing your paperwork, preparing a portfolio, and cultivating references. Chapters 6 and 7 show you how to write a resume and application letter, and what to include in thank you notes after an interview. Chapter 8 advises you about interviewing for and negotiating a paralegal position. We discuss what to wear to an interview, how the interview most likely will be structured, and what to do after the interview. This chapter also provides a brief overview of negotiating salary and benefits when a job offer comes your way.

The last chapters of the book provide advice about settling in and organizing your space and your time. Chapter 9 explains how to get off to a good start in a paralegal position and also concentrates on important time and billing practices. Chapter 10 addresses technology, including what to do when you are given older technology to use. Chapters 11 and 12 provide advice about organizing your time and your space. Chapter 13 addresses the tendency for paralegals to be perfectionists, while focusing on how you can use this tendency to build your reputation. Chapter 14 focuses on ways you can participate in the profession and build your career.

Core Features of the Book

Each chapter offers how-to advice for planning your internship, getting your first job, and starting your career. This advice is supplemented with the following features:

- **Checklists for Success:** Each chapter ends with a Checklist for Success that highlights the points of the chapter and reminds you of things to do.
- **Assignments for Preparing for Your Paralegal Career:** Each chapter includes questions for you to discuss in class and for you to ask working paralegals. This will enable you to start conversations about topics that are sometimes difficult or seem personal in nature.
- **Profiles of Paralegals:** Each chapter includes profiles of paralegals who are searching for jobs, who recently found positions, and who are recreating their careers. You will learn firsthand how paralegals navigate this economy and job searching.
- **In Practice:** Throughout the book, you will find resources, tips from seasoned paralegals, and advice to help you succeed in your internship, on the job market, and when starting a new job.

MYLEGALSTUDIESKIT FOR THE PROFESSIONAL PARALEGAL: A GUIDE TO FINDING A JOB AND CAREER SUCCESS

Online resources include video cases, interactive job search documents, video case studies, examples of resumes and application letters, frequently asked questions about interviewing, access to the Golden Personality Type Profiler, and Pearson's MySearchLab, which includes tools for conducting research, tools for improving grammar and writing, and access to the Longman Online Handbook. An access code can be packaged with the textbook or purchased independently at *www.mylegalstudieskit.com*.

- **Professionalism Video Cases** are presented allowing instructors to assign a video case outside the classroom to be viewed by students online.
- **Interactive Job Search Document Examples** include chronological and skills-based resumes and application letters, providing provide students with examples of properly constructed resumes with notes to help guide creation of their own documents.
- **The Golden Personality Type Profiler™** This popular personality assessment provides students with information about five fundamental personality dimensions: Where you direct your energy (introverted or extraverted), the way you gather and interpret information, how you make decisions, how you approach life (e.g., organizing versus adapting) and how you respond to stress. The Golden assessment is similar to the Myers-Briggs Step 1 assessment program. It takes about 15-20 minutes to complete and students receive an easy to use and practical feedback report based on their results. This tool helps students improve their self-knowledge and ability to work effectively with others by providing students with feedback on their leadership and organizational strengths, communication and teamwork preferences, motivation and learning style, and opportunities for personal growth. The *Golden* is typically used in a classroom setting to help prepare students for entry into the workforce or for career development. Instructional support materials are available so that instructors can guide students through their feedback report and help them apply their results to build personal and interpersonal skills.
- **Pearson's MySearchLab: Research, Grammar, and Writing Tips** gives students access to research tips, the EBSCO document database, writing and assessment and instruction and the Longman Online Handbook for Writers.

To order

The Professional Paralegal: A Guide to Finding a Job and Career Success Student Textbook value packed with the MyLegalStudiesKit Access Code Order ISBN: 0-13-305188-9

A MyLegalStudiesKit Standalone Access Code can also be purchased online at *www.legalstudieskit.com*

ACKNOWLEDGMENTS

I would like to thank the people who pushed my paralegal career forward from the beginning: Jody Mange Pearson, the first paralegal colleague and first mentor I ever had; Frances M. Whitaker, Esq. who challenged me to take the Certified Paralegal exam and then the specialty exam; the members of the National Association of Legal Assistants/Paralegals, and its Board of Directors who model professional excellence every day; Shary Lyssy Marshall, who pushes me to be a better writer; and my co-author Vicki Voisin, APC. I couldn't have written this book with anyone else; thank you for a great journey. John M. Lannon connected for me my work in litigation to the research I do now. I wrote earlier drafts of some material in this book under his guidance. Thank you, Tom, Mason, and Ava for giving me space to do this work and to Mom, for understanding why I haven't visited as often as I should. Much of the writing of this book occurred while Ava learned to talk, Mason played with Lego® bricks, and Tom kept us going. This book will always be proof that, as an infant, Ava slept at least a little bit.

—**Charlsye Smith Diaz**

As a paralegal working in a small town in a small law firm, I had to make my world large to experience the career success I have so enjoyed. That larger world included my service as President of National Association of Legal Assistants/Paralegals, with its Board of Directors and members who taught me that leadership is a privilege and excellence is the supreme goal. The friends and colleagues who have walked this path with me are too many to mention here, but please know that each of you has contributed to my achievements and I could not have done any of this without you! Special thanks to Karen M. Dunn, ACP who never doubted I could lead NALA and Vicki J. Kunz, ACP who has always been the consummate friend and confidante. This project could not have come to fruition without the talent and dedication of my co-author, Charlsye Smith Diaz, Ph.D. Thanks, Charlsye, for inviting me to join you in this endeavor! Last, but certainly not least, I so appreciate the love and encouragement of my husband, Don, and my children, Wendy and Vince, as well as their spouses and children, who have always supported my goals and had supreme confidence in my abilities.

—**Vicki Voisin, ACP**

We also thank the reviewers of this book for their thoughtful feedback and insights:

Christine R. Bork, Gloucester County College
Carol Brady, Milwaukee Area Technical College
Pat Burnes, University of Maine
Ernest Davila, San Jacinto College
Elizabeth J. Dibble, Southwestern Illinois College
Ronald A. Feinberg, Suffolk Community College
Jane B. Jacobs, Community College of Philadelphia
Jennifer Jenkins, South College
Brian McCully, Fresno City College
Joy O'Donnell, Pima Community College
Carole Olson, Dallas County Community College District
Alva P. Poole, Bryant and Stratton College
Julia O. Tryk, Cuyahoga Community College
John A. Whitehead, Kilgore College

Many people at Pearson Education provided invaluable professional support throughout this project. We especially benefited from the help and patience of Gary Bauer, Executive Editor; Linda Cupp, Editorial Project Manager and Tanika Henderson, Editorial Assistant. Holly Shufeldt, Production Manager at USHE Central Publishing, and her team, and Chitra Sundarajan, Project Manager at PreMediaGlobal, and her team, were instrumental in the production of this book. We appreciate their work on this project.

ABOUT THE AUTHORS

CHARLSYE SMITH DIAZ, PH.D. Charlsye was working as a paralegal when she discovered during an intellectual property dispute that she wanted to study communication to see if she could learn more about how miscommunication leads to lawsuits. She earned a Ph.D. in technical communication and rhetoric from Texas Tech University. Now the coordinator of professional writing in the Department of English at the University of Maine, Charlsye teaches courses in grant writing, technical editing, document design, and communication for small business and non-profits. She works with entrepreneurs and inventors to develop business plans, grant applications, and business pitches. Charlsye is an educational consultant for the National Association of Legal Assistants, where she works on the Advanced Paralegal Certification online training program. You can find Charlsye online at *www.charlsyesmithdiaz.com*.

VICKI VOISIN, ACP After enjoying a successful paralegal career that spanned more than 20 years and included intense involvement in a national paralegal association, Vicki wanted to share her love and respect for the profession with other paralegals and help them reach their full potential. First she became a nationally recognized author and speaker regarding ethical issues related to the paralegal profession. That led to her role as The Paralegal Mentor a web-based business where she delivers simple strategies for paralegals and other professionals to create success and satisfaction by achieving goals and determining the direction they will take their careers. She also serves as a consultant and expert witness in litigation related to paralegal issues. Vicki publishes a weekly ezine titled **Paralegal Strategies** and co-hosts **The Paralegal Voice**, a monthly podcast produced by Legal Talk Network. You can find Vicki online at *www.paralegalmentor.com*.

The Professional Paralegal

CHAPTER **1**

STARTING YOUR PARALEGAL CAREER

Welcome to the paralegal profession and to your paralegal career. This book will help you find your first paralegal job and will show you how to navigate your career.

Some people believe being a paralegal is a job that can be done by anyone, but this simply is not true. *Successful* paralegals need to arrive on the job with an openness to learning and collaborating. *Successful* paralegals must be willing to work hard to establish their reputations and to build their careers. The attitude, energy, and determination you bring to your internship and to your first job will set the pace for the career you build for yourself.

One of the best things about a paralegal career is that you can design your own career path. While studying the legal system and various practice areas, you gain skills that will help you in many areas of life and work. When you begin working in the legal profession, you will build confidence and develop skills that enable you to decide how you would like to shape your career. The truth is that as your career grows you can write your own story.

This chapter briefly reviews the basics about paralegal careers as we:

- Discuss the definition of "paralegal"
- Identify similarities and differences between paralegal work and attorney work
- Describe the various steps involved on the road to a paralegal career
- State the impact a good reputation has on a paralegal career
- Recognize the various training options for paralegals

- Define "certified" and "certification" and recognize the distinction of both
- Name the key elements in a paralegal's preparation to excel

The purpose of this chapter is to show you that you are entering an important profession that comes with purpose and responsibility.

■ OFFICIALLY SPEAKING: PARALEGAL DEFINED

National associations, bar associations, legislatures and supreme courts have addressed the definition of legal assistant and paralegal, often recognizing that the terms are synonymous and can be used interchangeably. Through discussions within each group, similarities in the identification and duties of legal assistants and paralegals are emerging with routine consistency. The common threads in these definitions and discussions are:

Legal Assistants/Paralegals

- have received specialized training through formal education or many years of experience;
- work under the supervision and direction of an attorney; and
- perform non-clerical, substantive legal work in assisting an attorney.

Despite these common threads, no universal definition of the terms paralegal and legal assistant exist, but many organizations adopt the one provided by the American Bar Association (ABA):

A legal assistant or paralegal is a person qualified by education, training or work experience who is employed or retained by a lawyer, law office, corporation, governmental agency or other entity who performs specifically delegated substantive legal work for which a lawyer is responsible.

Defining the terms paralegal and legal assistant is important because the definition separates the work that paralegals do from that of other law firm employees. State to state, the differences define the work for which a paralegal can bill clients, affect how paralegals are compensated and whether a paralegal can collect overtime, and set the limits for how a paralegal can interact with clients.

■ PARALEGAL WORK VS. ATTORNEY WORK

Paralegals work under the supervision of attorneys, and they perform tasks delegated by attorneys. These tasks can vary from office management to substantive legal work. Some states have made distinctions between the paralegal work that can be billed to clients and the kind of work that cannot. In general, paralegals bill clients for work that would be performed by the attorney if the paralegal had not completed the tasks. Tasks that are generally clerical in nature are usually not billable to clients.

Paralegal work is often limited by what paralegals *cannot* do. The ABA Model Guidelines for the Utilization of Paralegal Services, which are echoed in many states, limit paralegal work in the following ways:

- Paralegals are not permitted to establish an attorney-client relationship.
- Paralegals are not permitted to set fees for legal services.
- Paralegals are not permitted to give legal advice.
- Paralegals are not permitted to represent clients in court, unless specifically permitted, such as in front of an administrative agency.

For further limitations or exceptions to these rules, be sure to review the rules adopted by your state.

While most paralegals report directly to attorneys in an office setting, some paralegals establish freelance careers. These paralegals operate independently run businesses that provide paralegal services to attorneys. The New Jersey Committee on the Unauthorized Practice of Law issued an opinion that states that freelance paralegals are valuable and necessary but must work under the supervision of an attorney. In that opinion, the Committee stated:

> Given the appropriate instructions and supervision, paralegals, whether as employees or independent contractors, are valuable and necessary members of an attorney's work force in the effective and efficient practice of law. (In re Opinion No. 24 of the Committee on the Unauthorized Practice of Law, 128 N.J. 114 (1992))

With advances in technology, some attorneys are now establishing virtual offices with most, if not all, of their work and client contact taking place over secure Internet connections. Technology also allows paralegals to practice virtually. These paralegals are typically referred to as "virtual paralegals." They provide paralegal services both to attorneys who practice in a typical brick-and-mortar setting and to attorneys who practice virtually. Virtual paralegals work remotely, usually from their own home offices. Their work is not confined to one specific geographic area.

The common factor that applies regardless of employer or manner of working is that paralegals work under the supervision of an attorney.

■ STARTING OUT: THE ROAD TO A PARALEGAL CAREER

While states and associations may define the terms *paralegal* and *legal assistant* by the things that you can do on the job, your *paralegal career* will be defined by factors that have nothing to do with the tasks you perform at work. Understanding the difference between working as a paralegal (performing your job legally and ethically) and creating a career (embarking on a professional journey) is worth pausing to consider. Two factors that influence your career include geographical location and self-motivation.

Geographical Location

Your geographical location determines the kind of work available for paralegals. As you study the job opportunities where you live, you might decide to stay where you are or to move to a new area. If you live in a small town and do not want to move, you may have to search a little harder for opportunities to build the career you want.

For example, if you live in a small town that has mostly solo practitioners or small law firms, you might begin working as a traditional paralegal. As you gain skills and your career begins to advance, you might volunteer for a local non-profit organization. Volunteering could lead to a seat on the board of directors for this agency. You might find that working with non-profit issues fascinates you and take a position as paralegal/office administrator of a non-profit.

Your career will continue to advance, and you might be asked to serve on another board. Eventually, when your skills and experience working with non-profits are highly developed and well-known, you might be asked to lead a local agency, a position that no longer has the word "paralegal" in the job title. Your paralegal training and experience will have prepared you for this job.

Be sure you understand completely the realities and specific opportunities available in your geographical location when you begin your job search.

Self-Motivation

As a paralegal, you can have a job or you can have a career. Both are noble. As you read this section, think of people you know who have jobs and those who have careers.

A job is defined by the description of the work you do each day. People with jobs go to work, perform their tasks, and separate their work lives and outside-work lives fairly well.

A career is defined by the work you do at work and outside of work, to push yourself to a higher level. Two paralegals may work side by side at a large law firm. One of the paralegals sees the work as a job and another paralegal sees the work as part of a career. Both may give 110% at work, be well respected by colleagues, and do their jobs very well. They both attend lunch-and-learn continuing legal education programs. At a glance, they may seem to be comparable employees. Certainly, the firm where they work appreciates their expertise and dependability. Both have equal shots at being promoted to senior paralegal.

The paralegal who treats work as a job may leave for the afternoon, hit the gym, make dinner, and relax, all healthy and rational choices.

The paralegal who treats work as a career may leave for the afternoon, hit the gym, make dinner, and study for a certification exam or surf legal news websites to stay in touch with the field. This paralegal joins a professional organization or volunteers for a legal non-profit. This paralegal wants to explore options and see how far her paralegal education can take her.

Neither path is wrong, and both can be fulfilling. In each case, the paralegal must maintain her skills and stay on top of the job market. The volatile nature of the economy makes it imperative that employees be prepared for downsizing, layoffs, or closing of company doors.

Treating your paralegal work as a career may help you identify possibilities. After becoming a senior paralegal, you might move on to be the paralegal manager or work on special projects.

Even if you work for a solo practitioner in an office where you are one of three people—the attorney, you, and a receptionist—you can have a job or you can have a career. The paralegal who treats the work as a job will perform similarly to the paralegal at the large firm. From 9 to 5, this paralegal will use her skills and expertise to work hard for the supervising attorney.

But what about the paralegal who wants a *career*? Is there a place at a solo practitioner's office for this person? Absolutely!

You can still create a career for yourself and you do not have to change jobs to do so. Instead, create a plan that challenges you both in and out of the office. Become an expert in one or more of your supervising attorney's practice areas so that you can contribute to cases in increasingly complex and interesting ways. Expect more from yourself than anyone else expects.

Become certified. Join a professional organization, take continuing education classes, learn to network, and volunteer to help. During your first year of membership in a professional organization, you might be in charge of assisting with just one task, but as you become known within the organization, you might become a leader within it.

Write newsletter articles for other legal publications. Volunteer for a non-profit agency that uses paralegal services. If your supervising attorney does volunteer work for an organization that interests you, team up and make a name for the firm. As your career develops, accept invitations to speak, to mentor new paralegals, and to teach.

Whether you choose to think of your work as a job or as a career, remember that you are in charge of the route you take. Both paths require dedication and motivation to stay on top of your skill set and both can be rewarding.

Where Paralegals Work

The paralegal profession is unique in that paralegals can work in many environments. In Chapter 4, we detail options to explore when looking for jobs, but as you begin thinking about your paralegal career, remember that the best thing about being a paralegal is that you can write your own career plan.

Many paralegals work in the following areas:

- Law firms of all sizes
- Corporate legal departments
- Non-profit organizations

PARALEGAL PROFILE

Wil Antonides, ALS

Current position: Paralegal

Employer: Liggett & Ripley, PLC – Richland, MI

Years in this position: 1

Certifications: ALS – NALS...the Association of Legal Professionals

Years of paralegal experience: 1

Education: B.A., Psychology, Calvin College, Grand Rapids, MI, 1991

Post-Baccalaureate Certificate, Paralegal Studies, Davenport University, Grand Rapids, MI, 2010

Caught in the economic downturn, Wil Antonides found a new career as a paralegal.

Wil Antonides, ALS, had to admit that "starting over" at 40, a time when he thought he should have been striding along in his career, was difficult. As Michigan's economy declined in 2008, his leadership position in human resources with a healthcare provider was eliminated. Because positions were so few and the number of individuals looking for work so many, he spent a year depressed, discouraged, and feeling unwanted.

Wil decided to reinvent himself.

With the encouragement of his spouse, he looked at opportunities outside human resources. After taking a Legal Studies 101 course in 2007, his interest in the paralegal profession was piqued. Hungry to work again, he plunged in, making being a student his "job." Wil found himself reenergized and excited. As he slowly regained his confidence, others commented on the change.

During his final semester, he took the ALS certification exam from NALS. A board member from his local NALS chapter heard his story and nominated him for board treasurer. He was the first man to be elected to the board.

At his first statewide conference, Wil was the only man in the room. Breakout sessions and group lectures all good-heartedly opened with, "Good morning/afternoon ladies...and Wil..."

Wil reflects that what he learned working in other settings has only helped his career, not hindered it. "I have a lot of experience and confidence to draw from," he says, "even when faced with new challenges in the paralegal field. As a new paralegal, almost everything is a new adventure. I now see that being a paralegal fits my total career path. Beginning again has caused me to take a step back and see the larger picture that a career is a marathon, not a series of sprints."

- Governmental agencies
- Law enforcement entities
- Universities and school systems
- Banks
- Hospitals and other health care agencies
- Insurance companies
- Legal publications
- Litigation support consulting firms

This short list indicates where paralegals often *begin* a career. Once you gain skills and develop interests—even passion at times—job opportunities open up. You can develop skills by learning as much as possible on the job, joining professional organizations, volunteering for non-profits, and being open to taking on new challenges and listening closely to feedback and constructive criticism.

Choosing a specialty during school is not as important as being open to experiencing different areas of law. Once you begin your first or second paralegal position, you might find yourself following one path. When you see that you enjoy working in a particular area, then it is time to specialize.

Sometimes, paralegals leave their traditional jobs to take on new roles. For example, a paralegal might move from the legal department in a corporation to risk management. A paralegal specializing in intellectual property might move from a law firm to a university's technology transfer department, helping faculty secure patents and other intellectual property rights. Human resources, advocacy groups, and environmental agencies scoop up paralegals because paralegals are smart, have excellent analytical skills, and write and speak well.

The most important aspect of your paralegal career is to *begin*. Do not wait for the "perfect" job; it does not exist. Instead, make the most of the job you have and you will find new opportunities as your career progresses.

Specialties and Subspecialties

Paralegals specialize and sub-specialize in many areas. A paralegal who begins working in bankruptcy might specialize in Chapter 13 bankruptcies or Chapter 7 bankruptcies. This paralegal might sub-specialize even further and work only on creditors' rights in Chapter 13 bankruptcies.

Paralegals typically select specialties based on the needs of clients in their geographic region. Texas, for example, has firms that work only on issues involving oil and gas. While you certainly can choose an area in which to specialize, you may find that you develop a specialization gradually as you take on more and more work in a particular area, become familiar with that area, and take continuing legal education credits to learn the newest information. Without really thinking about it, you have developed a specialty.

At times, paralegals will deliberately change specializations. If you decide you want to change your specialization, it is always prudent to first examine the work available at your own organization and then examine the job market to make sure you can sustain yourself in that new specialization. Even if you do not plan to switch jobs, you *must* know that if your organization downsizes or closes its doors you will be able to support yourself in your geographic region. You do not want to specialize yourself out of a job, should you find yourself looking for one.

■ DEVELOPING A GOOD REPUTATION AT WORK

On the job, your reputation is *everything*. It is the commodity you "sell." You need to be known as someone who does good work, who is punctual and meets deadlines, who communicates well, and who understands how to collaborate with others.

On the job, your reputation defines how your career will grow. In a small firm or solo practitioner's office, your reputation reflects significantly on the attorney because you may be the only other person, or one of three or four, in the office. As the first person a potential client may meet, you need to represent the office in the manner the attorney wants it represented. The same is true in any position, of course, but your client contact may not affect the attorney-client relationship as significantly as it might in a smaller firm.

In every office, regardless of size, your reputation often determines the type of work you are assigned. You do not emerge from a paralegal program with an automatic good reputation, not even if you earned a 4.0. You still must prove yourself on the job. This means jumping in where you are asked and performing well.

If you are assigned labeling and photocopying exhibits, you need to do this work perfectly, double-checking that each exhibit emerges properly from the copy machine. Every task completed well contributes positively toward the working relationship you have with your supervising attorney and other colleagues. As you get to know your supervising attorney and other colleagues and demonstrate that you are reliable and dependable, the types of assignments you receive should increase in difficulty and complexity.

When you have a good reputation, you will find your workday to be more interesting and challenging. In some offices, your skills and reputation will earn you bonuses and promotions.

Organization

Paralegals must be organized. Even if you are the type of person who has to search for your cell phone, keys, and money every single morning before work, you need to be the opposite of that person at work. It is not fun (and not billable) to search for lost documents, misplaced files, and phone numbers.

Build good checklists for keeping your desk organized and your work moving. Develop a morning routine for when you arrive at work and an end-of-day routine to do before you leave. In the morning, check your calendar, respond to urgent requests, and prioritize your to-do list. At the end of the day, put things away, straighten your desk, jot a to-do list for the next day, and check your calendar so you know what to expect (and to wear) the next day. If you are going to court or meeting a client, you might dress differently than you would on a day you are going to a dusty warehouse to sort through and catalog contents of boxes.

Because every paralegal job is different, develop your own checklists and routines to keep your work moving forward. Chapters 11 and 12 focus on time management and office organization. Try these strategies if you are not sure where to start. In addition, read books about organization and experiment with different methods. Find methods that work for you and stick with them.

Communication (Written and Face-to-Face)

The most miserable law office to work in is one with little or no communication or communication that feels one-sided. Perhaps the attorney allows for few opportunities to ask questions or perhaps you are not reporting a case's status often enough for an attorney's comfort level.

As the paralegal, your job is to figure out and practice communication methods that are effective for each supervisory person (attorney, senior paralegal, office manager, paralegal supervisor, etc.) with whom you work.

The reason it is your job to figure out what works best is that you are supporting the attorney's practice. The attorney needs to hear you and communicate with you, but *you* must figure out the best method of sharing information.

IN PRACTICE

Try These Communication Strategies

Every time you begin working with a new supervising attorney, work hard to find a communication strategy that works best for both of you. If you are struggling to achieve clear two-way communication, try these methods:

E-mail updates and questions. Does the attorney use e-mail? A BlackBerry? An iPhone? If you need to get answers to questions, try sending e-mail messages with a very clear subject line and a brief question or request for a short meeting.

Draft a document and add a note. If you are waiting for your supervising attorney to draft a letter or other short document to go with something you need to send out, and you have asked for it repeatedly, try drafting the document yourself and leaving it on the attorney's desk with a note to review it.

Offer regular, face-to-face briefings. If your supervising attorney likes to go over things face-to-face, but is often out of the office, compile a list of your questions, and request by e-mail, by phone, by text message, the amount of time you need to go over these questions. Give a time frame, so that the attorney understands that you need information to move on with your work.

Interrupt. Sometimes, attorneys get so focused on what they are working on that they forget to talk to staff about ongoing projects. If you must get an answer, interrupt. Do not try this technique if the attorney is on the phone, with a client, or tied up in a meeting. Do try it if the attorney's usual practice is to work alone behind a closed door. Sometimes, attorneys simply do not realize you need a minute of their time. When you do interrupt, be prepared so you do not waste anyone's time.

You do not have to spy or resort to other clandestine methods to learn what the attorney prefers. Just ask. Recognize, though, that the attorney may not know, and you may need to try several techniques until you hit upon one that works.

Paralegals who have good analytical skills *and* know how to communicate both orally and in writing usually have a few tricks that support good communication habits. Once you develop good communication practices, your relationship as a member of the legal team will grow, become more interesting, and be much more challenging.

Collaboration

Working together, or collaborating, is required for a successful legal office or department. You can be a responsible collaborator by completing the tasks assigned to you. The attorney is the managing delegator but do not be surprised if a senior paralegal or paralegal project manager takes charge of elements of a case and delegates work to newer paralegals. That person reports to a supervising attorney, just as you do, so she will know the attorney's preferences and working style. Get to know senior paralegals or paralegal project managers because they might serve as excellent mentors for you.

■ TRAINING OPTIONS FOR PARALEGALS

This book assumes you are fully engaged in a paralegal education program. In the off chance that you have not yet begun your paralegal education and are looking for information about various program options, this section should help you.

Becoming a paralegal requires learning about substantive law and about the practical aspects of working in the legal system. At one point in time, this training did not occur in a classroom but on the job. The first paralegals started as legal secretaries and moved into paralegal positions, learning about different areas of law as they did their work. It is unusual today to land a paralegal position without first obtaining education in that field.

The choice you make about your paralegal education is important because in some locations you cannot work without a certain kind of paralegal education credential. The Supreme Court of South Dakota, for example, issued a rule that establishes the educational or training requirements paralegals need in order to enter the profession (Rule 92-5) in that state:

1. Successful completion of the Certified Legal Assistant/Certified Paralegal (CLA/CP) examination of the National Association of Legal Assistants; or
2. Graduation from an ABA-approved program of study for legal assistants; or
3. Graduation from a course of study for legal assistants which is institutionally accredited but not ABA approved, and which requires not less than the equivalent of 60 semester hours of study; or
4. Graduation from a course of study for legal assistants, other than those set forth in (2) and (3) above, plus not less than six months in-house training as a legal assistant; or
5. A baccalaureate degree in any field, plus not less than six months in-house training as a legal assistant; or
6. A minimum of three years of law-related experience under the supervision of a lawyer, including at least six months of in-house training as a legal assistant; or
7. Two years of in-house training as a legal assistant.

Now, the typical route to paralegal employment is through a formal paralegal education program, and potential paralegals have many options to choose from. Check to see if your state has educational or training requirements.

Sorting Out the Options

Multiple options are available for a good paralegal education, but your particular geographic area may have only a few. There are some things to look for that make paralegal programs stand out, but very few programs will have all of them, so do not despair if you

IN PRACTICE

American Association for Paralegal Education

The American Association for Paralegal Education (AAfPE) provides information on its website for sorting out the options for paralegal education: *www.aafpe.org*. AAfPE recommends paralegal educational programs meet the following minimum standards:

- Post-secondary coursework in substantive and procedural law, the American legal system, law offices and related environments, the paralegal profession, legal research and writing, ethics, and areas of legal practice such as those described in AAfPE's Core Competencies for Paralegal Programs
- No fewer than 18 semester credit hours (or the equivalent) of substantive paralegal courses
- The completion of a minimum of 60 semester hours (or the equivalent) of total post-secondary study

prior to graduation. A semester hour is equivalent to 15 classroom hours of at least 50 minutes in duration. The course offerings may be for credit or not for credit, but should meet these minimum time periods.

- The paralegal education program must be offered by an institution that is:
  - An institutional member of the American Association for Paralegal Education; or
  - A paralegal educational program approved by the American Bar Association; or
  - A paralegal education program offered by an institution accredited by an agency recognized by the U.S. Department of Education and offering courses at the post-secondary level.

cannot find a program that does. Use the characteristics described in this section to sort out what you need in an educational experience.

ABA Approval

The ABA offers a process through which paralegal programs can gain approval. This approval is rigorous, and each program must go through a re-approval process every seven years.

Programs that have successfully completed this process are called *ABA-approved* paralegal programs. Some employers look for paralegals who have completed ABA-approved programs.

ABA approval is voluntary and not all schools seek such approval. While ABA approval signifies that an education program meets guidelines set forth by the ABA, a program that is not approved may still meet or exceed the guidelines and be equally excellent and reputable.

Internship or Co-op Program

Look for programs that provide an internship or cooperative learning program. These programs put you in a law firm or other legal setting for a specific period of time so that you can gain some on-the-job experience before you leave school.

Many paralegal programs provide this experience. These internships sometimes turn into full-time jobs or good recommendations for full-time jobs.

Job Placement Center

A lot of paralegal programs use their internship placement network to build a job placement network as well. Programs that offer placement services are serious about guaranteeing you are prepared to enter the job market in your geographic region.

Some schools allow alumni to use the job placement service as well. Find out what your school offers and how you can tap into this resource.

Student Paralegal Organizations

Schools that have active paralegal organizations are tapped into a network of working paralegals. This is a great way to meet people in the profession and to network toward the kind of work that you want to do.

Lambda Epsilon Chi (LEX)

Lambda Epsilon Chi is the national honor society for paralegals. LEX was founded by AAfPE and inducts students for their outstanding academic achievements. Students who achieve this honor are recognized through a formal ceremony and awarded a special pin.

Only schools that are institutional members of AAfPE are permitted to have LEX chapters, so schools with a LEX chapter meet certain standards established by AAfPE (see the box about AAfPE's educational requirements).

■ BECOMING CERTIFICATED VS. CERTIFIED

A paralegal *certificate* is what you earn through many paralegal education programs, such as post-baccalaureate programs. The certificate shows that you have completed the specific educational requirements of that particular program. If you have a certificate, you can say that you are *certificated*, although few people use this word and it may sound odd. Most say, "I hold a paralegal certificate from City College of San Francisco."

When you are *certified* you have completed one of the voluntary certification processes offered by a national organization or a state bar. Certification offerings vary from state to state, so check with your state bar or your national professional association to see which options are available to you.

Note that some employers confuse certificated and certification. You may see an advertisement asking for a *certified* paralegal, but most likely, the employer wants a paralegal with a *certificate*.

Nationally, the National Association of Legal Assistants/Paralegals (NALA) offers a national Certified Legal Assistant/Certified Paralegal exam and a specialty certification education program with a multitude of specialty areas. The National Federation of Paralegal Associations (NFPA) and NALS...the Association for Legal Professionals (NALS) offer national certification exams.

A number of individual states have state-specific certification programs. Some states include: Texas, Florida, Kentucky, Louisiana, North Carolina, and California. Having state-specific certification in addition to national certification can enhance your career prospects. Check with your state bar association and the state paralegal association to determine the options in your state.

When considering a certification program, consider the following:

- National certification "travels" with you if you move to another state.
- Some certification programs are more popular in certain areas of the country. By getting the "hot" certification, employers will recognize your credential and you will have less explaining to do.
- Choose a certification program that provides the best value for your time. Pick one that will enhance your reputation, that provides you the opportunity to stretch yourself professionally and educationally, and that grows with your expertise.

■ PARALEGAL ORGANIZATIONS: YOUR PROFESSIONAL GUIDES

Use local and national professional organizations to provide an introduction to the professional community in your area. Most local professional organizations are linked to national organizations and also provide opportunities to network. Networking with members of these organizations can help you learn the landscape of the legal profession where you live and work.

If you are attending school in one location but hope to work in another, join an organization in the location where you hope to work. Even if you cannot attend meetings, you will receive mailings and e-mail messages from the organization. If you reach out to members, they are usually happy to respond and help you get settled when you finally make the move.

Many professional associations provide study groups to prepare for a certification exam. The South Dakota Paralegal Association reimburses members for the cost of taking the Certified Legal Assistant/Certified Paralegal exam. Others offer scholarships that cover the exam fee and, perhaps, some study materials.

■ PARALEGAL SALARIES

Paralegal salaries vary based on the size of the office, geographic location, and many other factors. Local and national paralegal associations regularly survey members about salary, benefits, and hours of work. NALA, for example, performs a salary survey and publishes the results on its website.

■ PREPARE TO EXCEL AS A PARALEGAL

To excel as a paralegal, you will have to spend the first months on the job proving yourself. You will need to display an attitude that demonstrates to others that you are willing to be a team player and to be excellent at your job.

Adapt to the Office Space and Equipment

Some employers provide paralegals with private offices. Others provide desks in an open-floor-plan workspace. Some offices have state-of-the-art equipment. Unfortunately, some have equipment that was state-of-the-art a decade ago. You must—especially during the early part of your career—take what you get and not throw a fit. *Adapt.*

If you need quiet space to think, ask to use an empty office, conference room, or library for an hour or so. Be cheerful in your request instead of complaining.

Learn how to use the technology, no matter how old it is. There are ways to work around its limitations. Once you overcome those limitations, share what you have learned with others on the job. This will result in everyone being more efficient.

Create the space you need to work efficiently by keeping your assigned workspace neat, regardless of its size. You will appear in control of your work and capable of managing space efficiently.

Be Willing to Do More

Never say:

> *"That's not part of my job description."*
>
> *"I didn't go to college so I could type file labels."*
>
> *"That's a waste of my time."*

At the beginning of your career, you really have very little say in the size of job or type of projects you are given. If you feel yourself sliding into the, "But this isn't in my job description," step back and think about whether the task you are doing will contribute to the professional trust you are building with an attorney or other colleagues, will lead to more challenging work later, or will show everyone at your new job that you have a can-do attitude and are willing to get things done, regardless of the size of the job.

Expect your first job to include work that you feel overqualified to do. Take it on and do it with gusto. If you cannot make five photocopies of a document correctly (or without whining), then it is unlikely you will be asked to work on a more complicated task. If you complain about having to make the photocopies, you may find that you are destroying any chance of developing a good relationship with co-workers.

PRACTICE NOTE

Your first job is not your career. Your career is the body of work you do over your lifetime. Start with the attitude that you will learn as much as you can and grow from there. Do not begin by thinking you already know the job.

Set Your Own Goals

Remember, your career is the body of work you do over your lifetime. An employer may meet with you annually and suggest you strive to meet certain milestones, but you should have your own goals. Yes, strive for those milestones set by your employer, but how about going *beyond* those milestones, too? How do *you* want to grow your career?

Your goal in the first or second year on the job may be to figure out what you want the first five years of your career to be. Always take time to figure out your own goals and to create synergy between your employer-driven goals and your personal professional goals.

For example, if paralegals in your area of the country tend to be certified by a state or national certification program, you might consider pursuing certification even if your current employer does not have any interest. You may have to pursue this goal on your own time, but if you believe it will serve your career in the long-term, you may find this to be a goal worth achieving.

■ LEARN TO BE YOUR OWN CAREER ADVISOR

Some jobs in the legal profession—especially at smaller law firms and small organizations—do not have job descriptions at all. Your job is to do what you are asked to do. Even without a job description, you can often create a position you love as the professional relationship between attorney and paralegal is established.

The reality is that lawyers are not trained in human resource management, so you have to take the initiative in your own career to pursue professional development through continuing legal education, certification, joining a professional association, or through volunteer work.

Keep a running list of your professional accomplishments. Record new skills you acquire, continuing education you complete, projects you do, and other details that show progression through your career. Log continuing education, meetings you attend, and volunteer work that you do. This information will be helpful to you as you plan your career, and will be critical if you find yourself looking for a new job.

Hold a meeting with yourself every six months and provide honest answers to these questions: Are you doing all that you can to succeed in this job? Are you excelling at this job? What should you do better? Do you need a new skill? How could you achieve one new thing within the next six months?

At this meeting with yourself, be your own career advisor and ask yourself if you are headed in the right direction. What are you career goals? What are your at-work goals over the next six months? Be specific so that you shine at work and are moving your career forward.

You are entering the paralegal profession and your career is just beginning. How high you fly or where you land is up to you.

CONCLUSION

Starting your paralegal career can be an exciting time if you embrace the idea that you are entering a structured profession that often allows flexibility in the way that you build and develop your career. To maximize opportunities, pay attention to the trends in your geographic location and begin thinking about where you might fit. You do not need to have a specific plan for your career at the very beginning. Instead, develop a good reputation at school and at work, learn as much as you can, and seize opportunities that come your way.

Checklist for Success

☐ Find the definition of paralegal in your state and understand how the definition and rules define how paralegals work.

☐ The career path for paralegals has many opportunities. Be open to opportunities that come your way.

☐ When you begin an internship or job, develop a good reputation. Your workday will be more interesting.

☐ Develop good organizational strategies so that you do not miss deadlines or allow tasks to slip through the cracks.

☐ Try different communication strategies until you find a system that works in your office. Good communication is very important.

☐ Learn to collaborate with colleagues.

☐ Think about how you will develop your career. What kind of education are you pursuing? Will you join a professional association? Will you become certified?

☐ At work, adapt to the office space and technology you are given.

☐ Always be willing to do more than is asked of you.

☐ Your employer may set goals for you, but set goals for yourself, too. This will make your work more meaningful.

☐ Be willing to evaluate your own work and always be your own career advisor. What can you do better? What do you want to do for yourself?

ASSIGNMENTS: PREPARING FOR YOUR PARALEGAL CAREER

Schedule

Finding an internship and your first paralegal job takes as much time as a part-time job. This assignment is to begin a career management notebook that can be expanded at the end of each chapter of this book. We recommend a three-ring binder with a pocket in the front and back.

Your first task is to create a weekly plan for job searching. Tasks that need to go on your list include the following:

a. Review job announcements, boards, or classifieds for open positions.
b. Apply for jobs by sending application letters and resumes or by applying online.
c. Create a spreadsheet where you record jobs you have applied for and the responses you get.
d. Plan to attend at least one networking event every week during the heart of your job search.
e. Use online social networks to connect with other paralegals.

Each of these tasks takes time. Plan a regular time for doing them each week.

Next, create a master career management calendar. You could print blank calendar pages for the next few months. Fill in the calendar with upcoming networking events, workshops, and continuing legal education opportunities.

Report

Before you begin working as a paralegal in a particular state, you need to know whether and how the state defines paralegals and if any special rules apply to paralegal work. Look at your state bar, legislature, and local organizations to determine which definition or definitions of "paralegal" or "legal assistant" apply in your state. In addition to definitions, some states have case law or legislation that applies to the scope of paralegal work and billing practices. What does your state have? Check with your state bar association, your supreme court, and online resources. Write a memorandum to your instructor that reports your findings.

Network

Check in with your academic or paralegal advisor to make sure you know which extra-curricular programs your program offers, if any. If your school does not offer such programs, ask about organizations off-campus that might offer networking opportunities, continuing legal education, or volunteer opportunities. Create a list of these opportunities and discuss it in class. During the discussion, identify at least one opportunity that is a "must" do, and then make time to do this work.

Prepare

Take time to think about the kind of career you hope to pursue. Use the form in Appendix C to help you create a list of professional organizations, people, and other resources that will help you develop your plan. Find out about organizations affiliated with your school and your local geographic region. Look at major national organizations to see if one stands out to you as more helpful with starting your career. Bring your form to class to discuss. Do you need to add any networking opportunities to your list?

INTERNET RESOURCES

Paralegal Gateway: *http://www.paralegalgateway.com*

The U.S. Bureau of Labor Statistics: *http://www.bls.gov*

American Bar Association's Center for Professional Practice: *http://www.americanbar.org/cpr*

American Association for Paralegal Education: *http://www.aafpe.org*

NALS...The Association for Legal Professionals: *http://www.nals.org*

National Association of Legal Assistants/Paralegals: *http://www.nala.org*

National Federation of Paralegal Associations: *http://www.paralegals.org*

REFERENCES

American Bar Association. (2004). Model Rules for the Utilization of Paralegal Services. Retrieved from: *http://apps.americanbar.org/content/dam/aba/migrated/legalservices/paralegals/downloads/modelguidelines.authcheckdam.pdf*

American Bar Association. (2008). Current ABA Definition of Legal Assistant/Paralegal. Retrieved from: *http://apps.americanbar.org/legalservices/paralegals/def98.html*

American Association for Paralegal Education. (2003). Statement of Education Minimums. Retrieved from: *http://www.aafpe.org*

South Dakota Supreme Court. (1992). Rule 92-5: In the matter of the adoption of a new rule relating to the utilization of legal assistants. Retrieved from: *http://www.sdjudicial.com/Uploads/sc/rules/92-5.pdf*

CHAPTER **2**

YOUR INTERNSHIP: A BUILDING BLOCK AND A STEPPING STONE

At some point during your paralegal education you may engage in an internship. An internship provides unpaid or paid on-the-job training for students. An internship is required in some programs, optional in others, and not even addressed in a few. Your advisor will have the details for your program.

By the end of this chapter, you should be able to:

- Define an *internship*
- Discuss the importance of an internship
- Identify sources of an internship
- Develop a strategy for applying for an internship
- Describe best practices for interns both during and after the internship

Many fields want to hire graduates with some on-the-job experience, and the paralegal profession is no exception. Make an internship a priority.

■ WHAT IS AN INTERNSHIP?

Generally, an internship is a work-related learning experience that should provide you with exposure to your career field and the opportunity to explore or gain relevant knowledge and skills, as well as insight into specialized areas of law practice.

The primary focus of an internship is to get on-the-job training, as well as to take what you learned in the classroom and apply it to the real world. You also will be able to determine if you have a genuine interest in a particular area of the law or working in a specific legal environment.

Most internships are short-term and temporary, lasting for a predetermined amount of time, such as three months, a semester, a term, etc.

There are usually supervisors for interns. These supervisors will assign specific tasks to you and evaluate your overall work. Paralegal interns must work under the supervision of an attorney.

If you are to receive credit for your internship, a faculty member will usually coordinate your experience.

Internships are an excellent way to begin building important connections that are invaluable in developing and maintaining a strong professional network for the future.

IN PRACTICE

Key Questions about Internships

Before you look for an internship, ask yourself these key questions:

- Do you have a preference about the area of law you might like to concentrate on during your internship?
- Where do you want to do your internship?
- Will your internship be for credit?
- Will you be paid? Do you *need* to be paid?

- Do you need to be on campus for classes or meetings during your internship?
- Do you have reliable transportation to an off-campus internship?

The answers to these questions will help you set the limits of your internship. Be very honest, but also realistic, in your answers.

An Internship vs. an Externship

Internships and externships are different.

Internships are designed to teach you actual job skills and offer you opportunities to practice these skills. Externships are designed to give you exposure to a job without much hands-on experience. An "externship" may also be referred to as "job shadowing."

Externships typically vary in length, but generally last one or two days. They offer no pay or academic credit. In fact, this may be an assignment for one of your classes. Usually externships are hosted by volunteers from various organizations to help students gain an insider's view of a career field. They may include interviews, a tour of the facility and perhaps, depending on the amount of time available, participation in office projects. Internships are longer term (a semester or for the summer), may involve pay and academic credit, and commonly support an organization's work function.

Externships offer participants the chance to "test" a specific area of the law or type of practice before making a long-term commitment to working in a specific area of law. An externship may also help you get your foot in the door for a competitive internship program or job.

An externship may be helpful to you; however, because you are probably most interested in long-term exposure, you will most likely seek an internship. This chapter focuses on preparing you for an excellent internship experience.

■ WHY DO YOU WANT AN INTERNSHIP?

There are many reasons why you would want an internship, and these reasons may vary from individual to individual. Do not worry about finding a "perfect" internship because you can gain skills and personal insight from any assignment. Instead, focus on why you want to obtain an internship and keep that reason in mind throughout your experience.

Your life circumstances may make completing an internship seem impossible. You may feel that you cannot afford to take time off from your full-time job to do unpaid work. Before you write off doing an internship, consider the benefits.

Internships Allow You to Network

One of the best reasons to do an internship is that you will have an opportunity to make connections and network. A lot of jobs are not advertised. Working in a legal setting will help you be in the right place at the right time.

Internships Give Hints About the Career Path You Will Take

During your internship, you will combine what you have learned in your paralegal program with practical work experience. This is an excellent way to determine what area of the law interests you and what type of legal environment appeals to you. Traditional law firm? Corporate legal department? Government offices?

Internships Help Develop Professional Work Habits

Internships provide an introduction to the culture of the legal profession and help you develop professional work habits. In many situations, you will have an opportunity to work with one or more experienced paralegals who can show you the ropes, but sometimes, you may have to work without the benefit of another paralegal's leadership.

Whatever your particular situation, you will gain practical work experience and expand your base of experience during your internship. You will also begin to see your own preferences and ways of doing things emerge, and may discover that you have some opinions about how you *do not* want to do things when you have a job to call your own. You will also come to understand the importance of being on time and meeting deadlines.

> **PRACTICE NOTE**
>
> Be open to internship opportunities in law practice areas you are not sure about. You might find yourself on an unexpected career path that you enjoy.

Internships Offer Career-Building Work Experience

Every internship offers benefits that cannot be denied. Internships look great on your resume. You will experience situations that you can discuss thoughtfully (no whining or complaining) in an interview. You will learn to think on your feet and to handle stressful situations. You will meet people who can help in your future navigation of the career field.

Internships May Lead to a Permanent Job

Sometimes, internships lead to full-time employment. Many firms and corporate legal departments offer employment to interns as full-time employees after successful completion of the internship.

Further, having this work experience on your resume can be a good way to make contacts that may result in more job offers as compared to individuals who lack the experience an internship provides.

PARALEGAL PROFILE

Janine Hanrahan

B.A., Political Science & Philosophy, Boston College,
Expected 2012

Janine Hanrahan used interning to explore career interests.

Janine Hanrahan is a senior at Boston College, where she is studying political science and philosophy and seeking a minor in women's and gender studies.

In 2011, Janine drew on skills gained from working with an orthopedics distributor to compete for one of ten summer paralegal internship positions at WilmerHale in Boston. She drew on the skills she believed would transfer to the legal profession—the ability to handle confidential information, her skill in talking with people, and her attention to detail.

Janine participated in a nine-week summer paralegal internship at WilmerHale in Boston as a way to see if she would enjoy a career in law. "Everything I knew about the legal profession I learned through television shows," Hanrahan explained, "so this has been an invaluable experience for getting to see what this life would actually be like."

Janine applied for the 2011 WilmerHale Paralegal Program during the Fall semester of 2010. The competition for WilmerHale's program is increasingly keen; of the many who applied, over fifty were interviewed for just ten positions.

The primary goal of WilmerHale's Internship Program is to provide the interns with insights that will help them make critical decisions about their career paths. The workload is an essential part of the program, but, there are other important pieces to the program as well. Janine's experience is a good example, in that her work assignments provided exposure to multiple practice areas; however, having served as a witness in WilmerHale's mock deposition and mock trial programs, she also gained appreciation for the role of an attorney in these proceedings. Also, she participated in "Insight Sessions" that offered the opportunity to meet and consult with the law firm's recruiters, summer associates and partners, all of whom provided a wealth of advice and guidance on a myriad of issues from crafting a resume to whether one should take time off before law school.

While she was asked to file and collect signatures, jobs that some might consider small, she believes "the mindset is the most important thing. The assignment might be a small task but it ultimately might be very important to the case or to the attorney."

Janine believes this internship has given her more confidence and a greater appreciation for attention to detail, an important aspect of the practice of law. She leaves the internship with an understanding of how even the smallest job can have an impact in the practice of law.

She advises interns to take on the mindset of the person assigning the task. "Think 'How would I want this to be done?' Put yourself in that person's shoes and have a willingness to please and overachieve to some extent."

IN PRACTICE

Organizing Your Own Internship Experience

You may find that you need to find your own internship experience. If this is the case, make phone calls to potential internship sponsors and speak to a human resources representative. If there is no human resources representative, ask for a person who might help you with an internship.

The following are examples of questions you should ask:

- Does the office have internships for paralegals? If not, would they consider having one?
- What do paralegals typically do during an internship at this office?
- What would the start date/end dates be? Expected hours? Any flexibility in those hours/dates to make room for potential interns' school schedules?
- Is the organization willing to send a brochure or other company information to you? If not, is there information available online?
- How do you apply?

Follow up with questions about whether the firm interviews candidates or whether candidates are selected by the school's internship program director or how to get your school involved in their internship program.

■ ALTERNATIVE TO AN INTERNSHIP

If you have evaluated your situation and truly believe you cannot complete an internship, consider changing your work situation altogether by getting one or two part-time jobs at a law firm, corporate legal department, title company, governmental organization, or other group. Work as a runner, a file clerk, a receptionist, or in another position. The position does not matter so much as the experience you will gain and the contacts you will make. For example, a person working as a runner will get acquainted with people who work in many offices and may hear about full-time employment opportunities that open up.

■ WHERE DO YOU FIND AN INTERNSHIP?

Paralegals work in many kinds of offices. Some of the employers who hire paralegals and might offer internships as well include:

- Government offices
- Law firms (all sizes)
- Corporate legal departments
- Courts and local government offices
- Title companies
- Insurance companies
- Accounting and engineering firms
- Banks
- Non-profit organizations
- Legal aid clinics
- Universities and colleges, including offices of general counsel, offices that manage a university's intellectual property, and offices that manage a university's compliance issues.

■ HOW DO YOU FIND AN INTERNSHIP?

Some schools require students to complete at least one internship, while others leave the internship experience optional. We recommend completing an internship, even if one is not required.

Begin planning for your internship early in your educational experience. You will want to complete your internship near the end of your paralegal education so, early on, find out whether your school requires an internship, has a placement program, and any other guidelines your program has regarding internships.

Your educational institution will have resources to help you locate an internship. Many paralegal programs have an internship coordinator who matches paralegals and law offices. Be sure to use every resource you have available at your school to pursue an internship. In addition, examine local resources yourself. You may find an internship through a connection your school does not have. Confirm that your school approves of the internship situation.

IN PRACTICE

Non-paralegal Jobs Provide Learning Opportunities

Non-paralegal law firm jobs are important because, as Zachary W. Brewer, CP, points out, you can get your start there.

He told us: "As for paralegal training, I can point to the courses I took at Tulsa Community College and the NALA CLA examination. However, I received a good deal of 'apprenticeship' training from the attorneys in my office during the time that I was file clerk/runner with the firm.

"All of the attorneys were helpful if I had questions, or was just curious about a topic. Luckily, they felt before I was even ready to be a paralegal, that I would be a good one."

Begin looking early for the right placement. If your internship semester begins in January, start looking for the appropriate position in September. If you are interning over the summer, begin your search in November. While summer may seem far away, most firms like to fill their internship slots by April. The semester break is the perfect time to prepare resumes and send out letters. Set a goal of having your internship position in place eight to ten weeks before you are scheduled to begin.

Meet the Internship Coordinator

If your school has a paralegal internship coordinator, begin your search by meeting that individual. This person will be the best connection you have to the world of work because internship coordinators do a lot of networking and know many potential employers.

If you are receiving course credit for your internship, ask how many hours per week you need to work, what the recordkeeping requirements are, and whether you meet as a class during the internship. Ask for written guidelines and be sure you understand your reporting requirements. Your school may have you keep a reflective journal, report your hours worked, or request that your supervisor report back to the school about your performance during your internship.

Ask for written guidelines and refer to them often. They will keep you organized as you begin your internship.

Visit Your School's Career Center

Your school may have resources for locating internships. The campus career center often has listings of local internships and subscribes to databases that catalog internships in other cities or states. These career centers also often have people available to students, who assist with preparation of resumes and application letters, interview preparation, and sometimes finding mentors in certain fields. Make an appointment to meet with a career specialist and explain what you hope to accomplish during your internship.

Some schools have mentor programs, where alumni from various professions offer to mentor students. You might find a paralegal or lawyer working in the area who is willing to meet with you to discuss your career possibilities, including ideas for internship placements.

Use Your Connections to Find an Internship

If you know of an office where you would like to intern, but no one has a contact there, call the office yourself and ask how you might apply.

Some students turn to parents or relatives or other students in their program to make contacts for internships. Ask relatives who work for employers that hire paralegals whether they have internship programs.

Tell everyone you know that you are looking for an internship. Tell your professors. Tell your English professor. And your math professor. Tell any professor who thinks you are a good student. They may know of an internship and be willing to recommend you if you are a good student-citizen in their class.

Join a Paralegal Association

If your school has a student association for paralegals, join. Also become a student member of a local or state paralegal association. Some national professional associations also have student memberships. These organizations sometimes have exclusive listings for internships and jobs that are made available only to members.

Be sure to attend the association meetings and take advantage of continuing education opportunities. You will be both learning and networking. Another bonus is that there are often discounts for students for these activities and some offer scholarships for paralegal students. As you get to know people, you can let them know you are looking for internships and job opportunities.

Another benefit of belonging to a paralegal association is that they usually present excellent educational programs. You may become acquainted with a guest speaker who knows of an internship or is looking for an intern for his or her office.

Attend a Job Fair

Some schools and towns have annual job fairs. Check with your school's career center for information on these events. Find out if anyone who hires paralegals will be interviewing. Some offices that hire paralegals may have human resource representatives on hand to answer questions.

Before the fair, go through the list of companies planning to attend. This list is usually available online before the event. Visit websites of any organizations that interest you. Try to determine if the organization hires paralegals.

Prepare a formal resume and print copies on nice resume paper. Do not skimp on the quality of paper or the number of copies you make. Your resume is the most inexpensive and most useful marketing document you can have at a job fair. You do not want to be the one scribbling information on a piece of paper. Those pieces of paper never make it back to headquarters. And if they do, no one remembers their purpose.

When you find an employer that interests you, introduce yourself to the representative, explain that you are a paralegal student, and say a sentence or two about working for that company as a paralegal. You could say, "I visited your website [shows you did your homework] and I noticed that you hire paralegals. I am very interested in doing…[fill in the blank with skills/tasks listed in a job posting on the website]." Show that you have true interest in the company.

PRACTICE TIP

Paralegal Associations
Paralegal associations sometimes award scholarships, so becoming a student member has multiple benefits.

■ HOW TO APPLY

Treat your internship application as seriously as you would a job application. Refer to Chapters 6 and 7 for information about designing a resume and writing an application letter. Your application serves as the first writing sample an employer will see. You want to make sure your materials make a good impression.

IN PRACTICE

Dress Up for the Job Fair and Other Events

Dress up for the job fair. Consider it one big interview. Even if the fair is in the student gym, put on your interview clothes. When attending other events that alumni or legal professionals attend, dress up.

You are starting a career and presenting your best self at these events creates a lasting impression.

■ WHAT YOU SHOULD KNOW AFTER YOU LAND AN INTERNSHIP

The truth about internships is that firms are often reluctant to bring interns on board because they cost law firms money in time, training, and supervision. In the legal profession, lawyers are responsible for an intern's mistake.

Paralegal interns in legal offices are bound by the same rules as everyone else in that office. In other fields, employers sometimes see interns as "free labor." For example, an employer may need to update its website, but may not have a web developer on staff. The employer may bring in a new media student as an intern to do the work. In this situation, the student has little or no mentorship and is basically serving as free or cheap labor for the employer. This is not a good situation for the intern. Interns need mentorship.

In law offices, paralegal interns—just like paralegals—must be supervised by an attorney. This supervision is required by Rules of Professional Conduct. Paralegal interns also need mentorship, which can be provided by a senior paralegal. This kind of mentoring costs law offices money, so some hesitate before taking on interns.

One of the most important reasons employers hesitate to hire interns is that they may be unpredictable. Even earning a 4.0 in every paralegal class does not guarantee that the paralegal intern will not make a mistake or be unwilling to learn or take criticism from others.

When a law firm decides to take you on as an intern, they are doing so to further your education, not to get free help. In return for their generosity, you need to be ready to learn as much as possible and take an active role in your experience by listening, accepting projects when asked, and asking for advice or help when you are unsure how to proceed.

Your internship is not simply a box to check off on your school requirements list. It is an opportunity to learn about the law office environment and to showcase your talents. You need to see it as a job interview that comes with a long audition.

■ BEST PRACTICES FOR INTERNS

Interns are different from employees. Employers expect interns to be eager and open to instruction and learning. They want enthusiasm but not overconfidence. Employers want you to be yourself and to assimilate to the practices of the staff. To be all of these things, you must adopt best practices for interns.

What Should You Wear?

Be sure to ask how you are expected to dress. If you are too embarrassed to ask the employer, ask your advisor or a favorite faculty member. When you do your internship, it is time to drop the "college casual" apparel and dress as professionally as possible.

Even if you will work in a dress-down office, dress up on the first day and most other days. Here is why: You want to dress for the job you want (paralegal), not the job you have (student intern). If you show up in jeans while most others are wearing suits or dressy office attire, you will not make a good impression on anyone you meet. Even if someone tells you it is okay to wear jeans because you are a student, do not. Adopt this mindset: *You might be meeting a future colleague, boss, or encounter an opportunity you never knew existed.*

Also, if you are dressed casually, you might miss an opportunity to accompany an attorney to court for a hearing or part of a trial. If you are dressed appropriately, you might

IN PRACTICE

Things to Remember During Your Internship

During your internship, remember these things:

- You know a lot but you do not know everything.
- Take copious notes.
- You will see how attorneys and their staff work, how they interact, make decisions and get their work finished.

- You will be able to apply what you have learned in the classroom, but be ready to add to that knowledge rapidly as you work in a real-time, real-world setting.

tag along to a deposition or meeting with a corporate client. An attorney may not think to invite you, the intern, along until the day of the meeting, so being ready to take on opportunities is important.

Make a Good First Impression

Once you land an internship, you still have first impressions to make. Always arrive on time, wearing business attire, and ready to work. Do the assignments you get quickly and accurately to establish that you can do the work and that you are dependable. Do not be upset if the first job you are given is working on a task that seems menial. Paralegals have to do these jobs, and starting with a rather menial job still offers exposure to the law firm.

Focus on the Work

Try to stay focused on the work. *If* you do a good job at this internship, which includes being responsible and professional, and *if* you are invited to work at the firm full time, you will most likely bond with someone at the office with whom you share common interests. *That person* will gladly listen to you rave about last night's concert, but until that moment, keep your stories to a minimum and focus on your work.

A pitfall you may encounter when trying to stay focused on your work is an employee who *cannot* stay focused. Just as no one wants to hear about your transportation problems, you do not want to hear someone else explain how they sang happy birthday to their cat last night or that they woke up to their neighbor's trash spread all over their driveway. As difficult as it may be, continue to bring your work back to being the focus of your time and energy. You might say, "I'd really like to hear about that but I need to get a grip on this project." Then, ask a direct question about your project. "This is how I'm organizing this notebook. Is this the way you would do it?"

Learn as Much as You Can

Be sponge-like. Listen to everyone. Take notes. Go on field trips anytime anyone asks you to tag along to the court or for other errands.

When you move from office equipment to projects with substance, take good notes and ask thoughtful questions. If you do not know how to do something, be sure to ask for direction.

Be Positive, Even When Others Are Not

While everyone else may be burned out and exhausted, this does not give you license to complain along with them. You can certainly commiserate and you can offer to take on

IN PRACTICE

What to Expect During an Internship

You can expect to work hard during your internship and to learn a lot. This is an invaluable experience and you can expect the following:

- You need to be energetic and positive toward the work.
- You may be asked to do things that are not even close to glamorous.

- Even the dullest task will help you with your career.
- You may have more questions than you expected. Ask questions and try as many new things as possible.

IN PRACTICE

Write Information Down

The minute you begin your internship, carry a notepad and pen everywhere you go, even on your first tour of the office. Jot down information such as how to use the copy machine, where the postage meter is, and who is in charge of dispensing office supplies. *Do not ask the same questions over and over.*

Do not assume you know how to use the equipment. Copy machines work differently in every office and many require client and user codes. Computers work differently, too. Just because you know how to open Microsoft Word and type a letter, does not mean you can do it as easily at this office. You may need to use a document management system, which tracks client documents.

Never wonder whether you should write something down. The answer is almost always YES.

tasks that will ease a workday, but stay positive and energetic. The legal office has an ebb and flow that sometimes creates tired, cranky employees.

Find Your Physical and Emotional Stamina

Work in law changes constantly. Stress levels often run high. The ability to remain calm throughout stressful times demonstrates that you are mature enough to handle the pressure of a law office.

Keep a Log or Journal of Accomplishments

You may be asked to record your time, even if it is not billed to clients. If this is not the case, take time each day to make notes about the new activities you experienced and any accomplishments you feel you achieved. Jot a list of questions to ask the next day. As your internship continues, set goals for yourself and try to leave with several projects under your belt.

Your notes will help you write your resume and craft ways to talk meaningfully about your internship with future employers.

Check Your Ego at the Door

No matter how smart you are or how well you have done in your paralegal program, it is impossible for you to know as much as a paralegal with years of experience. Do not even try to fake it, but do not be discouraged. First of all, you are not expected to have the knowledge of an experienced paralegal. Second, people will notice your good work.

You will only be working as an intern for a short amount of time—three months, a term, a semester, etc. Please remember that it will take more than this brief period before you will be given more substantive work. You may feel that the work you are given is beneath you. You may have to do work that requires a lot more patience than education. You may fax documents, you may type documents. You may put away or close files or take telephone messages. You may be "doing" more than "thinking." You will be proving that you can do the "little things" like making friends with the photocopier. Do this gladly and competently because these tasks pave the way to more challenging assignments and demonstrate your commitment to the business side of the legal practice.

Do the Brainless Work Brilliantly

When you are given boring work to do during your internship, do it better and faster. Prove that you can do the brainless work brilliantly. You may be ready and willing to draft an astounding pleading but you have to prove that you can do the filing, answer the phone, and take directions first.

These activities, which may seem simple, may have legal and ethical implications. The supervising attorney needs to know you can be trusted to work within legal and ethical boundaries. If you are thinking, "I am too smart to do this simple stuff," remember that if you do not do it well, your supervisor will be thinking, "She is not smart enough to do even this simple task. How can I assign her anything important?"

Master the Basics

Have you traveled to a foreign country where people speak a different language? When you first arrive, it is helpful to learn just a few simple phrases like "please," "thank you," and "where is the bathroom?" Knowing these basics will make your stay more comfortable. People do not expect you to speak their language fluently. They will be happy to help you.

The same goes for your internship. Start by learning the basics (How do they format their letters and pleadings? Where are the files kept? Do you have to record any charges for photocopies and postage? Is there an office procedures manual? Who is the contact person in relation to technology?) before you expect to jump into the complicated stuff. The ability to get things done, to be a self-starter and notice what needs to be done, as well as the ability to work independently, are qualities you will need as an intern if you expect to be given the more difficult work. Master the basics first.

Remember: If the Work Were Not Important, You Would Not Be Asked to Do It

You may think the work you are doing as an intern is not very important, but remember that it takes all kinds of work, done by everyone, to have a successful law practice. Practicing law is not just about going to trial. It is about correspondence, filing, photocopying exhibits, scheduling client meetings, etc. All the small things make up the whole: a successful law practice that provides outstanding service to the client. If the small tasks are not completed properly, bigger mistakes can occur. Attorneys know this and rely on paralegals to make sure these mistakes do not happen.

You May Supervise the Intern Some Day

Just as you have an experienced paralegal (or perhaps an attorney) guiding you through your internship, you may do the same for another intern in a few years. Remember that you cannot become the tour guide until you have been the tourist. Everything you learn as an intern, from the mundane to the exciting, will help you be a better paralegal when you are ready for your first job. It will also help you when and if you supervise an intern during your career.

■ SOME "DO NOTS" FOR YOUR INTERNSHIP

Your internship may be your first foray into an office environment. Naturally, you may be nervous and excited. Or, you may feel ready to take on the world after studying so hard and doing so well in school. We want you to be prepared for your internship experience, and so we are going to tell you about some classic mistakes interns make.

Do Not Appear Overconfident

Paralegal programs prepare you to work in legal offices, but they do not prepare you to work in a specific office. Every law office is different. When you begin working, you need to pay attention to what people are saying to you. Do not try to impress them with what you know or insist that you already know how to do a job that someone is explaining to you. Instead, impress your employer by listening, taking in what people say to you, and trying your hardest to do a good job.

Do Not Let a Bad Day Ruin the Experience

Working as an intern in a legal office can be intense. Sometimes things go wrong. If you make a mistake, admit it, apologize, try to correct it, learn from it, and move on.

Do Not Get Caught Up in the Drama

Do not talk badly about co-workers just because other people are. Stay out of the office politics and do your job.

ETHICS TIP

Client Confidentiality   You are bound by the same ethics rules as the rest of the staff. Be very careful when you participate in any online activities so that you do not divulge any confidential or privileged information. Also, many places of employment have policies regarding computer usage. Be sure you understand the rules.

Do Not Tweet Your Day Away

Your internship experience should not be reported hour by hour via social networking accounts. In addition to staying off Facebook and other social networking sites, also refrain from surfing the web or playing a quick game of Solitaire. Remember that some employers monitor online activity. More than one intern has not been offered a job because of web usage habits.

Do Not Be Too Informal

Do not start calling the partner by his or her first name or what appears to be a nickname unless you are invited to do so. You may be accustomed to calling your professors by their first names, but once you start working, err on the side of formality until invited to be more casual.

Do Not Ignore the Staff

In most situations, you will be working under the supervision of an attorney. However, as an intern you need to listen to others on the staff, not just the attorney. If the attorney suggests you ask a certain staff member questions, ask that staff member. Be respectful toward staff members as they can be immensely helpful to you in completing your assignments. Should an attorney consider offering you full-time employment, the staff will almost always be consulted about whether you are a team player.

Do Not Miss Opportunities

Do not turn down invitations to lunch, to sit in on meetings, or to observe in court. Take advantage of anyone's offer of time so that you can learn more about the office, about the work you are being asked to do, and about the profession in general. If you are invited to go to court, go! Even if someone is just going to file a document with a court clerk, take advantage of this opportunity to meet court staff and local government personnel, and to learn procedures. If necessary, be willing to stay beyond the end of the standard workday to help complete a task, since such conduct shows your commitment and dedication.

Remember that an externship is mostly for observing for a few hours or a few days, but an internship or practicum is meant to be hands on. As an intern, be sure to offer or to ask how you might help with a task or project.

■ WHAT TO DO IF YOU HATE YOUR INTERNSHIP

Most internship coordinators try to work with employers to ensure that internships provide the appropriate training and supervision, but occasionally, an internship turns out to be less than stellar.

Before you complain to the internship coordinator at your school, there are steps you can take. First make a list of the things that are working at your internship. Next, make a list of things that you feel are just not working. Once you have completed your lists, make an appointment with your internship coordinator at your school. Bring your lists to the appointment and discuss the things that are working and are not working with her.

During the meeting, your goal is to determine whether the internship should continue or not. An internship should be discontinued if unacceptable behavior has occurred. Unacceptable behavior that should be reported to the internship coordinator at your school includes:

- Lack of appropriate, ethical supervision of your work
- Being called names or disparaged publically
- Sexual harassment
- Being asked by other staff to lie or to do things without the supervising attorney's knowledge
- Being asked to perform tasks that are beyond the authority of a paralegal and amount to the unauthorized practice of law

If you truly want out of the situation, you need to have very good reasons. The legal world is a small one, and you will only get the opportunity to bow out of an internship once. An internship should not be discontinued if you simply wanted to work at a large firm and you are assigned to a solo practitioner's office or vice versa.

If you are unhappy with the placement because you wanted something different, ask your internship coordinator to help you set some personal goals to achieve while working in the current situation. Try to focus on these goals rather than the situation itself. Your goals should be in line with the work you are doing for your internship. If the placement is truly a wrong match, the internship coordinator will be able to help you make the appropriate changes.

By being proactive and taking charge of the situation, you can direct your internship toward a more productive conclusion. If you do need to bow out of an internship, your coordinator can help you make a smooth exit.

CONCLUSION

Your internship may be only a small part of your paralegal education, but it will play a major role in your career. Your internship will allow you to build upon your education and apply what you have learned to real-world situations. It will provide exposure to various legal environments and specialty areas that will guide you to future employment choices.

When you plan and implement a successful internship, you will meet new people and demonstrate your skills and competencies on the job. People will be able to see you in action. If they are hiring and are satisfied with your work, as well as your attitude and aptitude, you may find that your internship leads to full-time employment following graduation.

Checklist for Success

☐ Begin your search for an internship very early.

☐ Consult all resources available to you on campus, including a faculty internship coordinator, the school's career center, professional organizations, and other resources.

☐ Have copies of your resume available at job fairs and networking events. Resumes are the least expensive tool a job hunter uses.

☐ Look for internship opportunities beyond traditional law firms. Paralegals work for many types of employers.

☐ Prepare yourself for your internship by being ready and open to an intense but valuable experience.

☐ Dress professionally, have a great attitude, and work hard.

☐ Report any problems to your faculty advisor or internship coordinator immediately.

☐ Pay attention to ethical issues while at your internship, including posting status updates on social networking sites that give hints about the work you are doing. Your work as an intern is confidential and remains so even after your internship is completed.

☐ Use the experience to enhance your resume and to offer you things to talk about during future job interviews.

ASSIGNMENTS: PREPARING FOR YOUR PARALEGAL CAREER

Career Management

Update your career management notebook by locating all the resources available to you for finding a good internship experience. Create a list of organizations, people, and events. For example, list the offices and people on campus that will be helpful. Identify any events you should attend such as career fairs, meetings of professional organizations, and resume workshops. Make a master list of resources and include the following information:

- Name of person, place or thing
- Address, phone, e-mail, web address
- Dates of special events
- Notes

Add the dates of special events to your career management calendar and your daily planner. Compare your calendar to others' to identify events or opportunities you may have missed.

Report

Interview two working paralegals. (When you ask for these interviews, request an "informational interview.") Ask where they interned and how their internships prepared them for their first paralegal positions. If they did not intern, ask about their first month at work as a paralegal. Ask

for their advice for being successful during an internship or at work. Prepare a memo to your instructor that identifies who you interviewed, the questions you asked, and the advice the paralegals provided. Organize your memorandum using headings and sub-headings to make the document easier to read.

Network

If your school or program has a career center, placement office, or a person designated to help graduates find work, set up an appointment to visit that office or person. Find out which services are offered and how to take advantage of those services. Some larger universities will review your resume and hold mock interviews. Find out if your school or program has access to any databases that list jobs that are not advertised to the general public. Prepare a one-page cheat-sheet of the services, passwords, and other information provided to you. When designing your document, think of a page in a directory of services. Prepare your document so that it is easy to use in the future.

Prepare

In 100 words or less, write what you hope to gain from an internship. Read your goals aloud and discuss.

CHAPTER **3**

TRAITS PARALEGALS NEED TO SUCCEED

You really need to know what you are getting into when you pursue a paralegal career. Based on the number of lawyer jokes, late-night pundits who spew attorney satire, and the general poking fun that lawyers endure, you might imagine that law firms and legal departments often have a lively, pressure-filled culture. The most successful paralegals understand the culture and build careers around the dynamics controlling day-to-day work.

The most obvious way to identify with the culture of the legal profession and to learn the ropes of the paralegal profession is to watch a seasoned paralegal in action. If you are really lucky, when you start an internship or job you will have a paralegal who can be your mentor. Many paralegals, however, are the only paralegal in their law office. How do you learn the ropes if you have no one to show you?

By the end of this chapter, you should be able to:

- Identify the reason certain traits are important for paralegals
- Discuss the need to be confident, reliable, and organized
- Describe the practice of law as a business
- State the need for paralegals to be entrepreneurial
- Discuss the need for flexibility

■ FIVE TRAITS IMPORTANT TO PARALEGAL SUCCESS

As is true with any group of people, you may find that the situation in your office differs, but a survey of more than 200 legal professionals, conducted by the authors, suggests paralegals need five traits:

- Paralegals need to be confident.
- Paralegals need to be reliable.
- Paralegals need to be organized.
- Paralegals need to understand the business of law.
- Paralegals need to be entrepreneurial.

■ THE REASON THESE TRAITS ARE IMPORTANT

Lawyers and paralegals are educated differently, and each emerges from school with a different skill set. These skill sets influence the way that lawyers and paralegals work together on the job. These traits are important for a paralegal because they complement the skills and knowledge that lawyers bring to the job and alleviate some of the stress the practice of law creates.

Lawyers are traditionally immersed in legal doctrine and theory during law school. They are taught to take a set of facts and apply a legal framework. Some law schools offer clinical experiences and skills courses, but the fact remains that law school education leaves very little time for learning the practical matters of practicing law: accounting, human resources, project management, and in the very beginning, even which forms to use.

Paralegals, on the other hand, learn many of the practical matters related to the practice of law. In addition to courses in substantive areas of law—although not nearly as in depth as law school curriculum—a paralegal may leave school understanding how to organize a case, use software, which forms to use, and how to work well collaboratively.

Paralegals need to understand how a lawyer's education and on-the-job challenges affect the working environment.

During Law School, Law Students Are Taught to Argue

During law school, law students are taught to argue. This type of arguing is not bickering or fighting. This type of arguing is being able to quickly construct a logical, point-by-point discussion related to a specific question or problem. Deidre M. Smith, associate professor at University of Maine School of Law, explains that this arguing is very conscious for law students as they learn to do the type of analysis required to practice law. They stop and think about each step. For seasoned attorneys, however, the practice is unconscious. They go through this analysis automatically, often not realizing they are cycling through the fact pattern. In addition, lawyers are evidence-driven people and expect some "proof" to support assertions made, positions taken, etc.

Learning to argue like a lawyer changes people, according to Smith. "Once you go through law school, you really do see things differently. You are constantly analyzing situations." For example, a law student might think, "When I order a pizza, have I created a contract?" This ability has implications beyond helping clients. It means that lawyers are top-notch negotiators.

A lawyer's ability to negotiate *well* matches the results of a survey of approximately 200 paralegals, in which the most common response to the question, "What would you like to know more about?" was: *How do I negotiate my duties on the job.* Because of their training, attorneys know how to be tougher when negotiating salaries, more convincing when asking you to work overtime, and may seem to "cross examine" rather than "discuss" projects or status reports. The bottom line is that lawyers are professional fact finders and negotiators, and working alongside them means you must be an excellent communicator.

Lawyers (and Paralegals) Face the "Deadly Ps"

As much practice as lawyers receive in the art of constructing well-reasoned arguments, law students receive little education in the art of managing a law practice. This can make starting a legal career quite overwhelming. Lawyers, especially new lawyers, suffer from what Rebecca Nerison, Ph.D. describes as the "three deadly Ps: perfectionism, procrastination, and paralysis." These qualities plague lawyers, because, Nerison explains that the work lawyers do is important. Clients expect lawyers to know the answers and to achieve agreed-upon outcomes. If we are honest, lawyers like to be perfectionists. And so do paralegals.

Legal employers like to hire perfectionists. Consider the following job ad:

PARALEGAL—GENERAL PRACTICE LAW FIRM

General practice attorney seeks paralegal for 30 hours per week. The ideal candidate will be organized, detail-oriented, a perfectionist, and have excellent communication skills on the telephone and in person.

This law firm is advertising for the quality of perfectionism in a paralegal. Perfectionism is such an important trait to talk about that we devote an entire chapter to it later in the book. Clients desire this trait, legal professionals desire this trait, but as good as it is to agonize over the details, sometimes being a perfectionist can slow progress. Perfectionism has drawbacks. According to Nerison, perfectionism can cause you to

- Take more time on little or inconsequential tasks
- Lose perspective
- Spend time for which the employer cannot or will not be paid
- Continue working and reworking something beyond the point of diminishing returns
- Procrastinate

The desire to be perfect can cause you to procrastinate starting a project. New attorneys receive little or no training in law school regarding personnel management and do not learn routine tasks performed in a law firm, such as filing a lawsuit. They must figure out project and time management on their own. Add these issues to the pressures of practicing law and sometimes the following problems cause work to slow down or to stop:

- The lawyer does not have enough support staff.
- The support staff is not sufficiently trained.
- The lawyer simply does not know *how* to complete a task.
- The lawyer is working right up to the deadline, making every effort to produce a perfect result.
- The desire to produce a perfect result stops the lawyer from beginning the project until the deadline looms and the project absolutely has to be finished.

Recognizing that lack of training and on-the-job challenges affect lawyers' day-to-day behavior will help paralegals develop specific traits that benefit the lawyer's legal practice and that lead to a successful paralegal career.

■ PARALEGALS NEED TO BE CONFIDENT

Lawyers and paralegals need enough self-confidence to do their jobs well. Attorneys recognize that the people they serve—clients, in-house employees, citizens—have an expectation that the attorney and the office staff will be correct and be as near perfect as possible. Anything less is unacceptable.

Attorneys seek support staff who recognize the expectations that clients have and strive to do their best all the time. Like attorneys, paralegals can use their professionally written resumes, membership and participation in professional organizations, choice of clothing and hairstyle, and posture to provide a confident first impression. Beyond the first impression, paralegals and attorneys must reinforce this confidence with good skills.

Paralegals must have enough self-confidence to gain the trust of lawyers and of clients. Developing good communication practices and working relationships with colleagues helps build mutual trust and respect.

As you develop working relationships with your colleagues, you will develop communication strategies that make your styles mesh. Meshing communication styles means you are preparing yourself and the rest of the legal team to handle stressful situations and to avoid the loss of productivity when miscommunication occurs. The practice of law can be intense; not every day will be organized and structured. If you are able to present an attitude at work that others view as capable, organized, and open to collaboration, you will find that you handle high-pressure situations more easily than others who do not have a similar attitude.

When clashes of opinions occur—and they will—you will be prepared to calmly explain yourself or your work and to jump in and remedy the problem, because solving problems is the heart of the legal profession.

PRACTICE NOTE

Asking good questions is a sign of competence and confidence. If you never ask any questions because you are afraid of being wrong, your supervisors will never know if you truly understand the complexity of what they have asked you to do. **Taking notes** shows that you are preparing to do the work correctly and that you are properly focused on the task at hand.

■ PARALEGALS NEED TO BE RELIABLE

You can become a reliable paralegal by doing what you say you will do *when* you say you will do it. Never promise anything you cannot deliver.

Develop a reputation of reliability:

- Learn and stay on top of the trends and technology in your specialty area.
- Communicate regularly and clearly with colleagues, including supervising attorneys, other paralegals, support staff in every area, and vendors you hire to do specific tasks.
- Participate in professional organizations and take part in continuing legal education.
- Be proactive in identifying problems, communicating the issues effectively, and identifying solutions whenever possible.

As attorneys learn to trust that you will deliver on time what you say you will, that you will ask questions when you need more information, and that you will communicate progress and problems regularly, your reputation as a reliable paralegal will emerge.

■ PARALEGALS NEED TO BE ORGANIZED

For paralegals, being organized requires much more than knowing how to sort out a case file or keep a neat desk, although these things are important. Being organized is so important

IN PRACTICE

When You Have a "Dumb" Question

When you have a question that you are certain might make you appear "dumb" to someone in your office, call another legal professional you trust. The other person can provide the answer for you or give you the assurance that your question is one that needs to be asked.

Having another legal professional you can call when you forget how to do something seemingly simple is a good trick to maintaining a good reputation in your own office.

When you do call a friend, however, make sure that you never violate an attorney-client confidence or share proprietary information.

Be willing to reciprocate when that person or someone else calls you seeking the same kind of assistance. Be willing to give a little in order to get a little.

IN PRACTICE

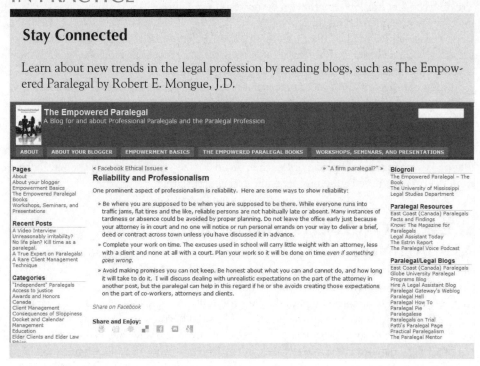

Stay Connected

Learn about new trends in the legal profession by reading blogs, such as The Empowered Paralegal by Robert E. Mongue, J.D.

that we provide two chapters about organizing your workspace and your time. But organization involves more than keeping a neat office and maintaining accurate billing records.

Being organized extends to two areas of growing importance in the legal profession: being a good project manager and knowing how to collaborate with others. These areas are growing concerns in legal practices nationwide, so be careful to watch for information about these trends in your specialty area.

Project Management

Paralegals are rarely in charge of a case, but they often *manage* significant portions of a case. Project managers plan, organize, and coordinate the resources needed to complete a task or project. Litigation paralegals manage document productions; corporate paralegals manage licensing activities; personal injury paralegals manage obtaining and reviewing medical records; and so on.

Project management requires the following steps:

- Developing a plan for achieving the goal
- Building a team, when necessary, to help achieve the goal or being part of the team that will achieve the goal
- Identifying weaknesses in the team's efforts and strategizing how to overcome these weaknesses
- Communicating to the team and to the supervising attorney

Paralegals who have good project management skills will emerge as leaders within large firms and as valued colleagues in solo or small law offices.

Collaboration

Paralegals and lawyers work collaboratively all day. Being able to get along with others and being responsible for your contribution to a collaborative project shows you are responsible and reliable. Collaboration, however, inevitably brings conflict, and paralegals need

PRACTICE NOTE

Part of your job as a paralegal may be to help keep an attorney or an office organized. Recognize organizational skills as something you must have to succeed in the legal profession.

to be able to distinguish between good conflict and bad conflict. Good conflict challenges a team to do a better job or achieve a better result for a client. Bad conflict causes bickering over inconsequential matters.

For example, good conflict usually involves the substance of a case: *What graphic is needed to illustrate a point? Which expert witness needs to be involved? How should our client's estate be structured?* Good conflict leads to a stronger result.

Bad conflict involves inconsequential matters: *Why are you putting Post-it notes on my desk when you know I am out of the office working on something else? You cannot roll into the office at 10 o'clock and then expect me to stay late.* Bad conflict is often personal.

Learning to work together and to stay focused on the substantive issues is important for successful collaboration. Letting go of the personal issues that create bad conflict makes a happier workplace, unless the personal issues are influencing the substantive work. If so, then those issues must be addressed appropriately.

■ PARALEGALS NEED TO UNDERSTAND LAW AS A BUSINESS

Many people think of the practice of law as a professional endeavor that helps society. This idea is lofty and may be why you chose to attend paralegal school, but the reality is that only one type of currency pays the monthly bills in a law office: cash. Lawyers and paralegals must understand that the practice of law is a business.

Law firms pressure associates to be profitable from the day they arrive at the firm, but other legal departments need to focus on cost and efficiency as well. An in-house legal department that becomes too costly may find its services outsourced. The district attorney's office has an ethical obligation to use tax money wisely. Non-profit organizations prefer to spend their money on services rather than legal fees. Regardless of *where* you work, paying attention to the bottom line is an important part of the workday.

A myth in the field is that paralegals save law firms money, but that is simply not true; paralegals are *profit centers* for law firms. Paralegals bill their time to clients, just as attorneys do. Clients save money. Organizations that hire paralegals save money. Paralegals bring efficiency to the legal practice. Attorneys specialize in case strategy, and paralegals specialize in case management, but always for the same goals.

Just because you are a *profit center* does not mean you should only accept work that can be billed to a client; you need to know and understand your employer's expectations. You may find that half your job is billable and the other half is administrative. For example, some paralegals work in the law library, maintain files, or prepare the outgoing/incoming mail each day. In smaller firms, the paralegal may be in charge of marketing, reception, mail, and other office management. These jobs are not billable to clients, but must be done in order for the law firm to function.

ETHICS TIP

Compensation Lawyers cannot share fees with someone who is not a lawyer; compensation cannot be calculated as a percentage of the settlement or a percentage of billable hours. Lawyers can and do take into consideration the value of a paralegal's contribution to a case or the general business of the firm when determining whether to award a performance bonus at the end of the year.

Law Firm Billing Practices

To get a sense of law firm billing practices, examine the American Bar Association's (ABA) Model Rules of Professional Conduct. The rules can be viewed online at the ABA's Center for Professional Responsibility website, http://www.americanbar.org/cpr. Your state will have its own variation of these rules, and when you begin working for a firm that bills time to clients, you need to understand these rules.

Missouri v Jenkins and *Richelin v Chertoff* allow attorneys to charge for paralegal time at market rates. Therefore, the law firm does not just recoup what they have paid the paralegal for salary and benefits, but also generates income for the firm. Firms are allowed to charge a higher hourly rate for paralegal time because paralegals perform substantive legal work that, without the paralegal, the attorney would have to do. This does not include work that might be considered secretarial in nature, such as typing documents and making copies.

How are market rates determined? The common method is by determining the cost of the paralegal's salary plus benefits and breaking that down into a per hour rate. This amount is then multiplied by three and allocated as follows: 1/3 for salary and benefits, 1/3 for overhead associated with the paralegal (such as office space, equipment and supplies), and 1/3 for profit. This method is known as the Rule of Three, and under this method, the paralegal should generate income for the firm at three times salary and benefits.

For example, if your salary is $42,000 annually, the firm might expect to generate billing of $126,000 per year, or three times your salary. By using a billing rate of $75 per hour and an expectation that you will bill at least 1,700 hours per year (35 hours per week for 50 weeks), you will bring in $127,500.

ETHICS TIP

Business Relationships Paralegals and attorneys cannot enter into business relationships if any activity of the business involves the practice of law. Partnerships and business interests not related to the practice of law are permitted (e.g., joint ownership of a building).

PARALEGAL **PROFILE**

Zachary W. Brewer, CP

Current position: Paralegal
Employer: Richards & Connor, PLLP
Years in this position: 2
Years of paralegal experience: 2
Certifications: Certified Paralegal – National Association of Legal Assistants/Paralegals
Education:
A.A., History, Tulsa Community College
B.A., History, University of Tulsa
Teacher Certification in Secondary Education, Northeastern States University
Paralegal Studies at Tulsa Community College

Zachary Brewer left a teaching career to become a paralegal. He shares what he learned along the way.

Zachary W. Brewer, CP, is a paralegal with Richards & Connor, PLLP in Tulsa, OK where he specializes in medical malpractice and insurance defense.

One of the riskiest moves Zachary ever made was leaving his teaching job to become a paralegal. It is a move he does not regret. Here are seven things he learned along the way.

1. If you are even entertaining the idea of a career change, odds are you are not enjoying your job. Changing careers is a very tough decision to make, and scary as well. I know, because I left the security of a teaching job (with government benefits) to go back to school to become a paralegal. I didn't even have a job when I decided to do it.

2. Once you make the decision to change careers, you have done the hardest part. It is not easy, but [cliché alert!] nothing worth doing ever is (or so I've heard).

3. Try to work in a law firm in some capacity, be it runner, file clerk, or even receptionist. The more you are around that environment, the more you can learn.

4. Go to a good paralegal training program and work hard. The teachers in these programs are often attorneys and experienced paralegals. Make an impression and make connections!

5. After you complete the coursework, study for and take either the NALA CLA/CP Exam or the NFPA PACE Exam. Those credentials are becoming the standard for paralegals in today's legal work place.

6. Join at least one professional organization; both national and local memberships would be ideal. You can network and learn valuable tips from fellow paralegals.

7. New paralegals should know that the first few months are a struggle and adjustment. Be confident in your abilities, but do not try to do more than you are ready to do or more than you are asked. Attorneys want you to do what they have told you to do. Less is never acceptable, but sometimes doing more can cause more harm than good. Be sure to clear "extra" tasks with your attorney before starting. They will likely be impressed with your initiative and agreeable to your doing them. If you develop a good working relationship with your attorney(s), work in the legal profession as a paralegal can be a rewarding and exciting career change. I'm glad I did it, and I would be willing to bet you will be too.

The current economic situation in the U.S. means that this billing formula might be modified somewhat, depending on the needs of the firm. Law firm management determines how to leverage the talent and skill of the staff to maximize resources. Maximizing resources is one way that a firm can remain profitable during an economic downturn.

■ PARALEGALS NEED TO BE ENTREPRENEURIAL

Forty years ago, young associates—and their paralegals—could expect to work for one firm until retirement, but now the schizophrenic economy causes law firms to downsize, merge, and constantly reinvent the firm's image and goals. According to *USA Today*, however, the newest generation of lawyers is not looking to adopt the old-school practice of depending on one firm for lifetime employment. *USA Today* reports that Generation Y, the so-called "echo boomers" are taking a very entrepreneurial approach to work.

Members of this generation, "...armed with a hefty dose of optimism, moxie and self-esteem...are becoming entrepreneurs" (Jayson). The underlying assumption is that instead of taking on the old-school firm and adopting its culture, this generation of lawyers is creating a new culture at work.

That lawyers are becoming more adventurous and entrepreneurial is good news for paralegals because the most successful paralegals *always* have been entrepreneurial. The most classic example is the paralegal who works for a traditional law firm but wants to switch practice areas. This paralegal seeks out opportunities to take on small tasks in new practice areas to build skills and expertise. The transition might occur slowly, but by proactively offering services to a different practice area, the paralegal can take advantage of an opportunity to move to that practice group should it arise.

Another example is a paralegal who becomes—literally—an entrepreneur by establishing a freelance paralegal business. This paralegal offers services to one or more law firms. In the new millennium, the freelance paralegal is redefining this role again. Today, we are beginning to see paralegals build very successful virtual practices. Virtual paralegals are available to assist law firms worldwide.

Paralegals have the opportunity to write their own career paths, depending on market conditions in the area where they live and/or work. This opportunity has positive consequences. A paralegal can begin as a paralegal but expand out of that role into other areas: law library management, paralegal/law office management, banking, insurance, risk assessment, court administration, and expert witness support, etc.

Initially, the lack of a set career path can be daunting, and figuring out how to fit in may seem overwhelming. If the firm does not have a paralegal career track—and most do not—you will want to use the advice in later chapters for setting your own goals and determining your own career track.

■ MOST IMPORTANTLY, BE FLEXIBLE

Successful paralegals learn to be flexible. Be open to learning new things and taking on new challenges.

Sometimes getting comfortable with an attorney or team of attorneys and developing a sense of confidence takes time, but during that time, you can build your reputation. As your reputation builds, so will your career.

CONCLUSION

Paralegals and attorneys work to achieve the same goals, but their education, roles, and expectations of each other are different. The stress of needing to achieve specific goals for clients as well as managing the business of law creates a high-stakes atmosphere that can be exciting and unpredictable. Paralegals need to be confident, reliable, and organized as well as understand the business of the legal profession. Knowing how to approach your own work entrepreneurially can lead to new opportunities at work and within the profession.

Checklist for Success

☐ Understand how lawyers are trained and what that means at work.

☐ Recognize that attorneys are not trained in office management or human resources.

☐ Appreciate the expectation that attorneys and paralegals need to be "perfect," but set realistic goals and help attorneys and yourself overcome the drawbacks to perfectionism.

☐ Be confident enough to ask good questions.

☐ Develop a resource bank of go-to people for questions that seem basic and you feel embarrassed to ask at work.

☐ Build a core skill set that complements your colleagues' working styles.

☐ If possible, learn about the firm's financial strategy and how your billable hours are calculated.

☐ Determine the firm's or department's pressures so that you can prioritize your work.

☐ Review the ethical rules for supervision in your state and make sure you are adequately supervised.

☐ Determine how your value is calculated. Is your time billed? Do you have to report or tabulate how you spend your time?

☐ As you begin to find your place at the office, look for a person who might serve as a good mentor.

☐ Become reliable by delivering work when you say you will.

☐ Bring an entrepreneurial mindset to your work and provide the best service you can to the attorneys you support.

ASSIGNMENTS: PREPARING FOR YOUR PARALEGAL CAREER

Career Management

Create a master list of blogs that you should read each week and place the list in a separate section of your career management notebook. Use tabs to keep information organized as your notebook grows. Prepare your master list with the following information:

- Blog title
- Uniform Record Locator (URL/web address)
- Author's name and credentials (Skip blogs that are written anonymously)
- Purpose: Write a 3-sentence description about the purpose of the blog.
- Write 1–2 sentences about why you are including this blog on your list.
- Mix up your list and choose paralegal and non-paralegal blogs.

Schedule time in your week to read blogs that have information useful to you as you begin your career.

Report

Find the ethics rules in your state (or the state where you plan to work) related to one paralegal issue: billing, types of work permitted, confidentiality, or another issue. Identify one actual or potential ethical dilemma that might occur and use the rules to determine how the dilemma should be resolved. Prepare a memorandum to your instructor that summarizes the ethical rule, describes the dilemma, and explains one potential resolution to the problem.

Network

Prepare for the inevitable—the day you do not know an answer. Sometimes, it feels embarrassing to ask questions at work. In the following situations, which questions are important to ask at work, and which questions can you ask someone you trust to help you so you do not appear clueless on the job.

a. You do not remember what a Motion to Quash is. Who would you ask? Why?
b. You have been asked to pull a key document in a case and mail it to several people. You are not sure whether you have the correct document. Who would you ask? Why?
c. You need to have a subpoena served this afternoon. The attorney says to use the usual delivery service. At lunch, a paralegal friend mentions a speedy hand delivery service that she loves—and they just brought her a box of candy. Do you use the speedy service your friend mentioned or do you ask someone at your firm who to call for subpoenas?

Prepare

Write a paragraph about the things that you do that help you feel confident. Which of these things will translate to showing confidence at work? What kinds of things can you do when you do not feel confident?

INTERNET RESOURCES

Paralegal Gateway: *http://www.paralegalgateway.com*
The U.S. Bureau of Labor Statistics: *http://www.bls.gov*

American Bar Association's Center for Professional Responsibility: *http://www.americanbar.org/cpr*
JD Bliss: Balancing Life and the Law: *http://www.jdblissblog.com*

REFERENCES

Nerison, R. (2010, May 12). "Three Deadly Ps: Perfectionism, Procrastination, Paralysis." ABA Book Briefs. Retrieved from: http://www2.americanbar.org/publishing/bookbriefsblog/Lists/Posts/Post.aspx?ID=153

Jayson, S. (2006, June 12). "Gen Y Makes a Mark and Their Imprint is Entrepreneurship." USAToday.com. *USA Today.* Retrieved from http://www.usatoday.com/news/nation/2006-12-06-gen-next-entrepreneurs_x.htm

CHAPTER **4**

SUCCESSFUL JOB SEARCH STRATEGIES

For several years, the paralegal profession has ranked among the fastest growing of all professions in the U.S. The following significant points were emphasized by the Bureau of Labor Statistics (BLS) of the U.S. Department of Labor when describing the paralegal profession in the 2010–2011 edition of its Occupational Outlook Handbook:

- Employment growth is projected, but paralegals should expect a competitive job market.
- Paralegals with formal training and experience may find the best employment opportunities.
- Most paralegals entering the profession have an associate degree in paralegal studies or a bachelor's degree in another field and a certificate in paralegal studies.
- About 7 out of 10 paralegals work for law firms; others work for corporate legal departments and government agencies.

Despite recent economic issues, the paralegal field is experiencing "faster-than-average employment growth" according to the BLS. However, because many people are trying to enter the profession, the job market will remain competitive. The BLS reports that "Employers are trying to reduce costs and increase the availability and efficiency of legal services by hiring paralegals to perform tasks once done by lawyers. Paralegals are performing a wider variety of duties, making them more useful to businesses."

The Bureau of Labor Statistics further states that "paralegals and legal assistants held about 263,800 jobs in 2008." If you are obtaining a degree or a certificate in paralegal studies, you are on the right track. According to the Bureau of Labor Statistics, "experienced, formally trained paralegals should have the best employment opportunities" in the paralegal field.

By the end of this chapter, you should be able to:

- Identify and discuss existing paralegal career opportunities
- Describe key elements of a job search
- Understand the benefits and methods of expanding a job search
- Utilize social media to increase networking efforts
- Recognize positive and negative effects of social media on a paralegal career

■ FINDING CAREER OPPORTUNITIES

To find a paralegal position in your area of the country, determine how jobs are advertised. Every region has its go-to place for finding up-to-date paralegal listings. Right away, before you finish school, you need to find out where the job postings are in your area. Some key places to look include:

- Your personal network. Friends, relatives, and other acquaintances often know of job openings and may be willing to recommend you for a job. Many law offices want to hire based on a recommendation from someone else.
- Your paralegal program or campus career center. You may find a database of job openings at the career center. Plan to check these listings regularly.
- Local paralegal association. Local paralegal organizations sometimes manage job boards or post jobs in their newsletters and on their websites.
- Legal news publications and their associated websites. Check, for instance, the Law. com Network at *www.law.com*
- Local newspaper classifieds and online job boards. Be sure to check these resources in your areas. For example, check *www.bostonworks.com* if you wish to work in the Boston area.
- Paralegal temporary agencies. Temporary agencies usually post opportunities online. For instance, *www.specialcounsel.com* maintains a database of paralegal positions.
- Governmental agencies. Federal positions are listed at *www.usajobs.gov*. You may also find job listings with your state governmental agencies at your state's website (such as *www.mich.gov*).
- Publications and websites that advertise jobs for various entities. These websites will have job postings for banks, corporations, universities, hospitals, and other employers who hire paralegals, such as *www.lawcrossing.com*

IN PRACTICE

Analyzing the Job Market in Your Region

To analyze the job market in your region, study job advertisements as if you are a scientist:

- Count how many positions are available during a given time period.
- Catalog the areas of law the positions are for: litigation, general paralegal, real estate, intellectual property, and so on.
- Make a list of the skills the jobs require.

Analyzing the Skills Employers Desire in Your Region

Collect five to ten job advertisements for positions for which you are (or soon will be) eligible. Use advertisements for jobs in your area. Do not pull advertisements for positions in other parts of the country for this analysis. Make a list of the skills required and preferred by each employer. Compare this list of skills to your own skills. Do you need to learn any new skills? What can you do now to prepare for the job market?

Where you find job listings will vary based on your geographic region. Ask working legal professionals for suggestions about how to start your job search. Use online search tools to help find information related to your location.

In every region of the U.S., one way to find jobs is by networking and via word of mouth. Some areas of the country *prefer* to hire through personal reference rather than advertising a position and having to sift through resumes. Because these positions are not advertised, getting to know (and maintaining contact with) your classmates, as well as people you meet at educational events and during volunteer or internship work, is very important.

Understand the Job Market in Your Geographic Region

Before you leave school—ideally before you even enter, but it may be too late for that—you want to examine very carefully the job prospects in your area. Working as a paralegal can be a vastly different experience in different cities. As you prepare for the job market, think about the kinds of jobs you might get as a paralegal in your area.

Consider other factors that will affect your study of the job market: Where do you live? Will you work in this area as well? What is the legal profession like where you live? If you want to relocate, where will that be? If you are a seasoned paralegal and you relocate, are you willing to start over at the bottom and work your way up?

Because law is a service industry, you need to watch trends and hone your skills to fit the "hot" areas because this is where hiring will take place. The practice sectors listed in Table 4-1 follow a trending cycle, according to the 2011 report by Robert Denney Associates, Inc., a firm that provides strategic management and marketing counsel to law firms.

Consider Your Options

If you cannot find the paralegal position you want right away, you may be able to transfer your skills to another industry, such as insurance, banking, or real estate. Any of these industries might provide the rewarding work that you are seeking, and your paralegal, research, writing and technical skills will help you break into these fields. Paralegal skills

TABLE 4-1 Practice Sectors In and Out of Demand

Hottest areas:	Getting hot:
• Healthcare	• Corporate
• Alternative Dispute Resolution	• Financial Services
• Federal and State Regulatory Law	
	Cooling off:
Hot:	• Patent Litigation
• White-Collar Crime	• Gaming
• Bankruptcy	• Real Estate
• Energy/Alternative Energy	• Patent Prosecution
• Labor & Employment	
• Public Finance	Getting cold:
• Litigation	• Tax, Trust, and Estate Planning
• Immigration	• Elder Law
• Emerging Companies/Entrepreneurial	

are among the most transferrable. Fifty jobs where paralegal skills transfer include the following:

- Auditor
- Bank officer
- Claims adjuster, appraiser, examiner, and investigator
- Computer forensic analyst
- Conflicts analyst
- Corporate or executive assistant
- Court clerk
- Designer and developer of visual exhibits for trial
- Employment benefits specialist or administrator
- Employment/temporary agency career specialist
- Equal employment opportunity specialist
- Estate administrator
- Evidence technician
- Grant writer
- Grants and contracts manager
- Insurance agent
- Investigator
- Jury consultant
- Law firm or corporate trainer
- Corrections officer
- Law librarian
- Legal secretary
- Legal technology specialist
- Legislative analyst
- Litigation support services representative
- Loan interviewer
- Lobbyist or advocate for public interest
- Mediator
- Mortgage processor
- Municipal clerk
- Occupational health and safety specialist
- Paralegal education specialist or instructor
- Parole or probation officer
- Patent database administrator
- Pharmaceutical sales representative
- Professional or trade association manager
- Public relations for law firm or legal services company
- Real estate agent, broker, or assistant
- Regulatory affairs for pharmaceutical research and development
- Risk management analyst
- Sales representative for legal software or litigation support
- Securities analyst
- Small business owner
- Tax preparer
- Technical communicator
- Technology licensing associate
- Title examiner, abstractor, and researcher
- Trademark search specialist
- Trust administrator
- Writer or editor for legal or business publisher

IN PRACTICE

Studying Job Ads

You May Have Transferrable Skills or You May Want to Mesh Two Career Paths

If you are completing paralegal school, but have had a career in another field, you most likely have what people call *transferrable skills*. These are skills that you gained in one field or job that can be useful in another field. The paralegal profession also provides opportunities to meld experience in one field with a legal career.

Compliance managers, for example, ensure that organizations participating in research and development are complying with the terms of grant funding and any local, state, or federal regulations that apply.

Some compliance managers focus on federal ethics rules that apply to research involving people or animals, while others concentrate on financial aspects of complying with research and development. They work for univer-

sities, research and development organizations, hospitals, and privately owned entities.

Qualifications for compliance managers include the following:

- Bachelor's degree
- Written and oral communication skills
- Ability to manage budgets
- Ability to draft clauses for agreements or contracts
- Negotiation skills
- Familiarity with federal laws related to research with humans and animals
- Ability to work independently
- Organizational skills and ability to multitask

A paralegal possesses many of these skills and would be a terrific hire for this sort of position.

To determine whether you are qualified for these positions, or to learn how to become qualified for these positions, examine the requirements that employers list in their advertisements. You may find that while you do not know much about a particular field, your paralegal education and experience make you a match for a position.

■ PREPARING FOR YOUR JOB SEARCH

When you gear up for a job search, you must organize your tools. For each type of job you would like to pursue, you need a resume, a goal, and a strategy. For example, if you are looking for real estate paralegal positions with law firms *and* with banks, you are conducting two job searches in distinctly different industries. For each type of search you conduct, you will need a resume tailored to that search. In this case, you would need a resume tailored for law firms and another tailored for banks.

The resume you design should be directly tied to your level of expertise and experience. The following guidelines are based on years of professional experience:

Entry-Level Job Seekers:

- Use a 1-page resume.
- Define your goal: Are you trying to break into the field? Will you do anything to make that happen?
- Figure out your salary/benefits requirements.
- Ask the people you know to answer your questions, including faculty, human resources departments, and professional organizations in your area.
- Figure out how your skills transfer. Be able to explain in 6 seconds and 20 seconds.
- Generally, the resumes for individuals falling into this category list the education section before the work history section.
- Play online games to practice interviewing and negotiating.

PRACTICE NOTE

THE JOB vs. *A* JOB

Before you start your job search, consider whether you are looking for *a* job or *the* job.

A job keeps you going. It allows you to pay for food, housing, and clothing.

The job, on the other hand, is the job that makes you so happy you get out of bed each day without an alarm clock.

IN PRACTICE

Seven Strategies for a Quick Start

Try these seven strategies for making your job search a success:

1. **Know your market.** Do some research to determine what employers want. Craft your resume and your job search so that you are the perfect candidate for those jobs.
2. **Prepare an inventory.** Make a detailed list of your skills, experience, accomplishments, interests, goals, and values. Be able to communicate, both verbally and in writing, how you are the unique and perfect candidate for a job.
3. **Develop a plan.** Begin with a clear, concise resume and a concise letter of application that states how your qualifications match job requirements. Avoid cluttered communication.
4. **Get the word out.** Let people know that you are looking for employment. Include friends, colleagues, neighbors, members of your professional association, former professors, and classmates. Your network is an important piece of your job search plan.
5. **Boost your network.** Register for job search newsletters and e-mail blasts. Post on social networking sites such as Facebook, Twitter, LinkedIn, and YouTube. Be sure to actively participate in Internet discussion boards and forums.
6. **Do not wait for opportunity to knock at your door.** Make your own opportunities by being persistent, assertive, and proactive. Make those cold calls to potential employers. As intimidating as that might be, it is important for two reasons: first, you need to beat your competition to the draw; and second, it demonstrates to the potential employers that you are serious.
7. **Keep track of your progress.** Maintain detailed records of the jobs you have applied for and the outcomes—interviews, rejections, offers, etc.

Job Seekers with 3 to 5 Years in the Legal Profession

- Still use a 1-page resume.
- Define your goal: Are you looking for *a* job or *the* job?
- Be able to recite your track record in 6 seconds, 45 seconds, and 90 seconds.
- Have a one-sentence wrap-up pitch: "I can offer your firm…"
- Generally, the resumes for individuals falling into this category list work history before the education section.

Job Seekers with a Decade or More in the Legal Profession:

- Never underestimate the power of a 1-page resume. Yours will look *very* different from an entry-level resume, but a 1-page resume will be a powerful tool for you. Depending on your experience, your resume may be a two-pager.
- Define your goal: Are you looking for *a* job or *the* job?
- Focus on your goal of getting a specific kind of position.
- Prepare your pitch. Your track record is clear or you would not be invited for an interview. Know how to finish this sentence: "I can offer your firm …"

■ ORGANIZING YOUR JOB SEARCH

Make your search easier by getting organized from the start. A good way to do this is to set up a system that will serve your career, not just this job search.

Set Your Goal

First, determine your goal. Do you currently have a job? Do you need *a* job? Are you looking for *the* job? Decide which kind of job you are looking for:

A Job: You will take any job because you are new to the profession and want to gain experience, you need a job because you are not currently working, or you despise your current work situation and will do anything to make a move.

The Job: You have a job or a situation that does not require a fast move toward employment, so you have time to find the job you consider ideal. When you are looking for *the* job, you may have to look long and hard for it. When you are looking for *the* job, you may have to take *a* job.

That Job: You see a job advertisement that interests you, and you want to learn more about this position. What is a typical day like? How much does this position pay? You might not have been looking for a job until you saw this position, but now you are considering applying. What should you do next?

Create One E-mail Account to Manage the Process

Set up a free web-based e-mail account (Gmail, Yahoo!, Hotmail) so you can check your e-mail from any location.

Do not use your school e-mail account for job searching. It is possible that when you graduate, you may lose access to your account so anyone who tries to reach you after the account is defunct may run into problems.

Never use your work e-mail account when job searching. Using your work account is unethical and unprofessional and shows that you use work resources for personal gain, even if you do all the work for your job search at home. Like students who graduate and move on, if you are job searching, you are preparing for your current work to end. When it does, your e-mail account will also end.

Last, pay attention to the name you use for the e-mail account you set up for yourself. Be professional. Our e-mail addresses, *charlsye.smith@gmail.com* or *vicki@paralegalmentor.com*, are better choices than these that we have seen:

redraiderQT@email.com

pianogod@email.com

PandSforever@email.com

These e-mail addresses are like vanity license plates: inside jokes to a few and confusing to everyone else.

Another common mistake in creating e-mail addresses is using your birth year:

JulieSmith1980@email.com

Do not do this. Even though employers are not supposed to discriminate based on age, do not offer up the information. Instead, try an e-mail address like this:

Julie.A.Smith@email.com

Create a Job Search Log

Only a few years ago, your job search would have consisted of writing a letter, photocopying your resume, and mailing the whole package to a potential employer. Now, you can apply for jobs by mailing a letter and resume or by applying online. Some companies are so sophisticated that you can complete a profile and then indicate with a click of a few buttons the positions for which you would like to apply.

To keep track of your job search, create and maintain a job application log that includes sections for the job title, company name, any contact you know there, and notes about results. Results might include telephone calls, e-mail responses, interviews, and follow-ups:

Position	Firm/Company	Contact	Date Applied	Results/Notes
Paralegal	Jones, Day	Beverly Lee	4/22	Interview on 4/29

Use a word processing program or Excel spreadsheet to set up your log. Excel offers filtering capabilities.

Follow the Rules

Some employers like to see if you can follow instructions, so follow their guidelines precisely when applying for a position. For example, when you see a job posting that says, "No phone calls, please," then, DO NOT CALL. If the ad asks for resumes to be mailed, do not send yours by fax or e-mail.

Define Your Face-to-Face Network

When should you begin developing a network of contacts? Immediately, of course. You began developing a network when you enrolled in school and introduced yourself. No, not paralegal school—kindergarten. Sure, the children you tracked Big Foot with may or may not be connected to the legal profession, but your network can be as wide as you want or need it to be. Even if you currently work in business, industry, government, etc., these people may have contacts in the legal community. To expand your paralegal network, try:

- Joining a paralegal association and attending their events, including their continuing education programs.
- Volunteering with organizations that use paralegals. In Connecticut, for instance, one of the power companies asks paralegals to help with its annual day-long event where people can negotiate the cost of their winter heating bills.
- Attending all continuing legal education events available to you, even if you are still in school.
- Reading *Lawyers Weekly* and other legal publications, especially publications that cover your local area.
- Using social networking sites to meet other legal professionals.

To maximize your network, you need to spend some face-to-face time with people as a volunteer, working on temporary projects, or even offering free labor. You want others to see what you can do. Being able to say, "I worked with Tina on a fundraiser and she's looking for a job," is a much better statement to a potential employer than, "I know someone who is looking for a job but I've never worked with her." The first sentence is positive. The second seems cautionary.

■ EXPANDING YOUR JOB SEARCH BY "TEMPING"

Temporary work, or "temping" is a great way to get yourself noticed at the beginning of your career and it enables you to taste life at different offices. By temping, you may find an office where you fit better than you would have by taking the first job you are offered.

Temporary work allows you to get your foot in the door of an office that might not hire a person without any (or much) experience. Instead of feeling like a victim of the I-can't-get-a-job-without-experience-and-I-can't-get-any-experience-without-a-job syndrome, you can take charge of the beginning of your career by temping.

Becoming a temporary paralegal requires being proactive. Temporary positions do not fall into your lap, so you must decide you are going to look for this work and then actively seek it out.

These are the steps to take to getting your first temporary paralegal position:

Update your resume so that you show your paralegal skills, even if you are just starting your career. Your resume should *look like* you want to be a paralegal, even if you are making a career change. You want to highlight skills that might transfer from one field to the next. For example, if you have a degree in literature, highlight your analytical skills. (Refer to Chapter 6 for more information about designing an effective resume.)

Identify temporary employment agencies that place paralegals. Include agencies that specialize in paralegal placement and agencies that work with many types of companies. These agencies are usually located in larger cities. Ask your advisors at school and members of your local paralegal organization for recommendations.

Agencies that place paralegals should offer their services to you for free. These are agencies that contract with law firms to staff large projects or to provide temporary paralegals for firms. These are not "headhunting" agencies that work for you on your behalf to find you a job. If you take a temporary assignment from an agency and develop a stellar reputation, the agency is likely to recommend you when a full-time position becomes available.

The employer pays the agency's fee. If an agency wants to charge you, check its reputation with other paralegals you know. You may also check with your local paralegal organization, or your school's career center or program director.

Special Counsel (*www.specialcounsel.com*) or Robert Half Legal (*www.roberthalflegal.com*) are agencies that places paralegals in temporary and permanent employment. Other agencies will have similar policies and procedures.

PRACTICE TIP

A Secret Benefit of Temping A secret benefit to working as a temporary paralegal early in your career is that if you find yourself laid off or extremely unhappy in a year or so, you can go back to temping or you can ask the agency to help you find new permanent employment. A good reputation as a temp makes the agency more than happy to help place you.

PARALEGAL **PROFILE**

Libby Pace, M.A.

Current position: Paralegal

Employer: Los Angeles County Public Defender, Public Integrity Assurance Section

Years in this position: 2.5 years

Years of paralegal experience: 5.5 years

Total years in the legal profession: 6.5 years

Education:

M.A., Organizational Leadership, Woodbury University, 2010

B.A., Business Management, Webster University, 2006

Paralegal Certificate, California State University, 2004

Networking with people you know can lead your career in interesting directions, as Libby Pace, M.A., has learned.

Before she found her place in law, Libby worked as a researcher for film, television, books, museums, visitor centers, and other groups worldwide. After being laid off from this position, she began a paralegal certificate program and applied to an employment firm specializing in the legal field. Her first position was as a temp interviewing plaintiffs in a pharmaceutical case at a class-action law firm.

While walking to her car after work, she would occasionally run into a classmate from paralegal school who worked nearby. One evening the classmate mentioned that his firm, a major brokerage house, was looking for a file clerk in the legal department. Libby's temporary assignment was wrapping up but she didn't yet have a paralegal certificate—a requirement in California, so she applied for the position. With her classmate's recommendation, she was hired.

After she received her paralegal certificate from California State University in Los Angeles, Libby was promoted to paralegal. When the attorney she worked for left the brokerage house to start a solo practice, he took her with him—for a salary increase.

Libby currently works for the Los Angeles County Public Defender, the largest criminal law firm in the country, with 750 attorneys and 75 paralegals in 40 offices covering 4,000 square miles. Her main duties are drafting motions; interviewing clients, family, and witnesses; and researching and writing mitigation reports for post-conviction sentence relief. In addition, she writes procedural manuals and grant proposals, and presents training seminars to paralegals and attorneys. She is a member of the Public Defender's Paralegal Training Committee, and Libby gives back to the profession as an adjunct instructor with the ABA-approved paralegal program at California State University in Los Angeles.

Research each agency. This can easily be done online. Pay particular attention to each agency's requirements and instructions for applications.

Follow up with a phone call after the agency has had time to receive your materials. Ask politely to speak to a recruiter and explain that you are looking for temporary work.

The next steps vary from agency to agency:

Expect to be interviewed. Follow the same standard of care in preparing for an interview with a temp agency that you would for a permanent job. (Refer to Chapter 8 for interviewing strategies.) Wear professional attire. If you are unsure, be conservative and wear a suit. Prepare extra copies of your resume. Bring your portfolio, if you have one.

Sometimes, the agency will interview you and then a potential temporary employer will want to interview you as well. Treat both interviews seriously.

Once you begin working as a temporary paralegal, stay in touch with your recruiter. Let the recruiter know when the position begins to wind down so that you can make a smooth transition to another temporary position.

It is okay to register with as many temporary agencies as you want or can find in your area. Once you begin working through one, though, you may earn certain benefits, such as paid holidays, if you stay with that agency. As you successfully complete assignments, your reputation will encourage the agency to offer you the best assignments—or permanent jobs—first.

Be nice to absolutely everyone. It is important to treat everyone well. This includes everybody from the receptionist you greet in the morning upon arrival to the last mailroom employee you see at night because they will help you when you need it—and trust us when we say, you will *always* need *something*!

■ USING SOCIAL MEDIA TO EXPAND YOUR NETWORK

Social networking sites, such as LinkedIn, Twitter, and Facebook, offer potential for getting acquainted with people who work in the legal field. This is not just limited to your own hometown, but across the country and around the world.

Your number of connections grows exponentially with each connection you make. For instance, if you have 20 connections and each of those has 20 connections who have 20 connections, etc., you can see that you have just increased your number of connections by far more than the original 20.

There are many social networking sites available, although LinkedIn, Twitter, and Facebook are considered the "Big Three." All social networking sites allow you to post information about yourself, including your education, work history, favorite music and

IN PRACTICE

Tips for Setting Up a Social Networking Account

Setting up a social networking account is fairly easy and straightforward.

First, determine your social networking goals. Will you be doing research? Are you interested in networking? What about learning? A job search? All of those? It is important that you know exactly what benefits you are seeking.

Next, go to the site you have chosen and set up your social networking account:

Twitter: *www.twitter.com*

LinkedIn: *www.linkedin.com*

Facebook: *www.facebook.com*

Choose your username. Unless you have a brand name that will identify you, your username should be your given name with no spaces or underlines, as in VickiVoisin. This will make the process of finding you much easier. If you are using Twitter, your username will be preceded by the @ symbol as this is placed before every name on Twitter. LinkedIn and Facebook do not use the @ sign. When you select a username, the site will automatically check to see if the one you have chosen is available.

Upload a picture. Try not to skip this important step. If you do not use a picture, you will be assigned a computer-generated faceless avatar. People are less likely to connect with someone if they cannot see what they look like.

Write your profile. The information you post should attract followers and reflect positively on your professional persona. Your Twitter profile will be quite short, so you have to get the most "bang for your buck" when you draft it. LinkedIn allows a more lengthy profile that really serves as an online resume. While your LinkedIn profile is not a true resume, you will want to include much of what is often put into a resume:

- Summary of your professional history
- Specialties
- Current position
- Highlights from your career (include awards)
- Significant volunteer activities, unless they are too closely related to politics, religion, or other information you prefer to keep private
- Any articles you have written
- Your education
- Any special activities

When you include a rich description, you will increase the likelihood that others will find you.

If you use Facebook, you can link your Twitter and Facebook accounts.

books, political leanings, religious preferences, and any other information you want to share with other people. You can upload pictures, post videos, join groups and causes and become a fan of many. The idea for most sites (and the thing that keeps you—and others—coming back) is reading "status updates" that offer information about how you are feeling or what you are doing right this moment.

Without a lot of effort, you are dropping clues right and left about yourself. Many companies, including law firms, use social networking sites to screen prospective hires. They may use them to check on the behavior of current employees. A simple entry of a name in the Google search box can reveal all kinds of information. Some of it may be embarrassing (refer to the section about career sabotage), but some of it may be impressive and a good way to market yourself.

Two sites that are particularly useful for paralegals are Twitter and LinkedIn.

Twitter (www.twitter.com)

Twitter is a social networking service that allows users to send messages (called "tweets") that are 140 characters in length to their friends (called "followers"). This 140-character format is unique to Twitter and allows for quick, informal sharing of information with people you would not normally include in e-mails or instant messages. By using Twitter, you expand your circle of contacts to a community of like-minded people.

Twitter offers tools that enable you to receive information about specific topics, such as paralegals, U.S. Supreme Court rulings, or quilting. There is also the capability of adding links to recent news items, stories, or articles.

Twitter can be used for both business and personal purposes. It is a great way to keep in touch with your friends and broadcast information about what you are doing. You can always share that you are eating a PB&J at your desk but, really, the BEST use of Twitter is for business purposes. Companies broadcast their latest news and blog posts. Individuals post links to their blog posts or ask for help and ideas.

When you need to make a career move, be sure to tell your Twitter friends. For example, a paralegal who was laid off from her job pulled out her cell phone and sent a tweet that said, "I need a job." She announced her need for work within a few minutes of her lay-off, even before she told her family. Before social media, laid off workers would share this news with just a few close friends and their family. Thanks to social media, the newly unemployed are able to jump-start the job search and emotional support and, perhaps, suggestions for a new job.

LinkedIn (www.linkedin.com)

LinkedIn is an online network of people all over the world. LinkedIn is probably the best known and most widely used business networking site. The concept of LinkedIn is that of "connections." Through LinkedIn you can search for jobs, easily make personal "inside" connections in relation to job opportunities, promote your qualifications, and be found and pursued for job opportunities. LinkedIn allows you to form relationships that are critical to your career success and progression.

Even if you are not conducting a current job search, any tool that helps you network more effectively and efficiently should be of great interest.

Six major benefits to using LinkedIn include the following (Alba):

1. The ability to be known and enhance your personal brand.
2. The ability to be found by recruiters or other hiring authorities.
3. The ability to find others and make important connections.
4. The opportunity to learn and share.
5. The ability to connect with group members.
6. The opportunity to show you are plugged in to current technology.

While LinkedIn (as well as Twitter) allows you to make connections, perform a job search, and be found by recruiters, the time to begin networking is BEFORE you need it.

PRACTICE NOTE

This book presents **social networking** as a way to foster professional contacts. If you have been using social networking sites for personal connections, you need to consider how you present yourself through the sites. Now is the time to declutter, defriend, and detag photographs, old status updates, and other information that does not present you as the type of professional you are. You might, for example, lock down Facebook to only your family and six closest friends and use LinkedIn and/or Twitter for professional contacts.

PRACTICE NOTE

Do not fall into the habit of updating your status with the minutia of your day. If you find yourself with nothing to say, respond to an interesting update (one with useful information) from someone else or "retweet" it.

You should begin now by setting up your account and building your network so that when you are ready to launch your job search or when you are looking for a new job, you have a network to get you started.

Both LinkedIn and Twitter are effective networking tools, but only if you use them to your full advantage.

■ WARNING: DO NOT SOCIAL NETWORK YOUR WAY TO CAREER SABOTAGE

While social networking is an important tool, it can cause problems if you are not careful. Please read the following and keep the information in mind as you post on LinkedIn, Twitter, and Facebook.

Social networking is not just about you. You really have little control over who sees your information. Your contacts have access to it. Their contacts have access. Those contacts have access. You can see how the web widens.

How much should you reveal about yourself? The answer depends on your circumstances. Does a recruiter need to know that you are 32, single, Catholic, have a mad crush on Hugh Jackman, and would throw your designer shoes at a political candidate if given a chance? Probably not.

IN PRACTICE

What to Do with Twitter and LinkedIn

Twitter

Keep your status updated on Twitter. Tweets, Twitter's name for status updates, are limited to 140 characters (including spaces and punctuation), so you must be brief and concise.

Your first tweet or two will feel strange but you will quickly get the hang of it. Just type in "Am a paralegal new to Twitter and hope to connect to others working in estate planning." Hit send and there goes your tweet. The response may surprise you. Once you get the hang of it, tweet about an article, an idea, or share a link of professional interest to your targeted followers. Many tweets will offer tips or links to articles or blog posts.

Twitter Followers: You can search for people to follow in the Find People link at the top of the Twitter page. Look for people with similar interests or experts who discuss things that interest you. Don't worry if the person you follow does not follow back. This is a terrific option with Twitter because if someone chooses to follow you, you do not have to reciprocate. You may want to ignore anyone whose profile is questionable or who is not writing about anything you are interested in reading.

You can follow topics, too. There is a search box on the Twitter page. Type in "paralegal" and all posts about paralegals will pop up. Type in "job search" and you will see all those tweets. From those tweets, you can select people to follow who are posting in an area that interests you—such as paralegal employment.

LinkedIn

After you set up your LinkedIn profile, begin adding contacts and joining groups. Perform a simple search to find people you know already and then people you would like to know better, as well as groups that fit your interests. You will have to wait for your new contacts to accept your invitation to connect. You can instantly join most groups, although some require the approval of an administrator. You will have the ability to enter your current status. You should update your status regularly—daily, if possible—as well as post statements for each group you join.

Consistency Is the Key

You will reap far more rewards from your social networking if you post often. You should set aside time every day to be involved with each social network you join. Remember that all social networking should take place outside the office and on your own time.

Tip: You can shorten any links you want to post by going to *www.snipurl.com* or *www.tinyurl.com*. The link: *http://www.paralegalmentor.com/ethical-technical-05-14-09.html* would become *http://snipurl.com/han90*. Twitter also has a feature that will automatically shorten links for you.

Information that you should keep to yourself:

- Medical information
- Plans to quit your current job
- Your love life/sexual preferences
- Politics and religion
- Salary/financial information
- Gossip
- Racially charged jokes and profanity
- Confidential work information
- Complaints about your current co-workers

Your online presence is a virtual resume. Craft your profile carefully so you reveal only positive information. Do not use a screen name that gives a poor impression. Do not post pictures or videos you would not want your mother to see. Do not work through the anger or emotional toll of a break-up with status updates. Delete any photos your friends might post that show you drinking alcohol. If any comments that can be misinterpreted are associated with your posts, delete them immediately. Choose your Facebook friends and followers on Twitter wisely. You do not have to accept every request.

Enjoy your social networking as a great way to connect with friends and colleagues. An inappropriate tweet (or post on any networking site for that matter) could hurt your career, cost you the job you have or take you out of the running for a new job. Do not say anything about anyone (especially your boss and your co-workers) that you would not say to them if they were standing in front of you.

Consider Setting Up a Website or Blog

A website or a blog can be used to showcase your skills and your expertise. You can use both to display professional information that you would be proud for a future employer to see.

Two popular (and free) blog sites are *www.blogspot.com* and *www.wordpress.com*.

If you are new to creating websites, try *http://www.weebly.com* for a free site and templates to use.

If you would like to buy a domain name, like *www.paralegalmentor.com*, two economical options are *www.godaddy.com* and *www.1and1.com*.

A blog or website is only as good as its last update. Once you have established a website or blog, be sure to set aside time for maintenance and updates.

CONCLUSION

Starting a job search may feel daunting; you are trying to make a major life shift. For some people this time is exciting; for others, it is an overwhelming time with too many possibilities and too many decisions to make. Get your job search started properly by polishing your online presence and by developing a networking strategy. Will you network online, in person or both? Organize your search and keep records of where you submit resumes. Meet people and make connections through volunteer opportunities, temporary work, and participating in social networking sites like LinkedIn.

Checklist for Success

☐ Understand the job market in your geographical area by studying advertisements for jobs.

☐ Consider traditional paralegal positions and positions where your skills transfer.

☐ Open an Internet e-mail account so that you can check e-mail anywhere.

☐ Create a 1-page resume (refer to Chapter 6).

☐ Define your goal: Do you want *a* job or *the* job. If you are looking for *the* job, expect your search to take longer.

☐ Create a job search log.

☐ Consider working as a temporary paralegal to gain experience and to expand your job search options.

☐ Develop a network through contacts, volunteering, attending educational events, and social networking.

☐ If you have social networking accounts, examine how your image may be perceived by others.

☐ If you do not have social networking accounts, consider setting up an account to expand your network.

☐ Consider setting up a blog or a website.

ASSIGNMENTS: PREPARING FOR YOUR PARALEGAL CAREER

Career Management

Use the list provided at the beginning of this chapter for locating job opportunities. Create a master list of resources for your career management notebook. Identify the following information:

- Resource (Publication name, website name)
- Uniform Record Locator (URL/web address)
- How often and when the information is available or updated, if provided

Place this list of resources in your binder. Schedule time in your master job search task list to regularly search for positions. Compare your list to the lists that others make.

Report

Find 10 job advertisements for similar positions (all for litigation, probate, general law office, etc.) and copy the descriptions into a table or spreadsheet. Identify the skills that these positions require. Do you see similarities? Differences? Write a memorandum to your instructor explaining your findings. In your memorandum, provide a general overview of what you found, list the skills that the positions require, and analyze your own skills—either learned in school, obtained in other work, or in combination—to show how you could do the jobs advertised. Last, identify areas where you could improve your knowledge or experience and try to identify one strategy for doing so. Attach your spreadsheet of job descriptions as Attachment A.

Network

Locate calendars of events for professional organizations for paralegals and legal professionals in your area. Also locate your school's calendar of events, as well as that of the placement office. Create a networking calendar for yourself for the next three months. Write a memo to your instructor with a networking plan that includes the goals you hope to accomplish while networking (meet three working paralegals; meet someone who works at a specific law firm or company; volunteer for one *pro bono* event or help one organization with something) and a list of events you plan to attend to try to accomplish these goals.

Prepare

Select one paralegal, attorney, or other legal professional who uses social networking regularly to promote the paralegal profession. Follow that paralegal's status updates, blog entries, and other participation for one week. Determine how you might use social networking to make contacts beneficial to your own career development. At the end of the week, write a memorandum to your instructor that describes your experience.

REFERENCES

Alba, J. (2009). "I'm on LinkedIn, now what: A guide to getting the most out of LinkedIn." (2nd ed.) Cupertino, Super Star P.

Denney, R. W. (2011). "What's Hot and What's Not in the Legal Profession." *Law Practice Magazine.* 37(1), 11.

Paralegals and Legal Assistants. (2010–2011). *Occupational Outlook Handbook.* Retrieved from: *http://www.bls.gov/oco/pdf/ocos114.pdf*

CHAPTER **5**

ORGANIZE YOUR JOB SEARCH PAPERWORK

Picture yourself at your first job interview for a paralegal position that you *really, really* want. That moment is not the time to scroll through your phone trying to find the names and phone numbers of three people who will serve as your professional references, especially three people you have not asked. What if someone calls them before you get a chance to warn them?

And then, while you are wondering if the interviewer will figure out that one of the people you listed is really your neighbor, you receive an e-mail message reminding you to bring two writing samples to your interview tomorrow. Which samples do you bring?

Your laser printer has toner, right? You have plenty of paper? Do you have a note card to send the person who interviewed you earlier in the day? And what *is* the correct spelling of that professor you had for the class in land use, anyway? He agreed to serve as a reference a couple of months ago.

The time to organize your job search paperwork is before you begin looking for a job. This chapter helps you to start your job search by showing you how to:

- Review and assess your online reputation
- Identify the supplies needed for your job search
- Understand the importance of maintaining confidentiality
- Prepare a professional portfolio
- Recognize the function and importance of references

■ ASSESS YOUR ONLINE REPUTATION

Have you Googled yourself? Now is the time. Clean up your online presence before you begin searching for a job. Human resources personnel are reporting that they Google candidates before bringing them in for interviews, so you want to know exactly what they will find. Refer to Chapters 4 and 10 for more information about cleaning up your social networking image.

Do not, however, let human resources find nothing. Use the guidelines in Chapter 4 to set up a LinkedIn profile that you use for professional purposes.

■ GATHER YOUR SUPPLIES

You need certain paper supplies for job searching and networking. Keep these supplies stocked even after your job search ends, because managing a professional career means producing resumes and other documents even when you are not job searching. For example, you might be asked to provide a resume to your employer once a year.

Resume and Application Letter Paper

Resumes and letters of application should be printed on good paper. Choose white or ivory. White paper is best, although a nice ivory is acceptable. Never use blue or gray, even if the box at the office supply store is labeled as resume paper. Recycled paper is becoming very popular, but some of it is flimsy. When applying for work in the legal profession, choose a quality paper.

Good choices would be linen or heavyweight resume paper. Linen paper is usually 25% cotton and 24 to 32 pounds in weight. (A paper's weight is determined by how much a ream of 500 sheets weighs.) Heavyweight resume paper should be 24 to 32 pounds. Paper that is heavier than 32 pounds is too heavy for resumes and would best be used to produce report covers. When you touch a nice paper, you will understand why it is sold in small boxes; this type of paper is not economical for everyday use. Resume paper is meant to show that the document you are sending is special. Your resume is very special.

Choosing good resume paper may seem over-the-top when most of your applications will be submitted electronically, but you will need it so choose carefully. You will want to print extra copies of your resume and take them with you to career fairs, interviews, and to places and events that offer networking opportunities.

Note Cards

You also need professional note cards to use for thank you notes and networking notes. Note cards can be purchased at an office supply store. Office supply stores offer printer-friendly card stock that can be personalized.

Use note cards to send thank you notes after interviews and to send notes after networking events. You can send a note to a speaker you enjoyed or to say you enjoyed meeting someone at a professional event.

The great thing about note cards is that they are an inexpensive way to make yourself memorable, regardless of the stage of your career. E-mail also works, and at times is more appropriate and efficient, but a handwritten note is very special in today's electronic blitz of information.

Choose note cards that are conservative in style and appropriate for the legal profession. White or ivory cards trimmed in navy blue, dark (really dark) green, maroon, or dark gray are acceptable. You can purchase plain or personalized note cards.

IN PRACTICE

A Note about Note Cards

We hear you saying, "But my instructor never had to use note cards during a job search." That may be true, but *your* job search is different and reflects the current economic and professional landscape.

In fact, most of your instructors will correctly advise you to send a formal, typed thank you letter (and we will, too, in Chapter 7 where we discuss job search correspondence and provide examples).

The problem with a formal thank you letter is that often timeliness is more important. You can neatly write out a thank you note and pop it in the mail a few minutes after a job interview is finished, and it might be received the next day. A formal letter that has to be printed and then mailed may be delayed by a day or more.

Write a formal letter if you have time. For example, the interviewer might tell you that they are interviewing more candidates throughout the week. If you do not have time or you are not sure, send a handwritten note. For example, you might be interviewing for a temporary position that will be filled the next day.

Business Cards

Business cards should never be used when searching for a job. A business card suggests that your professional allegiance is to the company name on the card. Because of this implicit understanding, even handing over a business card *without* a company name (such as one you designed yourself) is a mistake. It gives the appearance that you are working for yourself rather than seeking to align with an employer.

If you are not employed, or, if you have a side business or blog you like to promote, you probably use business cards with your home address, phone number, and e-mail address, but do not let lines cross. Never use or distribute these cards at your place of work and never give this card to a potential employer. If you are looking for a job, do not use this card at networking events. Potential employers and people who know potential employers do not want to have evidence that your allegiance may be split or that you are going to sell something during your lunch hour.

Locate a Laser Printer

Print your documents using a laser printer. At the University of Maine, students can take their resume paper to the Career Center and print at no charge. The Center keeps the laser printer toner stocked so that it prints in crisp black ink—never too light or smudged. Your job is to figure out how to access a laser printer that always has toner. If you have an inkjet printer, you *might* be able to use it occasionally to print a resume, but *never* send a resume printed in green or blue because your printer ran out of ink, and never send a resume that is too light or smudged.

■ PREPARING A PROFESSIONAL PORTFOLIO

The purpose of a portfolio in the paralegal profession is to show that you can write well and that you understand the conventions of different kinds of writing.

The person reviewing your portfolio will look to see if you know how to format a memo or a letter (so make sure yours is formatted perfectly), and whether you have learned how to format different types of legal documents. You will not be expected to include many different kinds of documents and, in fact, you should not, but if you include a pleading, you want it to be formatted properly. Most importantly, the person will use your portfolio to examine your writing skills. By handing over a portfolio, you are demonstrating your ability to communicate through writing.

A portfolio is rarely required at a job interview, but if you bring one, it provides something to talk about during the interview. If you decide to create a portfolio, create the best one that you can.

What to Include in a Portfolio

Choose documents that show your writing skills and your paralegal skills. Include documents you drafted for class, such as pleadings, letters, and estate plans. Also include your resume in your portfolio.

Choose your documents carefully. If you are interviewing for a real estate paralegal position, include the real estate documents you drafted in class that represent your absolute best work. If you are especially proud of a memorandum of law that you drafted for another class, go ahead and include it. The purpose is not to show that you know everything about real estate law, but to show that you can write well and that you have a sense of the types of documents lawyers typically draft.

Present only five to seven pieces, or fewer. Look for your best work. If you feel fewer than five pieces are absolutely excellent, include fewer. The thickest portfolio does not win. The *best* writing sample does. Make sure your best writing sample gets noticed and is not overlooked because you included too many documents.

Julia Tryk, Professor of Paralegal Studies at Cuyahoga Community College, requires students to prepare a professional portfolio as a class assignment. A portfolio provides all the information you need for a job search at your fingertips. Tryk recommends that a portfolio include copies of the following documents:

- Resume and application letter
- Letters of recommendation and reference lists
- Informal transcripts, awards, diplomas, and certifications
- Notary commission and continuing education documentation
- Document samples, including pleadings and discovery, a predictive legal research piece (usually a legal memorandum), a persuasive legal research piece (usually a brief in support of a summary judgment motion or appeal), a contract, and any form or item specific to that position. Watermark the document samples as STUDENT WORK so that they do not appear to violate rules of confidentiality.
- Work product or samples of work from a job placement, redacted and approved by the supervising attorney

How to Present Your Portfolio

Present your portfolio in a professional folder. We recommend a black, three-ring binder, with a 1- to 1.5-inch spine. Anything larger will provide too much information, and your best work will be lost in all the paper.

Provide a Table of Contents in the front of your binder. Some people choose to put the Table of Contents in a clear sheet protector. Use tabs to separate each document listed on the Table of Contents. After an interview, check to see that your portfolio does not look too worn and that no one wrote on your samples. Repair or replace whatever you need.

Never put original documents into a portfolio. Occasionally, a firm may ask you to leave your portfolio behind. More than one portfolio has been lost, never returned, or forgotten on a shelf. If you leave your only copy, you risk losing it.

■ CHOOSING AND CULTIVATING REFERENCES

Professional references are people who can talk about your character, your communication skills, and your paralegal or other professional skills. You may have one reference who can describe what a great paralegal student you are and another who can talk about your professional character and communication skills. References develop over time, so it is never too early to begin cultivating those references.

ETHICS IN PRACTICE

Maintaining Client Confidentiality in Your Portfolio

If you want to include documents you worked on during your internship (or even a professional job) in your portfolio, you must obtain permission from the employer or internship sponsor. Most likely, these documents are confidential.

Sometimes, an employer will let you include a document you have written if you *redact* (cover up or white out) all identifying information (client's name, certain facts, firm name, etc.).

When an employer agrees to allow you to use a *redacted* version of a document in your portfolio, be sure to ask the employer to look over the document to ensure you have removed enough information.

Include a note at the top of your document that explains you have used the document with permission from your employer, with confidential information redacted.

The interviewing firm will appreciate your attention to detail, including maintaining client confidentiality.

Tip: You can use Adobe Acrobat (the latest professional version) to redact a .PDF of your document. Your computer lab at school may have this version of Acrobat.

Start thinking about references during the classes you are taking this semester. Your paralegal class instructors are an excellent place to begin cultivating references, but look in other places, too. If you take a business communication course and do really well, the instructor may be happy to serve as a reference. That instructor could say a lot about your work ethic, communication skills, and how quickly you pick up new skills. Any instructor who knows you well can comment on your work ethic and commitment to doing a good job, so do not be afraid to use references who are not related to the legal profession.

The manager for your current job may also be a terrific reference, especially if you have held the same job for a period of time. This manager can describe your at-work attitude, your working style (do you do what it takes to get a job done?), and how well you get along with colleagues.

Maintain Contact with Potential References

Once you ask someone to be a reference for you, stay in touch throughout your job search. Give the person a heads-up whenever possible that a company or person may be calling. Remind them of the job and why you applied for that job in the first place. Your phone message or e-mail could be as simple as this:

> "The Logston Corporation may be calling you for a reference. I applied for an entry-level paralegal position in their corporate legal division. I interviewed last week, and a lot of the job has to do with identifying products that are counterfeit but have the Logston logo on them. I took several forensic science classes as an undergraduate, so I'm really excited about this position."

What you are doing is offering your reference some points to mention during the phone call, and letting the person know to expect a call. It is much easier to be prepared for a phone call than to receive one without notice.

References who agree to speak on your behalf are willing to take phone calls without a heads-up, of course, but if they take too long to figure out why the person is calling, "Oh, Joe MORGAN…oh, yes, Joe. I know Joe," your reference may sound a little out of the loop and bring doubt into the phone conversation. Job searches have very little room for doubt.

PARALEGAL **PROFILE**

Anne Hughes, ACP, FCP

Current position: Litigation Paralegal

Employer: Roper & Roper, P.A.

Years in this position: 1.5

Years of paralegal experience: 7

Certifications: Advanced Certified Paralegal in Discovery (NALA), Florida Certified Paralegal (PAF) and Florida Registered Paralegal (Florida Bar)

Education:

A.A., Legal Studies, Seminole State College

B.A., Legal Studies, Specializations in Trial Advocacy & Litigation and Corporate/Transactional Law, University of Central Florida

In addition to working as a litigation paralegal, Anne Hughes, ACP, FCP, has been an adjunct instructor and remains active in her local paralegal association, Central Florida Paralegal Association, Inc. She has served as NALA Liaison, President, Student Relations Chair, Webmaster and has coordinated and taught the CFPA Annual CP Exam Review Course.

Q&A about Portfolios with Anne Hughes, ACP, FCP

We asked Anne Hughes, ACP, FCP, for advice about preparing a portfolio for your job search.

What kind of portfolio do you recommend?

I chose a regular 3-ring binder for my portfolio because attorneys are familiar with them and it's simple. I use a white binder, though, instead of black so it will stand out. I use color-coded, tabbed dividers so that it gives the appearance of a Trial Notebook.

What kinds of documents do you include in your portfolio?

The first divider includes work that demonstrates my proficiency with word processing programs, specifically Word and WordPerfect samples that have been carefully redacted and clearly define my personal work product from collaboration or boilerplate language.

Next are sections that include Excel spreadsheets and PowerPoint slides I have created. The spreadsheets are also redacted and the slides are ones I have used in teaching that are law-related. Next is a section for Recognitions & Awards in which I include letters of recommendation from past employers and color copies of current certification certificates such as my Notary Public certificate and paralegal credentialing letters and certificates.

Finally, are copies of Certificates of Attendance for all CLE courses I have attended in the past reporting period (3–5 years) and a summary of my current CLE status from both NALA and the Florida Bar.

What advice would you give to job seekers about creating a portfolio?

I would strongly recommend a job seeker to take his or her portfolio to the first interview. If asked for a writing sample, the candidate will be prepared. Also, I slip a skills resume and a personal business card in the inside front pocket so that, not only is my portfolio clean on the outside, and clearly identifiable on the inside cover, the reviewing hiring manager/attorney has an opportunity to see a skills summary while he/she is reviewing the portfolio.

Of course, I present a standard chronological resume at the time of my interview, but I find that tucking a skills resume and personal business card in the portfolio is a helpful way to put my contact information and skill summary in front of the hiring manager/attorney again. Be certain not to use a business card from a past/current employer at the interview or in your portfolio. There are low- or no-cost ways to have a personal business card made up with a professional look and your personal contact information.

Prepare Your Reference List

Your reference list should *not* be included on your resume, but provided as a second document and given to an employer only when asked. Before you make this list, confirm that your references agree to serve as contacts. Format the reference list the same way you formatted your resume, as shown in Figure 5-1. Use the same heading style and typefaces as your resume.

Include the following information about each reference:

- Full name and credentials:
  - Jennifer H. Smith, Esq.
  - Lindsey K. Marks, CP
  - Adam Lee, Ph.D.
- Address, including city, state, and ZIP code
- Phone number, including area code
- Fax number, including area code
- E-mail address

Ask for Reference Letters

You may need a reference letter for some positions. If you need a reference letter, you should do everything you can to minimize the work that the letter writer must do. Print any instructions and provide your resume. If the letter writer needs to send an accompanying

---

Scott Westerly

123 Washington Lane, New City, TX 75555
Phone: 222-333-4444
E-mail: scott.westerly@email.com

References

Martin Allen, Esq.

Lawler & Lawton, LLP
14 North Parkway
Dallas, TX 75555
Phone: 214-333-7777
Fax: 214-123-4567
E-mail: Martin.Allen@email.com

Bob Billings, Ph.D.

Chair, Department of Communication Studies
University of Texas
Parlin 4
Austin, TX 75555
Phone: 512-122-3333
Fax: 512-122-4444
E-mail: Bob.Billings@email.com

Rhonda Santiago, Esq.

Corporate Legal Department
Medical Technology Corporation
124 Main Road
Ausitn, TX 75555
Phone: 512-888-9999
Fax: 512-454-9999
E-mail: Rhonda.Santiago@email.com

FIGURE 5-1 Reference List. Format your Reference List using the same heading style and typefaces that you use for your resume.

IN PRACTICE

Filling Out Applications at Job Interviews

When you go to a job interview, you may be asked to fill out an application, just like the one you might fill out at McDonald's. This routine gets really annoying because you will have already sent in an application letter and a fabulous resume (how else would you have gotten the interview?), and now, when you are most nervous, a receptionist will give you a clip board, a leaky pen, and a four-page application to fill out and sign.

That application will ask for your work history AND your references. Here is our advice: Take out your resume and your reference list and use them to fill in the blanks

of the application. By making sure both documents match, you will know that you have provided accurate information. Your reference list will be invaluable at this moment because few people can remember the names, addresses, and phone numbers of their references.

The reason for this application-filling-out routine is that by signing the application, you are attesting to providing accurate and true information. Your resume is not signed and does not provide that personal guarantee that it is true and accurate. (Trust a law firm to figure that one out!)

form, print the form and fill it out. Address an envelope. Affix postage. Do not simply ask for the letter and provide a link to the instructions and forms. No one has 24/7 Internet access and your letter may need to be squeezed in during a long airplane flight. If the letter writer has to spend time looking for additional information or cannot access that information, the time allotted to writing your letter will be cut short and the letter may not be as good.

Use our checklist to provide details about yourself to the letter writer. You do not want the letter writer to make a factual mistake about you or to write a vague letter because details about your academic or professional work were not readily available.

IN PRACTICE

Checklist for Reference Letters

Provide the following to the person who will write a letter for you. You may not need all of these things, but use this checklist to determine which items you will use:

- Instructions provided by the organization requiring the letter.
- Any required forms, filled out and signed.
- Name of the person who will receive the letter. If you can, identify whether they are male or female. Even if the name seems obvious—like Michael—go ahead and confirm that Michael is male. Traditional names are now used for both men and women.
- Address where the letter should be sent.
- An addressed, stamped envelope.

- Your updated resume.
- A brief description of why you want the letter and what you hope the letter will help communicate to the employer. Be as specific as you can because you will be helping the letter writer shape the letter for the work you want to do.
- Some reminders about yourself. List the courses you have taken from the person you are asking, the grade you received, and any special projects or stand-out things that happened during the course. Mention any special information about yourself that you think the instructor might comment on as well.

CONCLUSION

Once your job search begins, you need to have your paperwork ready to go. Build your portfolio, write your resume, and purchase resume paper and thank you notes. Set up a workstation to handle incoming and outgoing information related to your job search.

When a potential opportunity arises, you can act immediately instead of needing to stop by the office supply store to buy a new toner cartridge or get in touch with one of the people you hope to use as a reference. If your life is already busy and especially if you are finishing school or working at another job while you search, being organized will decrease some of the stress job searching brings with it. Being organized allows you to act as soon as an opportunity comes along.

Checklist for Success

☐ Make a list of supplies you need for your job search.

☐ Remember to choose note cards that you can use to send thank you notes and networking notes.

☐ Choose white or ivory resume paper. Do not use gray or blue.

☐ *Never* use business cards during your job search.

☐ Locate a laser printer that you can use to print excellent quality documents.

☐ If you create a portfolio, carefully choose the documents you include.

☐ Present your portfolio in a black or white, 1- to 1.5-inch three-ring binder.

☐ Identify possible references and contact each one to ask them to serve.

☐ Confirm that each reference is willing to serve.

☐ Confirm the spelling of names, titles, mailing and e-mail addresses, and phone numbers of your references.

☐ Provide enough information when you ask people to write letters of recommendation.

☐ Prepare a reference sheet to take with you to job interviews.

☐ Clean up your social media profile (refer to Chapter 4).

ASSIGNMENTS: PREPARING FOR YOUR PARALEGAL CAREER

Career Management

Prepare your reference list. Confirm with each person that they will agree to serve as a reference. Write a memorandum to your instructor explaining why you asked specific people. What do you need each person to discuss? Your work ethic? Your knowledge or skill? You ability to communicate?

Prepare

Bring five documents to class that you might include in a portfolio and discuss the pros and cons of including each document. Proofread the documents for each other and make suggestions for improvements.

Prepare

Prepare a portfolio that includes copies of the following documents:

- Resume and application letter
- Letters of recommendation and reference lists

- Informal transcripts, awards, diplomas, and certifications
- Notary commission and continuing education
- Document samples, including pleadings and discovery, a predictive legal research piece (usually a legal memorandum), a persuasive legal research piece (usually a brief in support of a summary judgment motion or appeal), a contract, and any form or item specific to a position for which you are applying. Watermark the document samples as STUDENT WORK so that they do not appear to violate rules of confidentiality.
- Work product or samples of work from an internship, redacted and approved by the supervising attorney

CHAPTER **6**

PREPARE YOUR RESUME

Twenty years ago, human resource personnel said you had less than 60 seconds to catch a potential employer's attention with a resume. Today you might have 10 seconds, if you are lucky.

Thanks to the Internet, people are able to apply for almost any job anywhere. Consider Vicki and Charlsye, the authors of this book. We are not computer programmers, but we could apply for programming jobs at Nintendo if we wanted to waste some time. The ability to apply for any job without paying the postage to mail an application letter and resume has resulted in potential employers being bombarded by applicants who are only marginally qualified or not qualified at all. Employers must determine quickly whether the applicant is qualified.

Even if you are still a student, your skill set must be very clearly communicated so that a potential employer can *digest* it in fewer than 10 seconds. Consider that word *digest*. We like to think people examine resumes closely—and they do, but not on the first review. When your resume arrives at a potential employer's office, it is either filed electronically for the appropriate position or a paper copy is placed in a pile. Your goal is for your resume to stand out on the screen or to rise to the top of the pile.

Someone—an attorney, a human resources representative, a paralegal, an assistant—will go through resumes looking for a specific skill set. If you have it, your resume makes the second cut. Because so many resumes arrive at one time, the reviewer rarely has time to *read* the resumes. Instead, the reviewer scans each resume for key words; therefore, the key words on your resume must send a clear message that you are a match. This is a difficult job to ask of a single sheet of paper, and exactly why writing a good resume takes time and planning. Your resume may be one of the shortest documents you ever write and one of the most difficult.

Your resume is a visual representation of yourself. Like the paper you wrote for your English class, a resume needs a "thesis"—a point of view that makes the reviewer say, "Here is a paralegal who can do X."

This chapter will show you how to:

- Determine the type of resume you will need
- Describe how a resume is written to both show and sell
- Understand that people read differently on paper than on the computer screen
- Understand the importance of making the first 11 characters of a bullet point count
- Define and structure the "F-zone" on your resume
- Identify when to use an electronic resume and when to use a scannable resume

■ YOUR RESUME REPRESENTS YOU

The Pamela Cooper resume, Figure 6-1, was submitted for a temporary position coding documents for potential litigation. Because the position was temporary, the employer did not need to hire a paralegal, *per se*, but intended to interview people who demonstrated good analytical skills and who could work independently to extract information from documents and enter it into a database. Pamela Cooper applied for the job. Her resume was immediately rejected. Can you figure out why?

If you said that Pamela's resume did not offer any skills the employer sought, you might be right. Continue reading this chapter to see a revision of Pamela's resume that might have landed an interview. We will return to the resume saga of Pamela Cooper at the end of the chapter.

■ THE TYPE OF RESUME YOU NEED

The legal profession prefers resumes that *look like* traditional resumes. To make your resume stand out, it must first look like a resume, but with information strategically placed on the page to catch the attention of the reviewer. For jobs in the legal profession, avoid creative resumes. Only graphic designers, artists, or advertising professionals benefit from a truly creative resume.

The One Page Power Resume

Your resume should be no more than one page. Exceptions are rare: logging a decade or more *in the legal profession*; publishing extensively; bringing special skills (a degree in chemistry and a desire to become a patent agent); entering the paralegal profession after doing something that makes you more qualified than others (such as being an excellent nurse). But, nothing says powerful and in control like a resume that has been condensed carefully to one page.

IN PRACTICE

Resume Reminders

1. Remember that your resume represents you.
2. Write a one page power resume.
3. Choose an organizational format that accentuates your strengths: either an experience-based resume or a skills-based resume.

4. Develop a "thesis" for your resume. After someone scans your resume, they should be able to fill in this blank: This person would be good at _____ _____.

5. Use guidelines for on-screen writing to prepare a resume that can be read *fast*.

Pamela Cooper

124 Washington Lane
New City, TX 75555
222-333-4444

Summary

May college graduate with marketing and public communications experience. Can bring strong organizational, office, communications, and people skills to fast-paced environment.

Work Experience

| 2010 | The Coffee Pot | Austin, TX |

Trained and functioned in all aspects of gourmet coffee roaster and retailer. Provided counter service and prepared specialty coffee drinks.

| 2009 | PMC Cleaning Services | Austin, TX |

Residential cleaning, errands, child care, and miscellaneous client needs.

| 2008 | The Bar Hop | Austin, TX |

Waitress and bartender in fast-paced restaurant and bar. Responsible for balancing cash register at the end of each shift.

| 2007–08 | The Sandwich Shop | Austin, TX |

Made sandwiches and worked as cashier.

| 2006–07 | Government Regional Associates | Austin, TX |

Performed field surveys, prepared reports, proposals, and marketing materials. Answered telephones, made appointments and travel arrangements.

| 2005–06 | Melody's, Inc. | Austin, TX |

Coordinated special store events, fashion shows, media advertising, and created store promotions.

Skills

Type 60 words per minute
Working knowledge of Microsoft Word and Excel
Excellent communication skills

Education

B.A., Political Science, 2010
University of Texas at Austin
References available upon request.

FIGURE 6-1 Cooper Resume. This resume is ineffective as written and designed. A redesign of Cooper's resume is provided later in the chapter.

PARALEGAL **PROFILE**

Ann Callahan, SPHR

Current position: Human Resources Manager

Years in this position: 4 (with 14 years in HR in another industry prior to this)

Certifications: Senior Professional in Human Resources

Education:
B.A., English, Western Washington University
Certificate, Human Resources, University of Washington

Q&A about Resumes with Ann Callahan, SPHR

We asked Ann Callahan, SPHR, human resources manager, to explain the hiring process and what she thinks paralegals can do to be good employees.

When interviewing, what do you look for in a person who has no experience as a legal professional?

I generally interview for behavioral aspects. I ask for and want to hear *specific* examples of how an applicant solves problems, works with clients, strategizes with attorneys, etc. For our firm, the next interview is with the attorneys, who then ask more questions regarding specific abilities. For candidates with little or no experience, I caution them to keep in mind that, just as with brand new law school graduates, they are really only beginning their training. Applicants new to the legal profession need to be open to other positions as entry-level options, while being clear about their long-term goals.

What do you look for in a person who has many years of experience?

For candidates with many years of experience, I generally assume a body of knowledge exists, but I am likely to investigate whether their tech skills have kept pace.

What are some things that new law firm employees should do to stand out?

As the roles played by paralegals and legal secretaries continue to shift, and with the implementation of flat fees, paralegals need to be skilled at tracking their billable hours and be crystal clear about how the two functions differ. In the billable hour setting, keep the focus on the activities you can bill for and assign the rest out.

Cultivating a good working relationship with the legal secretaries in your office is vital. Be clear with them, appreciate them, and they will have your back.

Knowing the working styles and typical cases of the attorneys with whom you work will make you stand out. When you are new to a position, err on the side of annoying in the number of questions you ask. It's the fastest way to get established. Make your questions smart, and, if possible, offer a possible answer or two to show you have done some analysis, and make notes that you can refer to in the future as you build this knowledge base.

Continue to sharpen your knowledge and skills externally also. Know what is happening in your field and share that with your colleagues and attorneys. The highest praise I hear attorneys give is that someone is engaged and passionate, and that they have enough of a sense of the trajectory of a case to either anticipate or ask about next steps.

Work to manage the case on a basic level by providing status updates, even if not asked. The cycle for those will vary with the situation, but to the extent that you can free the attorney to focus on the work at hand that day rather than to be sifting through all the currently active cases, you will have made a significant contribution.

The Full Resume

You are the only person who should ever see your full, complete resume. As you begin your career, keep a running resume that includes everything from the summer job you held when you were 15 to the work you are doing right now. Whenever you switch jobs,

Whitney M. Franklin
932 Keeley Lane
Manchester, NH 03103
(603) 123-4567 • wmfranklin@email.com

Objective

To secure a full-time paralegal position where my skills in communication, organization, research, and writing are used.

Education

Paralegal Certificate, Rivier College, Nashua, NH, 2010
GPA: 4.0

B.A., French, Siena College, Loudonville, NY, 2006
Minor: Spanish
GPA: 3.96

Legal Experience

Intern for Attorney Harold Akin, Chelmsford, MA, August 2009–present

Answered interrogatories
Drafted interrogatories
Drafted "demand letters" pursuant to M.G.L. Chapter 93A
Organized and maintained files

Employment History

House of Pizza, Dedham, MA, 2006–present

Manager, 2009–present

Manage shifts of 3–15 people
Schedule management and crew members
Order and inventory all food and paper products
Train management trainees
Hire and train crew members

Shift Supervisor, 2007–2008
Shift Worker, 2006–2007

Skills

French and Spanish, speak and read
Microsoft Office
AbacusLaw for time and billing
CaseMap for case analysis
TimeMap for time graphing

FIGURE 6-2 Franklin Resume. This is an experienced-based resume.

update this full resume. When you are asked to volunteer at a professional function or you win an award, add that to your resume. Then, when you are ready to look for a job, you will not have to start from scratch or try to remember what you did and when you did it.

Because your full resume includes everything you have done, it will probably provide too much information. After a certain point, no one will care how many children you taught to swim or whether you were the valedictorian of your high school class. Frankly, no one will care that you went to high school, which makes all the drama that happened there not so important after all. What matters about your resume is what it shows about you *right now*.

To shape your resume into a visual and descriptive representation of yourself as a professional, choose a resume that accentuates your strengths: a skills-based resume or an education-and-experience-based resume.

The Experience-Based Resume

The experience-based resume is the most traditional. This resume highlights your education and experience, in that order. In an experience-based resume, your work is relevant to the profession and really speaks for itself. You show that you have been there/done that.

As a college student, you might have a terrific experience-based resume for a job in retail sales. But, you are now looking at your work-life in a different way. You now want entry into a field where you may or may not have *any* work experience.

You need to show an employer what you can do. You may have only your education and a little bit of experience. Great! Firms need entry-level employees, too, so do not try to make yourself *not* look entry level by trying to disguise your newness. You will look less qualified. In fact, some firms even prefer to hire entry-level personnel because, even though new hires may require more supervision at first, the firm can be reasonably confident that the person can be trained to do things the way the firm wants them done and that the firm will not be hiring a new employee who has someone else's bad habits.

Look at Whitney Franklin's sample resume, Figure 6-2. Whitney has several years of experience working at House of Pizza, and she has completed one internship as a paralegal. Her experience-based resume highlights that experience by separating her Legal Experience from her Employment History. Whitney's job is to make herself look like an entry-level paralegal rather than a pizza queen. She achieves this successfully.

The Skills-Based Resume

The skills-based resume (sometimes known as a functional resume) is a great option if you are entering a profession with little experience related to that profession. In a skills-based resume, what you can do is more important than the jobs you have held. In your paralegal courses and at jobs where you worked previously, you developed skills that are *transferable*. This resume should include skills that will be appreciated by the legal profession.

Applicants using a skills-based resume organize their abilities into meaningful chunks of data. When similar skills are grouped together, an employer can see the depth of your talents in those areas. A paralegal seeking a corporate job might begin a skills section in this way:

> CORPORATE PARALEGAL SKILLS
>
> **Corporate Documents:** Certificates of incorporation, bylaws, and organizational documents
>
> **Corporate Minute Books:** Minutes, stock certificates, board consents
>
> Proficient with Microsoft Word, Excel, and Lotus Notes

Annilee Hanson's resume, Figure 6-3, provides an example of how a skills-based resume showcases paralegal skills. Annilee attacks this problem by featuring skills attorneys needed by attorneys in her geographic area. Annilee learned about these skills at an

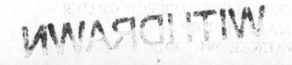

event where the keynote speaker was a prominent local attorney. By finding what employers are looking for *right at that moment*, Annilee is able to gear her resume for the current market.

Annilee's resume features legal research, writing, and technology skills because these are skills she has *and* skills that are important to the profession.

PARALEGAL QUALIFICATIONS

Legal Research: Westlaw, Lexis-Nexis, Internet, and law library research

Writing: Drafting correspondence, memoranda, motions, wills, and contracts

Technology: Microsoft Office, time and billing software, CaseMap, and databases

---

Annilee Hanson
84 Fifteenth Street
Medford, MA 02155
(617) 123-4567 • ahanson@email.com

Education

B.A., Paralegal Studies, Expected 2012
Newbury College, Wakefield Campus
GPA: 3.92

A.A., Criminal Justice, Spring 2008
Quincy Junior College, Quincy, MA
GPA: 3.20

Paralegal Qualifications

Legal Research: Westlaw, Lexis-Nexis, Internet, and law library research

Writing: Drafting correspondence, memoranda, motions, and wills and contracts

Technology: Microsoft Office, time and billing software, CaseMap, and databases

Office Skills

Leadership and Collaboration: Work well in team or independently; can assume leadership role when needed

Office Procedures: Filing and typing skills; fax, copier, postage meter, and accounting calculator

Employment History

Office Clerk
Law Office of Harold M. Peters, Boston, MA, 2009–2010

Trader's Assistant
Merchandising America, Dedham, MA, 2008–2009

Data Entry
Allen, Jenkins & Jones, Boston, MA, 2006–2008

Sales Associate
J.C. Penney, Los Angeles, CA, 2004–2006

Barista
Starbucks, Los Angeles, CA, 2002–2004

References available upon request.

FIGURE 6-3 Hanson Resume. This is an example of a skills-based resume.

Figure 6-4 shows the resume of Jason Pellman. Jason wants to change his career path from paralegal to litigation technology specialist. Jason has four years of experience working in law offices. To change his area of specialization, he focuses his resume on the skills he has that a litigation technology specialist needs to do this job well:

PARALEGAL TECHNOLOGY

Legal Research: Westlaw, Lexis-Nexis, Internet

Document Management: Case Manager Pro, Verdical, relational databases

Case Analysis: CaseMap, West Case Notebook, Discovery ZX, LiveNote

Office: Microsoft Office, Excel, Access, time and billing, document management software

---

Jason S. Pellman, CP
1812 Autumn Ave., Apt. 11B
Somerville, MA 02143
(617) 123-4567 • jspellman@email.com

Education and Certification
Certified Paralegal (CP) Exam, 2010

B.A., Paralegal Studies, Suffolk University, May 2009
GPA 3.20

Paralegal Technology
Legal Research: Westlaw, Lexis-Nexis, Internet

Document Management: Case Manager Pro, Verdical, relational databases

Case Analysis: CaseMap, West Case Notebook, Discovery ZX, LiveNote

Office: Microsoft Office, Excel, Access, time and billing, document management software

Professional Experience
Paralegal
Glenn and Lawson, Boston, MA, 2009–present
- Draft letters, motions, and affidavits
- Document analysis to identify key documents in litigation matters
- Investigate facts and law of cases to determine causes of action
- Interview potential witnesses

Case Clerk
Law Office of Helen M. Satarre, 2008–2009
- Trial preparation assistance for medical malpractice caseload
- Medical records requests by writing letters and obtaining forms for client
- Trial notebook preparation

Data Entry
Levonwitz and Jordan, Boston, MA, 2007–2008
- Typed and proofread documents from dictation and handwritten drafts
- Excel spreadsheet design and data entry
- Billing analysis and proofreading

Professional Organizations
National Association of Legal Assistants (NALA)

Association of Litigation Support Professionals (ALSP)

FIGURE 6-4 Pellman Resume. This is an example of a skills-based resume that is being used to show knowledge in a specific specialty area.

IN PRACTICE

How to Choose Your Resume Type

If you are not sure which resume you should use, this chart might help:

Situation	Resume to Use
Class of 200X and the job market is horrible	Skills-based resume. Use this resume to get a job—a temp job, a lateral job, an entry-level job-job.
You are going for the job—the job that makes you want to get up and go to work each morning. The problem is that during the middle of your job search, you got laid off from your current job. What do you do?	Create two resumes: • Experience-based resume. Use this resume to keep looking for the job. • Skills-based resume. Use this resume to get a job—a temp job, a lateral job, a job-job.
You have more than three years experience and you have been laid off. You need a job. Any job. Right now.	Skills-based resume. This resume will put your skill set right in the "F-zone." Experience-based resume. If you had an awesome three-year work experience that will really stand out on your resume, choose an experience-based resume to highlight that position and experience.
You might want a new job. You definitely want to see what is out there for someone with your experience. You have some wisdom and things to offer. During this job search, you are going to be very picky.	Experience-based resume. Use this resume to highlight your wisdom and to show that you are doing or are capable of doing exactly what the firm wants you to do.

Remember that everyone is in the position of being entry-level at least once in their career. A skills-based resume can help you position yourself to get your first job in the legal profession.

■ FOR RESUME WRITING, SHOW AND SELL

The body of your resume needs to describe you and your skills. If you are beginning your career, you do not need to know the area of law you want to specialize in yet; however, you want people who look at your resume to think, "This is a paralegal student who is serious about working as a paralegal."

First and foremost, make sure your resume makes you look like a paralegal or paralegal student. As you move through your career, you can refine your resume so that you look like a real estate paralegal or a patent prosecution paralegal or however you want to position yourself. For now, though, focus on looking like a paralegal or a paralegal student who is ready for the job market.

Develop Your "Resume Image"

Some people rely only on the objective or summary to communicate their professional goal, but this is a mistake. If you want a job as a paralegal, you want people to see an image of a paralegal or a paralegal-in-training when they view your entire resume. If you are trying to get two different types of jobs, you may need two images and, therefore, two resumes.

For example, some people make the classic mistake that Georgia Lincoln makes with her resume in Figure 6-5. Georgia has worked her way through college working with horses. Georgia's professional goal is to be a paralegal. The version of her resume below focuses on her experience with horses, including her position as the university's dressage club treasurer.

Her resume shows lots of good things: that she can be trusted, that she is responsible, that she would make a great camp counselor. But what does it say about her paralegal career? Her resume makes everyone think "horseback riding instructor" and "great with children." Potential employers may envision a woman in stable clothes and riding boots rather than a suit and office footwear, decreasing her chances of getting an interview for a paralegal position.

Georgia can help herself by focusing on the courses she has taken and internships or projects she has completed. She can list skills and focus on transferable skills, like teaching.

Georgia Lincoln
24 Lawrence Lane, Bangor, Maine 04401
Phone 207.123.4567   e-mail georgia@email.com

Education

Husson University

B.A. in Paralegal Studies, May 2012

Major GPA: 3.96/4.0; Cumulative GPA: 3.66/4.0; Dean's List 5 semesters

Work Experience

Stable Hand [September 2011–present]

Penobscot Farm, L.L.C (Newburgh, ME). Care and maintenance of approximately 30 horses.

E-Marketing Intern [May–August 2011]

Max Industries *(Freeport, ME)*. Completed competitor website analysis for consideration of new web features; aided in customer-interview exercises for website redesign; maintained product pages; and worked on both organization and maintenance of paid search information.

Camp Counselor [Summers 2008, 2009, 2010]

Arlington Camp & Farm (Temple, NH). Mentored young riding students; taught lessons; managed barn staff.

Equine Working Student [May 2008]

Ellis Farm (Orange, MA). Worked with high-level event trainer with daily lessons and schooling of sales and client horses. Traveled to clinics and acted as a groom.

Stable Hand [August–December 2007]

Bolton Equestrian Center (Manchester, NH). Care and maintenance of approximately 30 horses.

Equine Working Student [November 2004]

Marshall Farm (Red Hook, NY). Schooled and assisted in the training of young sales horses at top hunter/jumper barn.

Works-Related Skills

- Microsoft Office (Word, Excel, PowerPoint)
- Creative Suite (Illustrator, Photoshop, InDesign)
- Basic HTML and CSS
- Managing financial accounts and budgeting
- Excellent written and verbal communication skills
- Learn new tasks quickly and perform efficiently

FIGURE 6-5 Lincoln Resume. This resume shows a good work ethic, but does not show the skills that could be brought to a paralegal position.

If you are finishing your paralegal program and want to get a paralegal job, you want a resume that makes you look like a paralegal. If, on the other hand, you are finishing your paralegal program and want to apply to the FBI, you should scour the FBI's website, find the description of the job you want, and create a resume that reflects an image that fits *that* role.

The following ad is for a general paralegal in a small law firm:

> Small law firm seeks hardworking, detail-oriented, enthusiastic team player for full-time paralegal position. Ideal candidate is a demonstrated self-starter and multiple task manager with an excellent academic record, strong interpersonal and organizational skills and superior writing and communication skills. Must be proficient in Microsoft Office applications.

You want your resume to make you look like a detail-oriented person with good communication and computer skills.

If you wanted to apply for an internship at the FBI in the Records Management Division, according to the FBI's website you would need to meet these qualifications:

- Students must be enrolled at least part-time in an accredited high school, college, or university
- High school student must have a minimum cumulative grade point average (GPA) of 2.5 or above on a 4.0 scale, and be in good standing with their academic institution
- College student must have a minimum cumulative GPA of 3.0 or above on a 4.0 scale, and be in good standing with their academic institution
- Candidates must have strong writing skills and analytical abilities
- Candidates must be citizens of the United States
- Candidates must be at least 16 years of age
- Candidates must meet all FBI Employment Requirements, be able to pass an FBI background investigation, and receive an FBI top secret security clearance

Paralegal students certainly could demonstrate analytical abilities and writing skills through courses taken, writing samples, and other internships or experience. If you wanted a job with the FBI, however, your paralegal training provides some critical skills, but your resume would need to look different from the one you use to find a general paralegal position.

To create the image you want, strip away the facts about you that are not relevant. Sometimes, you feel like you are deleting some important aspects of your life. Journalists call having to delete their favorite sentences to get the story right "killing their darlings." When you write a resume, you may have to "kill your darlings" in order to make yourself look like a paralegal.

For example, you may have been involved in a sport or an art since you were a child. Perhaps you performed with a dance troupe that toured Europe while you were in college. Unless you are planning to work *only* for an organization that specializes in dancing, this experience is not relevant to your job search. You may have to relegate this experience to one line toward the bottom, giving it just enough space to demonstrate you handled coursework and an intense extra-curricular activity.

As you strip away facts that are not important, think about how these facts can take up less space, but add to the image you want to convey. For instance, if you worked your way through college, include that experience on your resume to provide evidence you are responsible and you can juggle competing priorities.

Annilee Hanson's resume, reviewed earlier in this chapter, highlights her paralegal education, skills, and office abilities. She includes her work experience to show that she can hold a job responsibly, but lists it at the bottom and omits descriptions.

Your entire resume must support the image you want to convey and the thesis you want to communicate.

Consider Objectives and Summaries Carefully

The most frustrating thing about writing resumes is that if you put 50 resume "experts" in a room, you will get 50 different opinions about how your resume should be written. One area that experts cannot agree on is whether you need an objective, a summary, or neither on your resume.

You do not need an **objective**. The *firm* has an objective: to hire a person to carry out *their objectives*. Why would they hire someone who has other objectives? Many times, the objective sounds canned and corny. Do not succumb to peer pressure; you absolutely do not need an objective unless you can write one that perfectly fits you and the job for which you are applying.

There are instances when an objective might be helpful. For example, if you attend a job fair with the goal of gaining an internship for the summer, having an objective that states your goal will remind the recruiter later. This example demonstrates that if you do use an objective, you must be sure it describes what you hope to accomplish with your resume.

This objective will remind a recruiter you are looking for an internship:

OBJECTIVE
To obtain an internship in a corporate legal department.

Even though the objective can be helpful, the problem is that the objective in this case is broad and limited. Corporate legal departments do many things. What if the reason you want to work in a corporate environment is that you want to avoid working on litigation at all costs? Some corporate departments focus only on litigation. Others focus only on intellectual property. Some do a little bit of everything, although, even in these departments, paralegals often specialize.

If you use an objective, tailor the objective for each job application. If you plan to take your resume to a career fair and hand it to as many recruiters who will take it, *omit* the objective. You do not need one.

Another approach that many people use is writing a summary.

A **summary** *sells* something. It is your pitch for what you can offer the firm. A summary can be dangerous because a summary is just like a package label: you will not buy a lawn mower that does not meet your needs based on reading a tiny description on the box. Most of the time, you will not even open the manual to look for the details. Neither will the resume reader.

Your summary also limits you, as it should. You cannot claim to be everything to every legal employer, but deciding that you want to market yourself as a bankruptcy paralegal may prevent an employer that you would love to work for from calling you at all.

Once you have thought about the image you want to portray in your resume, learn to use document design techniques to make your resume easy to read on screen and on paper.

■ UNDERSTAND HOW PEOPLE READ ON SCREEN AND ON PAPER

Your resume has the best chance of getting noticed if you prepare it thinking about how people will read and use your resume. A lot of people will look at your resume on a computer screen. They open e-mail attachments or scan paper resumes into a database. Because you do not know how the employer will use your resume, you need to prepare your paper resume as if it will be read on a screen. By designing your resume so that it appeals to the way people read on a computer screen, your resume has a better chance of getting noticed.

Jakob Nielsen, an expert who focuses on the usability of online documents, contends that most people **do not read** documents on a screen. Instead, they **scan** them, looking for key words and phrases.

If you submit your resume via e-mail—or if the company scans it and passes it around electronically, you must make sure your resume can be **scanned for key words and phrases** rather than **read**.

We scan instead of read because "[m]odern life is hectic and people simply do not have time to work too hard for their information," Nielsen explains. He also explains that reading from a computer screen is tiring.

This means you have only a few seconds to communicate your skills. The following tips should help you write a resume that does not need to be "read." Instead, your best qualities should stand out immediately.

Make the First 11 Characters Count

Nielsen reports that people tend to read the first 11 characters of headlines on a website. This tendency suggests that the first two words of a line on a resume really count. What do you want those words to say?

Given that readers tend to look at headlines briefly, readers tend to skip long blocks of text. Areas of a resume that look "gray" are similar to long blocks of text. For example, the job description in Figure 6-6 is too "gray."

Instead of "gray" blocks of text, use bulleted lists and bold to highlight important information. You may bold your job title or the employer's name, depending on which might get more attention.

Create an "F-Zone" in Your Resume

Eye tracking studies show that people tend to read in an "F" pattern when they view documents online. Examine the web page in Figure 6-7. In this example, typical readers tend to first scan the header (ParalegalGateway). Next, readers go to the title "Links of Interest" and the headline "How a Paralegal at Microsoft Uses Access 2010 Web Databases" and may glance at the photo. Next, readers tend to glance at the list of links down the left side. Readers may or may not read the article in the middle.

After that, typical readers might (or might not) look at the Facebook ad on the right side and may have to focus on the words in the white box with the Subscribe button in order to figure out what that box is for. This reading pattern is known as an "F-pattern," and information that falls into the "F-zone," tends to get the most attention.

This reading practice does not hold every time for every website, Nielsen points out, but we can learn something about preparing resumes from Nielsen's work. We would not, for example, want to include information on the right side of the page in an area that is least "scanned" by the on-screen reader. Doing so might cause people to miss important information.

Examine Figure 6-8, the employment history section of a resume. What do you look at first? Second?

For most people, the eye moves to the area where the city, state, and dates of employment are because that area has more white space and is less cluttered. Unfortunately, this is the least important part of the resume. If your eye scrolled down through the bulleted list, did you read the entire bullet point or did you read the first couple of words? Notice that the first two or three words are verbs that are not very concrete or meaningful. They do not really describe law-specific skills.

Employment History
Jackson, Willet, & Moore, PC, Scottsdale, AZ

Paralegal   June 2009–present

Reviewed and summarized medical records in medical malpractice cases; reviewed documents for attorney-client privilege; prepared notebooks and exhibits for trial; drafted questions for attorneys to ask at depositions; attended depositions with attorneys; conducted pre-interviews with perspective clients; helped clients identify important information and documents needed; assisted with opening and closing files and file maintenance.

FIGURE 6-6 Employment Description. Job descriptions written as one block of text are difficult to read.

FIGURE 6-7 ParalegalGateway. ParalegalGateway.com provides an online community for paralegals and offers news and recognition of paralegals who are making a difference professionally and in their communities. Experts blog for ParalegalGateway's Weblog at http://paralegalgateway.com/category/pg-weblog/.

Now, look at Figure 6-9, the revised employment history of the same resume. In the revised example, your eye should travel straight down the left side of the resume and pick up key words and phrases without much effort.

When you prepare your resume, try to place your most important information in the "F-zone," as Figure 6-10 shows.

Employment History
Jackson, Willet, & Moore, PC   Scottsdale, AZ
Paralegal   June 2009–present

- Reviewed and summarized medical records
- Reviewed documents for attorney-client privilege
- Prepared notebooks and exhibits for trial
- Drafted questions and attended depositions

White & Lowe, LLP   Scottsdale, AZ
Case Clerk   April 2007–June 2009

- Created and maintained client files
- Located documents requested by attorneys
- Ordered files from central storage
- Retrieved copies of documents from state and federal courts

Law Offices of Erin Hatch   Scottsdale, AZ
Intern   March 2007

- Made photocopies and files of exhibits
- Observed and assisted at real estate closings
- Learned law firm filing system

FIGURE 6-8 Employment History. Aligning the location and dates on the right draws a reader's eye away from the job descriptions, which are more important.

Employment History
Paralegal
Jackson, Willet, & Moore, PC, Scottsdale, AZ
June 2009–present

- Medical records review and summarization
- Attorney-client privilege document review
- Trial notebook and exhibit preparation
- Deposition questions preparation and attendance

Case Clerk
White & Lowe, LLP, Scottsdale, AZ
April 2007–June 2009

- Client file opening and maintenance
- Fulfill attorney requests for documents
- Access central storage files upon request
- State and federal court document retrieval

Intern
Law Offices of Erin Hatch, Scottsdale, AZ
March 2007

- File and exhibit photocopying
- Real estate closing observation and assistance
- Law firm filing system knowledge gained

FIGURE 6-9 Revised Employment History Section. These job descriptions make the first two or three words count.

Choose Typefaces Carefully

When choosing typefaces for your resume, consider the preferences of the field. Legal professionals tend to use Times New Roman (TNR) for almost everything. Legal professionals can read TNR *fast*. Sometimes different typefaces slow down and frustrate readers who read quickly. When submitting resumes in the legal profession a good combination of typefaces is Verdana Bold for headings and Times New Roman for everything else:

Education
B.A., Paralegal Studies, Suffolk University, Expected May 2012
Minor: Chemistry

Never mix more than two typefaces in a single resume: a bold san serif font (one without the little squiggles or "feet") for headings and a serif font (one with the "feet") for everything else. The squiggles help our eyes stick to the text, while typefaces without the squiggles allow our eyes to fall through the text, not really sticking to the words. You want eyes reading your resume to see the important words and phrases.

Describe Job Functions Strategically

The rule used since the late 1970s has been to use active words to describe the work you are doing right now:

> Prepare for and assist with civil litigation matters relating to contract dispute; assist with reviewing and organizing document productions, preparing indices

Bold Name

356 Cyprus Avenue, AnyCity, AC 03200 999-888-7777

boldname@email.com

The most important information that you want people to remember about you should go in the gray areas of the page.

FIGURE 6-10 F-zone.

to document productions, summarizing depositions, and preparing witness kits for depositions. Responsible for managing witnesses, research, and documents for hearings.

This description works if we rely on past resume advice; in fact, many publications suggest resumes be written this way today. Instead, though, edit the description using the first-two-words rule, so the description might be edited to be a bulleted list that reads:

- Civil litigation case management relating to contract disputes
- Document production organization and indices preparation; deposition summaries; witness kit preparation
- Hearing preparation, including witness management, research, and documents

Remember to include the most important information in the "F-zone." You want to maximize your chances of your resume being noticed so paying attention to its design is important.

The Alex Z. Price resume, in Figure 6-11, offers a summary that limits who will consider him for a job, but he has designed the entire resume to show off his skills as a paralegal specializing in real estate. Notice the words that appear in the F-zone. The most important information appears in that part of his resume.

After you have gained five to seven years of experience in the legal profession, you will want to use descriptions that provide more detail about your accomplishments on the job.

Alex Z. Price
113 Pine Street
Detroit, MI 01234
(123) 456-7890   alex.price@email.com

Summary

Paralegal specializing in commercial real estate transactions from the initial contract through closing.

Professional Experience

Paralegal

Real Estate Department, Jones & Bailey, Detroit, 2008–2011

- Commercial real estate transactions from initial contract through closing
- Create legal entities and draft entity agreements
- Review purchase and sale agreements
- Assist clients in due diligence, monitor transactions in escrow, and close transactions
- Draft and review commercial leases and financing documentation

Paralegal

Laughton & Laughton, Detroit, 2006–2008

- Prepared contracts, deeds, and leases
- Researched statutes, rules and case law related to real estate disputes
- Maintained client files

Education

Certificate in Paralegal Studies, 2006
Eastern Michigan University

Bachelor of Business Administration, 2006
University of Michigan

FIGURE 6-11 Price Resume. Price uses a summary to limit his job search to positions in commercial real estate.

■ THE ELECTRONIC RESUME AND THE SCANNABLE RESUME

Companies are using technologies to review and to search resumes. A paper resume can be scanned using an OCR scanner and then searched for key words. An electronic resume can be uploaded into a full-text database and scanned.

An **electronic resume** is one that is prepared without any formatting. The benefit of this kind of resume is that its look will not change when pasted into an e-mail or submitted through a corporate form. A **scannable resume** is one that is prepared with careful thought to font choice and the words you use. A resume can be both electronic and scannable.

Font choice is especially important because optical readers cannot read all typefaces equally. Times New Roman, Verdana, Georgia—typical and plain typefaces—are always good choices. The words you use also make a difference. If a firm is looking for a paralegal who can draft answers to interrogatories, a resume that says, "Prepares discovery documents" may not make it through an electronic search engine. Note, however, that very few employers use resume scanners. Most resumes are reviewed one at a time.

PRACTICE TIP

E-mail your resume to yourself or to a friend to check the formatting. You may discover that sections of your resume re-align incorrectly or that you have hanging pages that you did not know about.

When to Use an Electronic Resume

An electronic resume should be used when you are asked to paste it into the body of an e-mail or into the form of an online application. If you are asked to attach or upload a resume, use your well-designed version, saved in the format the employer prefers.

Tips for Preparing an Electronic Resume

An electronic resume does not have any special formatting. When submitting text through an online form or in the body of an e-mail, the format coding is usually stripped away. This coding is what tells your document to make something bold or to tab over or to insert a table. Because the formatting is lost, you want to make sure you send a very "clean" document that has no special formatting.

The guidelines for preparing an electronic resume include the following:

* Use only one column.
* Do not use tabs or other ways of spacing text on a line.
* Do not use tables. The table formatting may be lost and the text in the tables will bunch together incoherently.
* Use a regular font, such as Times New Roman. Most electronic forms strip the font codes. If you use an unusual font, some of your letters may be translated into unrecognizable characters.
* Use all caps for section headings.
* Use only one font.
* Boldface sometimes works.
* Do not use italics.
* Do not use "rules" (the line that can be inserted above or below text), like this one:

    This is a rule. It was made with the "border" tool in Word.
    _____

    Instead, use a line created with hyphens like this one:
    ----
* Do not use bullets. Instead, use asterisks.

The Alex Z. Price resume, in Figure 6-12, has had all the formatting removed. Alex relies on all capital letters for headings, the asterisk, and hyphen keys to make this resume easier to read.

ALEX Z. PRICE
113 Pine Street, Detroit, MI 01234
(123) 456-7890
alex.price@email.com

SUMMARY
Paralegal specializing in commercial real estate transactions from the initial contract through closing.

PROFESSIONAL EXPERIENCE

PARALEGAL
Real Estate Department, Jones & Bailey, Detroit, 2008-2011

*Commercial real estate transactions from initial contract through closing
*Create legal entities and draft entity agreements
*Review purchase and sale agreements
*Assist clients in due diligence, monitor transactions in escrow, and close transactions
*Draft and review commercial leases and financing documentation

PARALEGAL
Laughton & Laughton, Detroit, 2006-2008

*Prepared contracts, deeds, and leases
*Researched statutes, rules and case law related to real estate disputes
*Maintained client files

EDUCATION

Certificate in Paralegal Studies, 2006
Eastern Michigan University

Bachelor of Business Administration, 2006
University of Michigan

FIGURE 6-12 Price Resume, Electronic Version. Price stripped the formatting from his resume. He used capital letters, asterisks, and hyphens to format his resume.

This type of resume could be pasted fairly easily into an online form, such as that shown in Figure 6-13.

When pasting a resume into an online form, make sure that your text does not take any metadata with it—extra information about formatting that makes the resume look junky. You want to have as clean a letter as possible. Proofread your resume again to be certain all the characters are correct and the spacing is good. Most paralegals pay attention to the tiniest of details, and providing a resume that has not been checked over for odd characters and spacing shows a lack of attention to detail.

Applicants often are asked to paste a resume into a small box, like this one:

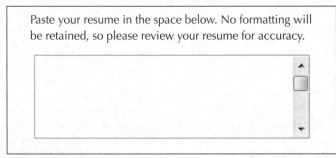

FIGURE 6-13 Online Form.

■ THE RESUME SAGA OF PAMELA COOPER

The story of Pamela Cooper's resume should have ended, but Charlsye rescued it from the files and used it for years as a "DON'T" during resume-writing workshops (redacted to hide the person's name and all identifying features, of course). At every workshop, Charlsye pointed out these problems:

- The summary is too vague. What kind of fast-paced environment does this applicant prefer? An office? Retail sales? McDonald's? It is not clear what sort of work this applicant wants to do.
- The experience as a waitress overwhelmingly suggests fast food or perhaps Starbucks.
- The skills section starts well with a real skill, even though most paralegal positions and other professional positions (with the exception of some administrative positions) do not have typing speed minimums.

Pamela Cooper
124 Washington Lane
New City, TX 75555
222-333-4444

Education

B.A., Political Science, 2010
University of Texas at Austin

Professional Experience

Government Regional Associates, Austin, 2006–07
- Performed field surveys
- Prepared reports, proposals, and marketing materials
- Answered telephones, made appointments and travel arrangements

Melody's, Inc., Austin, 2005–2006

- Coordinated special store events, fashion shows
- Coordinated media advertising
- Created store promotions

Other Experience

The Coffee Pot	Austin	2010
PMC Cleaning Services	Austin	2009
The Bar Hop	Austin	2008
The Sandwich Shop	Austin	2008

Skills

Microsoft Word and Excel
Type 60 words per minute
Report and proposal writing
Creative marketing campaign designs
Survey and data analysis

References available upon request.

FIGURE 6-14 Revised Cooper Resume. This resume shows off relevant skills. She might revise this resume again by adding a technical skills section or relevant coursework section.

- The phrase "Working knowledge of…" is a signal that the person has *heard* of and/or opened these software applications, but probably is not proficient. Charlsye has a working knowledge of car engines, household plumbing, and the lawn mower, but she is not qualified to be a mechanic, plumber, or landscaper.
- This recent college graduate lists education last. At this point in her career, her education is the most important bit of information and should appear at the top.
- If potential employers took a quick glance at Pamela's resume, they would clearly see that she has a four-year degree from a good school and worked throughout her college career. However, she does not seem like a good candidate for a job as a document analyst.

And then, one day, perhaps the 20th time Charlsye used this resume in a workshop, she saw something new.

This applicant actually *was very qualified* to be interviewed for the position of document analyst, but Charlsye had simply missed the good stuff in this resume the first 19 times she had looked at it.

Charlsye revised the resume to highlight the things that qualify this person for the document analyst position.

The revised resume, as shown in Figure 6-14, reorganizes Pamela's skills so that her analytical skills are highlighted. This resume shows the following:

- As a recent college graduate, Pamela might be open to temporary work.
- She has a four-year degree.
- Two positions required her to use analytical thinking and written communication skills.
- These positions required her to work independently.
- She worked her way through college, so she probably has a good work ethic.
- She ends the resume by summing up her skill set, which includes skills a document analyst needs to have.
- The resume could be further improved if Pamela provided some details about the field surveys she conducted or the special events she coordinated.

No one will get a 20th reading for a resume! If Pamela had submitted the resume in its revised form in the first place, she probably would have gotten an interview.

The design of your resume affects the way people read it and interpret the person you are. When they look at your life on paper, you want them to see a person who has the potential to become an outstanding paralegal.

CONCLUSION

A resume is the most inexpensive marketing tool you can have for your job search. To be effective, though, your resume must make you *look like* the type of professional an organization wants to hire. At the beginning of your career, this means that you may need several resumes—one for a general paralegal position, one geared for a corporate position you saw online and desperately want, and another one for the job working for the district attorney's office.

Your resume and letter of application (next chapter) may be two of the shortest documents you ever write, but they may take the longest to get just right. Take time to represent yourself well through these documents.

Checklist for Success

☐ Remember that your resume is a visual representation of you.

☐ Never use a resume template. Resumes show that you can format documents, an essential skill for paralegals.

☐ The first 11 characters of a bullet point are the most important.

☐ Choose typefaces that are easy to read online and on paper.

☐ Examine your resume to be sure the important information falls within the "F-zone."

☐ Highlight your experience, education, and skills for the job you want.

☐ Write a one-page power resume.

☐ Choose the resume format based on the job you want and the experience you have.

☐ Maintain an electronic version of your resume.

☐ E-mail your resume to yourself to make sure the formatting is not altered during the transfer.

ASSIGNMENTS: PREPARING FOR YOUR PARALEGAL CAREER

Career Management

Use a dark-colored sheet of paper to create an "F-zone" template and place your resume on top of it. Trace the F-zone. Does the most important information fall into that space? Rewrite your resume so that you place the most important information in the F-zone.

Prepare

Format your resume three different ways using different typefaces to change the effect. Print the different versions and bring them to class to discuss. Write a memorandum to your instructor explaining your design decisions.

Prepare

Find two job ads for positions you are either qualified for now or will be upon completion of your paralegal education program. For each job, write your resume two ways, trying skills-based and experience-based resumes to show your strengths. Bring all four versions to class to discuss. Write a memorandum to your instructor explaining your content and design decisions.

REFERENCES

Nielsen, Jakob. (2006, Apr. 17). "F-Shaped Pattern for Reading Web Content." Useit.com. Online: *http://www.useit.com/alertbox/reading_pattern.html*

"First 2 Words: A Signal for the Scanning Eye." (2009, Apr. 6). Useit.com. Online: *http://www.useit.com/alertbox/nanocontent.html*

"Email Newsletters: Surviving Inbox Congestion." (2006, June 12). Useit.com. Online: *http://www.useit.com/alertbox/newsletters.html*

CHAPTER **7**

JOB SEARCH AND NETWORKING CORRESPONDENCE

When Marcy was still a relatively new paralegal working in Baltimore, she had the opportunity to help sort through applications for a vacant associate attorney position. She met with the office manager and an associate attorney in the firm's conference room to review 122 applications for the position.

Marcy watched as the associate attorney and office manager began sifting through the pile of application letters without reading them. Instead, they sorted them by how the application letters looked:

- The letter and resume printed on blue resume paper? Out.
- The application letter that included a headshot? Out.
- The application letter that included a business card paper-clipped to the top of the letter? Out.
- The application letter that *went on* for six pages? Out.
- The application letter that was not formatted perfectly? Out.

And so it went. At least 25 percent of the stack was dismissed because the application letter did not *look like it should*.

At a family reunion a few months later, Marcy described the meeting to her cousin, Rebecca, who had taken a temporary job at an engineering consulting firm in New York City. Rebecca, a dancer, had broken her ankle and took the temporary job while she recovered. Her job was to review incoming applications. Marcy wanted to know how she could make decisions about the applications since she knew nothing about engineering.

"I scan the letters for key words," Rebecca explained. "If I see a word or two that matches the job description, I look at the resume."

"And if you don't see the keywords?" Marcy asked.

"I go on to the next."

You certainly do not want your application letter and resume to be tossed out because it does not look right or because you did not clearly define your skills.

Application letters are a key component of your job search and serve many purposes, including:

- Communicating that you want to apply for a specific job
- Serving as a writing sample that shows you know how to write a letter *and* you know what a proper letter looks like
- Showing how your skill set fits the job opening the company needs to fill

By the end of this chapter, you should be able to:

- Understand the importance of your resume and application letter looking "right"
- Recognize the purposes of an application letter
- Identify the basic formula for an application letter
- Know the different types of application letters
- Realize the importance of thank-you notes
- State how networking correspondence may help with your job search

In all of these types of correspondence, remember what Marcy and Rebecca learned: Your application letter needs to *look like* an application letter and needs to *be about the job* you are applying for.

■ WRITING THE LETTER OF APPLICATION

A good letter of application (often called a cover letter) follows a very basic formula *that gets results*. Because this is the first writing sample an employer sees, you want your letter to be formatted perfectly, grammatically correct, and rich with content.

There are three important rules for writing your letter of application.

First, your letter must look like a letter of application.

Formal application letters should be submitted on paper appropriate for a resume and include the formal elements of a letter. As you will see later in this chapter. E-mail letters and letters that you paste into a tiny little box in an online form are formatted differently because they are not submitted on paper.

However, *all* application letters have the same content.

For example, when you practice drafting a pleading for class, you want it—above all else—to *look like* a pleading. The content may be excellent. The grammar, perfect. The argument, persuasive. But, a pleading that does not *look like* a pleading may be regarded as another kind of document and misfiled by the court. An application letter that does not *look like* an application letter may be tossed out before it is even read.

Second, your letter must be reviewed carefully for accuracy. Always ask someone else to read your letter for you before you send it out to ensure all the words are there, the grammar is correct, and you have not missed a typographical error.

You should ask someone else to proofread your letter because our eyes are superefficient and fill in missing letters or words as we read. When we look at a second or third or twelfth draft of a letter, our eyes sometimes base what they are seeing on an earlier draft and may make us think we see entire words that are actually missing. Writers often suggest you put the draft down for a while and come back to it later. The reason for this is to give your eyes a chance to "forget" what they have seen so you can look at the document with "fresh" eyes.

PRACTICE TIP

The advice that an application letter *must look like* an application letter will be repeated throughout this chapter. You may think this advice is obvious. Unfortunately, many books recommend writing creative letters of application and give a lot of suggestions for doing so. We recommend writing *only* the type of letter described in this chapter when applying for jobs in the legal profession.

Third, follow the advice in this section for preparing the content of your letter of application. A letter that is rich with content will get attention. The content should be relevant and specific.

■ LETTER FORMAT: MAKE YOUR LETTER OF APPLICATION LOOK LIKE A LETTER OF APPLICATION

Format your application letter carefully and choose a typeface that matches your resume so that the two documents appear to go together. Figure 7-1 shows what a letter of application should look like.

April 24, 20xx

32 Hill Street
Dallas, TX 98765

Hiring Committee
William & Jones, L.L.C.
123 Main Street, Suite 8
Dallas, TX 98765

Dear Hiring Committee:

I am writing to apply for the bankruptcy paralegal position advertised in *Texas Lawyer's Weekly*. My education and internship experience have prepared me to work in a bankruptcy practice.

During my paralegal internship at Adkins Law, P.C., my work focused on one Chapter 7 personal bankruptcy matter and one Chapter 11 corporate bankruptcy reorganization. In the Chapter 7 matter, I learned how to assist clients with identifying their assets and debt. In the Chapter 11 reorganization involving Union Street Jewelers, Adkins Law represents the Trustee. This bankruptcy also has litigation pending, and my job was to review, distribute, and file incoming correspondence, pleadings, and other documents. I also assisted with document analysis and helped prepare the attorney for a hearing by creating a notebook of relevant documents.

I am completing my post-baccalaureate paralegal certificate at Southeastern Paralegal Institute, where I have a 3.75 GPA. Prior to that, I earned a B.A. in psychology from the University of North Texas. At Southeastern, classes in bankruptcy and litigation prepared me for my work at Adkins Law. During the bankruptcy class, I learned to draft bankruptcy petitions, to identify types of bankruptcies, and to create client checklists to manage each client's case.

My resume is enclosed. I look forward to hearing from you soon.

Sincerely,

Abby Lerner

Abby Lerner

Encls.: Resume

FIGURE 7-1 Letters of application follow a standard business letter format.

PRACTICE TIP

If you do not have time for anyone to proofread your letter, you can trick your eyes by making the font larger or smaller or by selecting a typeface that is much different from the one you have been using.

Use a standard letter format. Notice how the letter spacing is balanced on the page.

The date is typed out. Do not abbreviate the month. The proper format is 24, 20xx, *not* 24th, 20xx.

Abby Lerner's return (inside) address does not include her name.

After each element is one double space. To create this space, hit enter twice at the end of the element.

Each paragraph is single spaced with one double space between paragraphs.

The correct spacing for the signature block is to type "Sincerely," and then press enter FOUR times.

The last line is the "enclosure" line and tells the recipient what is enclosed. If you are sending an e-mail, you would use an "attachment" line: Attch.:

■ CONTENT OF LETTERS OF APPLICATION: THE FOUR CRUCIAL PARAGRAPHS

The overall conservative nature of the legal profession requires a conservative approach to letters of application. Even if you are applying to a firm that has a reputation for bucking trends, you still want to take the approach to letters of application that we recommend.

An application letter that looks like an application letter gets a second glance; a well-written letter gets attention. Looks + content = interview.

Application letters should have four paragraphs. That is it. Long letters or letters with cute openings are rarely a big hit. Short letters, especially letters with only one paragraph, are not very successful either. The four paragraphs should be composed as follows:

Paragraph 1   Identify the position you are applying for and include a "thesis" sentence that foreshadows the next two paragraphs. This paragraph usually has two sentences. In the following example, the applicant identifies the position to which she is applying and mentions internship experience and paralegal education:

> I am writing to apply for the real estate paralegal position advertised in the March 15 issue of *Texas Lawyers Weekly*. My internship experience at the Law Office of Sharon Larson and my paralegal education qualify me for this position.

> The last sentence in this paragraph serves as a "thesis" sentence. It will provide the organizational structure for the rest of your letter. In other words, the reader will expect your letter to focus first on internship experience and then education.

Paragraph 2   Discuss the first topic mentioned in the thesis sentence. This paragraph should be longer than the first paragraph and should provide details that show your qualifications for this position.

Paragraph 3   Discuss the second topic mentioned in the thesis sentence.

Example of Paragraphs 2 and 3

> I believe my internship experience solidified for me the skills I learned in my paralegal education program at South Paralegal Institute, an ABA-approved program. The class in real estate law focused on contracts for the sale of real estate, deeds, title examinations, security for real estate transactions, zoning ordinances, brokerage contracts, leases, and landlord and tenant rights and liabilities. I earned an A during this course, where I drafted different types of documents. This course prepared me for an internship in real estate law.

> During my six-week internship at the Law Office of Sharon Larson, I worked very closely with Ms. Larson's paralegal to prepare closing documents for more than a dozen clients. I drafted deeds, ordered title searches, and prepared title abstracts. I learned how to prepare amortization tables, coordinate escrow arrangements, and prepare escrow instructions. I assisted with proofreading, photocopying, and assembling documents and I had the opportunity to attend several closings. Toward the end of my internship, I was assigned the task of independently preparing for a closing.

Paragraphs 2 and 3 are all about you and your qualifications. They need to be written carefully so that you describe what you can do in terms of what the job requires. If you are applying for a corporate position, do not go on and on about your great work in an area that the company did not mention in its job advertisement.

These two paragraphs are really about showcasing your skills so that the employer thinks *We could really use this person.*

Paragraph 4   Conclude. Do not provide extraneous information.
My resume is enclosed. I look forward to hearing from you.

IN PRACTICE

Resume Wisdom

The following guidelines are not completely right or completely wrong, but are based on wisdom from those who know best. In this case, these guidelines are based on feedback from employers with experience reviewing resumes:

- Make your application letter *look like* an application letter.
- Do not write a chatty letter or a "creative" letter.
- Never use an exclamation point in your letter. Ever.
- Do not say, "I have excellent communication skills." When you do, you invite the reader to make a judgment about your communication skills, and the slightest odd wording or error will stand out. In this instance, *no observation* about your communication skills shows that you do, indeed, have good communication skills.

- Never explain how you *feel* about yourself. No one cares. They want to know what skills you have. For example, *never* write:
  - I feel my skills have prepared me to work at your firm.
  - I feel your firm is a perfect match for me.
  - I feel I will make an excellent employee for your firm.

There are no alternatives for these sentences. Just omit them. Your letter needs to *demonstrate* your abilities through descriptions of projects, education, and work experience. Employers like to believe they have made the perfect match by finding you.

■ TYPES OF APPLICATION LETTERS

Application letters (often called cover letters) take one of these forms:

- Solicited letters: letters responding to job advertisements
- Unsolicited letters: letters sent to potential employers who have not advertised a specific position
- Letters of inquiry: letters asking for information about the company, its hiring practices, and potential opportunities, such as an internship program

The key difference between these types of letters is whether you are responding to a specific request for an application, such as a job posting, or whether you are writing with the hope that your resume might get attention.

Solicited Application Letters

Solicited application letters respond to an advertised position or program. For example, as shown in Figure 7-2, WilmerHale in Boston offers a summer paralegal internship program. By advertising its internship program on its website, the firm is *soliciting* applications from students. A solicited letter of application would be the correct response to this request. Figure 7-3 shows a letter of application to an established paralegal internship program.

Unsolicited Application Letters

When you want to apply for a job at a company that has not advertised a specific need, you will write an *unsolicited* application letter. This is a letter no one has asked for so it must be drafted with care.

White & Case, an international law firm, provides detailed information on its website about the career path of legal assistants, but it does not *solicit* letters by inviting you to apply (Refer to Figure 7-4.). If you decide to send your resume to express interest in a position with the firm when no position has been advertised, you are submitting an unsolicited letter.

When you write an unsolicited application letter, you must specify why you are applying, as the letter in Figure 7-5 shows.

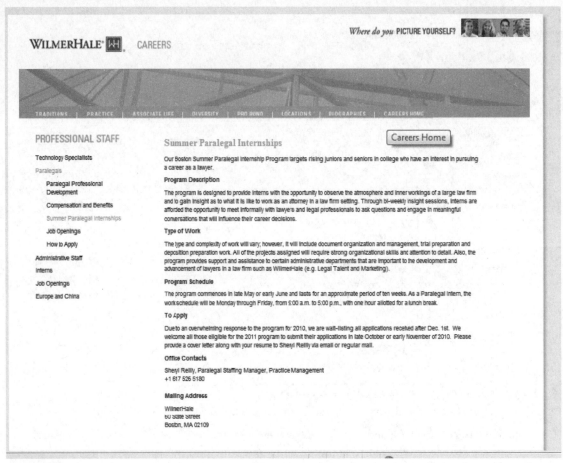

FIGURE 7-2 WilmerHale offers a summer internship program for paralegals.

Formatting Your E-mail Letter and the Online Box

This section explains how to format application letters submitted through e-mail or copied into a small online box. In both cases, the four core paragraphs remain the same. Sending a letter via e-mail or using an online box is not an excuse to write a one-paragraph letter.

E-mail Application Letter

An e-mail application letter should be written in the body of the e-mail. Do not attach a separate letter unless one is requested. An e-mail letter looks differently than a formal letter because it does not include the firm's name or address. The content of the letter remains the same. At the end of the e-mail, you should include a signature block with your personal information: name, address, e-mail address, and phone number.

E-mail Signature Blocks

E-mail should always include a signature block. This immediately gives the impression that you are polished and that your e-mail is complete. The purpose of the signature block is to provide contact information.

When you work for an organization, you include the business address, e-mail address, phone number, and fax number in the signature block. This is standard procedure.

April 26, 20xx

12 First Street
Somerville, MA 01222

Paralegal Internship Program
Wiley, Abrams, and Long LLP
60 Main Street
Boston, MA 02109

Dear Hiring Committee:

Please accept this letter and resume as application to your paralegal internship program. I believe my prior experience working at a small law firm, as well as my paralegal education, have prepared me for such a position.

While attending school, I worked part-time for two years at the Law Office of Jessica Jones, a trial attorney. At Ms. Jones's office, I learned to prepare trial notebooks, organize discovery documents, and to maintain a law office filing system. I have attended two trials and worked closely with Ms. Jones on preparing answers to interrogatories.

During my paralegal education at Suffolk University, I have taken classes in litigation, the American justice system, and discovery. I also took a class in e-discovery and learned how to use technology, such as CaseMap, to organize and analyze documents. My education and the skills I have gained working for Ms. Jones have prepared me for paralegal work.

My resume is enclosed. I look forward to hearing from you.

Sincerely,

Matthew Brown

Matthew Brown

Encls: Resume

FIGURE 7-3 A letter of application for an established paralegal internship program.

When you are searching for a job, you need to use your personal information. If you are writing an e-mail and applying for a job, use your personal address, phone number, and e-mail address. You will need an e-mail account that is separate from your work account to use when applying for jobs.

You can easily program your e-mail account to automatically include a signature block. For e-mailed applications, your signature block might look like this:

April L. Smith
123 Long Road
City, ST 07777
E-mail: *april.smith@email.com*
Phone: 999-888-7777

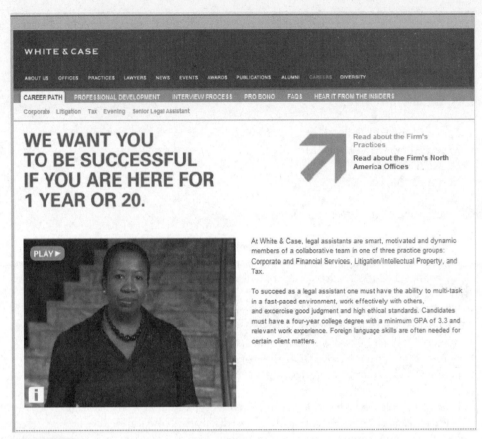

FIGURE 7-4 White & Case has a defined paralegal track.

Caution: Be very careful when you set up this automated function if you use this e-mail account for any other purpose. You should not send your personal address and phone number to everyone. For example, your day-to-day e-mail signature might simply be:

Julie Howell
Julie@email.com

In this case, Julie is including contact information, but not enough for anyone to find her at her personal residence. Some students choose to include more information:

Julie Howell,
President,
Paralegal Student Organization
Julie@email.com

By adding one more line, Julie has told us she is probably responsible and possibly a good leader because she can run an organization and has been elected to office. We do not know where she lives or what her home phone number is, which is good for security purposes. Some students feel it is safe enough to include a cell phone number, but that is a personal decision.

When using an e-mail signature, opt for a full signature, with name, address, and phone number, for job applications and a shorter signature for day-to-day e-mail correspondence. The shorter signature provides a layer of security. Figure 7-6 shows how an e-mail application letter should be formatted.

April 26, 20xx

32 Fern Street
Miami, FL 33131

White & Case LLP
Wachovia Financial Center
200 South Biscayne Boulevard
Suite 4900
Miami, FL 33131-2352

Dear Hiring Committee:

Please accept this letter and resume as application to White & Case's legal
assistant program. I am interested in working in the corporate transactions
section of the firm, and my education and internship experience have
prepared me for such a position.

> In an unsolicited letter, the first paragraph is generally the only paragraph that is different from an application letter.

During my paralegal education at Miami College, I have maintained a 3.75
GPA, and I have taken courses in corporate law. I especially enjoyed working
on projects involving drafting contracts.

Last summer, I worked as an intern at York Corporation, where I assisted attorneys with reviewing transactional documents including leases, purchase-
and-sale agreements, and other contracts.

My resume is enclosed. I look forward to hearing from you.

Sincerely,

Macy Brooks

Macy Brooks

Encl: Resume

FIGURE 7-5 An unsolicited letter of application must specify why you are applying.

Online Form Application Letter

Sometimes, you will be asked to upload your application letter and resume, as shown in
Figure 7-7, or to copy and paste the content of these materials into an online form so that
the documents can be saved into a database.

Sometimes, the instructions suggest that an application letter is *optional*. We believe
you should always exercise this option and supply a letter. Adding a well-written application letter separates you from other applicants who do not submit one.

In Chapter 6, we pointed out that you must pay attention to formatting when you
paste a resume into a form. The same is true for pasting an application letter into a form. You
want to make sure the letter does not have odd characters or spacing.

The subject line should include the title of the position or other identifier. Never send an e-mail without a subject line. Employers hate that.

To: *hiringcommittee@lawfirm.com*
From: *Julie@email.com*
Subject: Bankruptcy Paralegal Position
Date: April 24, 20xx

Dear Hiring Committee:

With three years of legal secretarial experience and a 3.96 GPA in my paralegal program, I write to apply for a bankruptcy paralegal position at your firm.

Note which areas are double-spaced and which are single-spaced.

At Mavis and Johnson, LLP, I worked as a legal secretary in the bankruptcy section. In this position, I prepared correspondence, service lists, and finalized documents for filing with the court by making copies and arranging for filing. In this position, I assisted staff at the corporate Trustee's office, maintained files, ordered supplies, and made travel arrangements.

The content of an e-mail application letter should be the same as the content of a formal application letter.

This year, I will complete my B.S. in Paralegal Studies at Kaplan University, where I took classes in bankruptcy and litigation. These courses have prepared me to work in bankruptcy and to work on cases involving bankruptcy litigation. I learned trial procedures and studied the Bankruptcy Code.

My resume is attached. Please let me know if you have any questions. I look forward to speaking with you soon.

Sincerely,
Julie Howell

Instead of Encls., use Attch.: when indicating a resume is attached.

Attch: Resume

The signature block gives contact information. E-mailed applications should *always* include a signature block.

Julie Howell
1234 Dove Street
Davenport, IA 52805
E-mail: *Julie@email.com*
Phone: 123-456-7890

FIGURE 7-6 E-mail letters of application should be formatted slightly differently, but the content of the four basic paragraphs remains the same.

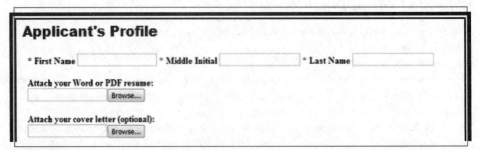

FIGURE 7-7 To apply for a paralegal position online, applicants are often asked to fill out an online form and upload their resumes and application letters. When attaching a letter appears to be optional, you should always exercise this option.

PARALEGAL **PROFILE**

Kisha Washington

Current position: Paralegal & Director of Legal Administration

Employer: Teach for America, Inc.

Years in this position: 1 year

Years of paralegal experience: 5

Education:

B.A, Political Science with Emphasis in Public Administration, Northern Illinois University, DeKalb, IL

Paralegal Certificate, Emphasis in Corporate Law, Institute for Paralegal Studies, Loyola University, Chicago, IL

Kisha Washington gives her perspective on hiring from a non-profit organization's point of view.

Kisha Washington works for Teach for America, a non-profit organization that works to close the achievement gap by placing excellent teachers in under-privileged schools and training these teachers to help their students make significant academic progress every school year. Kisha shares what she looks for when hiring paralegals to work for this non-profit organization, which is mission-focused rather than profit-driven.

What gets an immediate "No, thanks," when you are screening applications?

I immediately reject all applications that come to my desk without a cover letter. There is no way to gauge why an applicant is interested in working for our organization if they do not include a cover letter.

If an applicant has a history of service and the applicant's interest in our mission is evident in the cover letter, I then review for grammar and typos. The resume is reviewed for the same things. I reject all applications with grammatical errors, typos, and formatting errors.

Which applications get your attention?

Before experience, before certifications, before recommendations, I screen for fit with Teach for America's mission. I look for an interest in education and for a history of volunteering. I search for volunteer interests of any type, but I prefer a history focusing on education or involving children. I search for personal connections to our mission, such as an individual's experience with their own education or that of their children's or a member of their extended family, or I search for that "Ah ha" moment, in however they choose to express their recognition that something in our country's education system needs to change.

In essence, I want to see if the applicant has done any research about the organization and can connect their interests to our mission. I search for people dedicated to, or interested in, the movement, not just to the legal world. If an applicant does not show any connection to our mission, the applicant will not be invited for an interview.

What do you look for during an interview?

Applicants who are interviewed are evaluated on their fit with our mission, our core values. I also query for concrete examples of how they have built positive working relationships and evidence of their being able to communicate effectively with people across the organization at all levels. I search for evidence of an ability to organize, plan and execute without having to constantly be monitored, a willingness to constantly learn new things, and a comfort with making decisions and demonstrating good judgment. Since no one is perfect, I also search for evidence of accepting, examining, and learning from mistakes.

When you use an online form, be sure your text does not take any metadata with it—extra information about formatting that makes the letter look odd. You will know if your letter has metadata if it has strange characters or spacing. Two common symbols that show up in your pasted text include a ° and a ?. Your text might appear this way:

Dear Mr. Young: °

I° have worked on°°°°° the Big Project for six years.?? °As°°°°°°°°

Your letter needs to be as clean as possible. Metadata takes away from its appearance.

Attaching a Letter: If you decide to attach a letter, it should be a formal application letter. Take the time to scan your signature and learn how to insert it into the signature block on the letter. Your school computer lab or career center may be able to help you accomplish this task. *Not* pasting in a signature is acceptable, given that you are uploading the letter to a server. However, once someone prints your document and photocopies it several times, it begins to look like a formal letter that you mailed without a signature. You do not want anyone to wonder why you sent a letter without a signature.

Pasting the Letter into an Online Box: If you paste your letter into an online box, you can use a formal letter format and include all elements of a letter. In the alternative, you can use an e-mail letter format and start with "Dear Hiring Committee."

■ AFTER THE INTERVIEW: THANK YOU NOTES

After you attend an interview, you will want to follow up with a thank you note. You have three choices and must make your selection carefully. You can send a formal letter (always appropriate), a handwritten note (appropriate and you can send this one fast) or you can send an e-mail (sometimes appropriate).

Sending a formal letter is always appropriate. Everyone appreciates receiving such a letter. However, sometimes, you might learn during a job interview that a hiring decision will be made within one or two days. In this case, sending thank you notes by e-mail would be appropriate. If you are not sure—and it is not always appropriate to ask when decisions will be made—write thank you notes the day you interview and mail them. They will be received within one or two days. Employers remember the people who send thank you notes, like the example shown in Figure 7-8.

If you want your message to be received quickly, you can pen a handwritten note and place it in the mailbox right away. This technique works well if you do not live near the interview site. For example, if you drive an hour or two to the job interview—with the idea that you will relocate if you get the job—you can write a thank you note before you go home and mail it in the city where the company is. You will shave a day or so off the time that it takes for the letter to make it from your home post office.

This technique also works when you do not have a computer or laser printer readily available to prepare a formal letter. Use your best handwriting and make sure all the words are legible and spelled correctly.

April 26, 20xx

Martha Jackson, Esq.
Babson & Leeman, P.C.
426 Lexington Street
Scottsdale, AZ 76555

Use the name of the person who interviewed you.

Dear Ms. Jackson:

Thank you for taking time to talk to me about the paralegal position at your firm. I enjoyed meeting you and other members of the litigation department.

I am very interested in working on the intellectual property litigation matters you described. I believe I can learn a lot as well as bring energy and enthusiasm to the projects.

Sincerely,

Macy Brooks

Macy Brooks

FIGURE 7-8 Thank you notes should be sent after job interviews.

Your third option is to send your thank you by e-mail. This technique, while less memorable than a formal letter or handwritten note, also shows that you follow through and pay attention to detail. Make sure that your e-mail has a clear subject line and that you run the e-mail through a spell checker before you send it.

■ NETWORKING CORRESPONDENCE

When you meet someone you would like to stay in touch with, hear a good speaker, or want to reinforce a connection you made at a networking event, an e-mail message or handwritten note are great ways to tell a person you enjoyed the interaction.

Sometimes, you might meet someone on an airplane that you find interesting enough to stay in touch with. You may not know why the connection is important, but you exchanged business cards with the person and you want to keep the connection open. An e-mail message, such as the one shown in Figure 7-9, is appropriate.

You also could write a handwritten note, like the one shown in Figure 7-10.

Following up an interesting meeting with a note could open a door for you later when you are job hunting, trying to find people to contribute articles to a newsletter, looking for a speaker, or needing a bit of information about a subject. The connections you make expand your network of information.

```
To:       ann@bigcompany.com
From:     allie@email.com
Subject:  Book we discussed
Date:     April 24, 20xx
```

Dear Ann:

I enjoyed chatting with you on our flight from Detroit to Dallas. I wanted to send you the author's name of the book that we were discussing on the flight: Dan Ariely. The title of the book is *The Upside of Irrationality*. I hope you enjoy it as much as I did.

Best,
Allie

Allie Lillie
allie@email.com
Cell phone: 123-456-7890

Notice that Allie's signature includes only her e-mail address and cell phone number. She should *never* give a home address to a stranger on a plane. A business phone and address would be okay, especially if they traded business cards, which include this information anyway.

FIGURE 7-9 Sending a note after meeting someone helps solidify the connection.

Dear Jane,

I enjoyed your talk about alternative dispute resolution at the North Texas Paralegal Association meeting last week. I was able to take some of the strategies you presented and use them right away.

Thanks again. I really enjoyed the talk.

Lois Andrews

FIGURE 7-10 Handwritten notes are not used as often, and therefore, when you send a handwritten note, chances are it will be remembered.

CONCLUSION

The application letters and networking correspondence that you write show others that you care about your profession and your personal work within it. Your letters serve as a writing sample and show that you are personable. Prepare your letters, e-mail, and handwritten notes with care to show that you want to be taken seriously in the profession.

Checklist for Success

☐ The first rule of writing an application letter is that your letter *must look like an application letter*.

☐ Use proper letter formatting.

☐ Use the same typeface for your resume and application letter, so that the documents "match."

☐ Use a four-paragraph format for your letter. Prepare the content for your letter very carefully.

☐ Learn how to maintain formatting and submit letters using online forms whenever necessary.

☐ Write thank you notes after your interview to reinforce a good impression.

☐ Formal thank you notes are always appropriate, but handwritten or e-mail notes are acceptable and better than not sending a note at all.

☐ Use networking notes to extend and maintain connections with people you meet.

☐ Remember that any time you send an application letter, a thank you note, or a networking note, you are providing people with a writing sample.

ASSIGNMENTS: PREPARING FOR YOUR PARALEGAL CAREER

Career Management

Find an advertisement for a job you would be interested in upon graduation. Write a formal letter of application for this position. Reformat the letter for e-mail. Turn in the job ad, the formal letter, and the e-mail version. Last, write a paragraph about the choices you made related to the information you decided to include in the letter. Place the letters you draft in your career management notebook to serve as your templates, to be modified as needed.

Prepare

Write a paragraph that you would include in your letter of application that describes your internship experience.

Write the same paragraph four different ways. How do the paragraphs highlight different areas of your experience?

Prepare

Write a paragraph that you would include in your letter of application that describes one project you did during school. Write the same paragraph for two different projects. How do the paragraphs highlight different areas of your experience?

CHAPTER **8**

INTERVIEWING AND NEGOTIATING

Landing a job interview is exciting and sometimes feels like you have cracked a secret code. The real test comes with the next step: the interview itself where you will have an opportunity to impress a potential employer. This chapter focuses on interviewing for a job and negotiating salary and benefits when a job offer comes in. By the end of this chapter, you should be able to:

- Know how to prepare for an interview
- Plan answers to difficult questions that may be asked in the interview
- Describe the things you should consider when you receive a job offer
- Assess what to do when you do not receive a job offer after an interview

■ PREPARING FOR AN INTERVIEW

You only get to make a first impression once during your initial interview. To get ready for that interview, organize yourself and answer these questions:

- How will you dress?
- Which business accessories will you take with you to the interview?
- Which printed materials do you need take with you?

How to Dress for an Interview

The legal profession offers work in many environments, from offices that require dressing up every day to offices that find jeans and sneakers more productive. The legal profession is conservative at its roots, and even in dress-down offices, suits are required on special days. When you arrive for your interview, people will think that you are dressed the best you will ever be. With that in mind, even if everyone in the office is wearing jeans, you need to be wearing a suit.

Women

Women should dress conservatively. Wear a suit that includes a jacket and pants or skirt made from the same fabric. Wear a conservative blouse in a conservative color. Showing cleavage is not conservative, so we advise against it. Some experts advise against wearing red to interview at a law firm. Their thinking is that red signals over-confidence and may indicate to others that you may not be willing to defer to others or to work as a team player.

Your shoes should be closed toe and conservative. Pumps are always a good choice. If you cannot wear shoes with a heel, wear dress shoes with a wide, 1-inch heel. Flat shoes should be reserved for business casual attire. Shoes should be black, dark blue, dark gray, or brown, depending on the color of your suit skirt or pants. Never wear shoes in bright colors or white to a job interview. Make sure your shoes are clean and polished and that your heels are in good condition. Some people look at shoe heels to make a judgment about how you handle small details. If your heel taps (the rubber bottoms on the heels of your shoes) are starting to wear, you can have them replaced at a shoe repair shop, sometimes while you wait. The shop usually shines your shoes and smoothes out any nicks or scratches, making them look gorgeous again.

More and more women choose not to wear nylon hosiery to work; however, choosing to wear hosiery to a job interview is always appropriate, and a good decision if you are unsure. Hosiery should match your skin tone. Never wear a dark skirt and white hosiery, for example. Invest in good quality hosiery because it will not snag as easily. After you begin a job, you can observe your colleagues and follow the trend in the office.

Limit accessories. More is not better. When interviewing for a job, some women choose to wear one ring, one watch or bracelet, one necklace, and earrings. You should remove hardware from visible body piercings other than your ears, and tattoos should be covered, if possible.

Do not wear perfume or scented body mists. Many offices are fragrance free, which makes any perfume stand out even more (and not in a good way).

Men

Men should wear a suit in a dark color—navy or black. Suits with pinstripes or that are charcoal gray might be appropriate, depending on the fabric, width of the pinstripes, and overall look of the suit. Always opt for conservative.

Men should wear a crisp white shirt that has been professionally pressed. The shirt should be a business-style shirt. Oxford-style shirts (with the buttons on the collar) are often appropriate but are not as formal.

A tie in a conservative style and color is expected. Avoid red ties because some experts advise that red signals over-confidence and that you may not be willing to defer to others or to work as a collaborative team player.

Shoes should be black dress shoes. They should be polished, and the heels should be in good condition. A worn heel suggests that you do not pay attention to details. A shoe repair shop may be able to help you curb the wear of your shoes, and, at the very least, can polish away any nicks or scratches. You should wear socks that match your shoes or your suit.

Jewelry should be limited. For interviews, men tend to wear only a watch and one ring. You should remove hardware from visible body piercings, and tattoos should be covered, if possible.

IN PRACTICE

Interviewing in Inclement Weather

If you live in an area where you need to wear rain or snow gear to your interview, plan to change (sort of Superman style) once you arrive. For example, if you take public transportation and typically walk from a central station, you may need to wear more foul-weather gear than you would like.

Wear your snow gear to the door of the building. Once you step inside, you have some options, depending on the building. If you enter an office building, but are not yet to the reception desk of the potential employer, you can step off to the side and change your shoes. Bring a backpack or a black canvas shoulder bag (with a plastic grocery bag inside) to stow your wet boots. Black is the most inconspicuous color.

When you get to the reception area for the company or firm where you are interviewing, ask to hang your coat. Feel comfortable enough to leave your shoe bag and/or umbrella with or near your coat. Most offices have a coat closet or area for stowing these things.

After you have your coat and boots stowed, ask to use the restroom if you are worried about your hair or smudged make-up. You certainly do not want to begin an interview with mascara running down your cheek or your hair sticking up or out in places where it should not.

After your interview, be sure to gather your shoe bag and coat. Stop in the lobby to change shoes quickly before going back out into inclement weather.

Do not wear cologne or scented body spray. Aftershave usually has some scent to it and should be worn sparingly. Many offices are fragrance free, and you do not want to stand out because of your cologne or aftershave. In this situation, less is best.

Business Accessories

You could easily pack a briefcase of materials to carry to a job interview: portfolio, pocket folio, electronic organizer, paper calendar, extra resumes, and other materials. But please do not. You will look disorganized.

It is acceptable to carry a small attaché case or briefcase to hold your portfolio, your calendar, and a notepad. Go for small and conservative when considering which bag/briefcase to carry. Briefcases with right angles tend to look more professional than squishy bags like messenger bags, backpacks, or hobo-style handbags. In all cases, eliminate bling—no big shiny hardware.

Some people choose to carry a portfolio of work with extra copies of their resume and reference list tucked into the front pocket. Others choose to bring only a folio—a leather-type folder that has a notepad on the right side and a pocket on the left for extra resumes and reference lists.

Bring a pen, and if you do not carry a folio that includes a notepad, tuck a small notepad inside your portfolio.

Bring a calendar. You want your materials to be efficient and easy to use without feeling clunky. While you do not want is to look like a traveling side show, you do want to make sure you have all the materials that you need.

All of these materials—your portfolio, folio, calendar, pen—need to be in conservative colors. If you like to use a Dilbert calendar for fun (and we are all for fun) leave it at home. Instead, find a small black pocket calendar to use during your job search. Be sure all your important dates are on that calendar. You do not want to schedule a second interview on the day you are supposed to be at an event that cannot be rescheduled.

Always take extra copies of your resume (printed on good quality resume paper), as well as copies of your reference list prepared as directed in Chapter 5. Taking extra copies of your resume and reference list is a good idea because you may be asked to complete an application and need to refer to your resume to provide accurate dates of employment. Or you may be asked to provide references' names, phone numbers, and addresses. If you have your list, you can provide this information right away.

PRACTICE TIP

Cell Phones You do not want your cell phone to ring during a job interview. In fact, you do not want a potential employer to even see you scrolling through your messages while waiting in the lobby. Doing so makes you look like you would rather be somewhere else, and you do not want to leave that first impression with the employer. If your phone rings during an interview, you should quickly silence it. Do not look to see who is calling, and do not acknowledge that it rang. Focus on the interviewer as if that person is the most important person in your life at that moment.

Voice Mail/Answering Machine   Make sure that the message on your voice mail or answering machine is very professional, such as:

"You have reached _____. I am unable to take your call right now. Please leave a message, and I'll return your call as soon as possible."

If you use an answering machine, get one that uses a personal message, not a pre-recorded computer voice. The pre-recorded digital answering machine makes people unsure of where they are leaving a message.

While potential employers will already have your resume, they may not treat it as carefully as you would. Their copy may have been folded, photocopied, highlighted, or written on. Sometimes, another person may join the interview but does not have, or did not bring, their copy of your resume with them. You can smartly hand a copy to anyone who needs it.

Good manners require that you turn off your cell phone before you enter an interview. You might even leave it in the car. If you are using an mp3 player while walking to an interview, put the player and your headphones away before you enter the building. Do not fumble with them later.

Your Pitch

Before you interview, you want to prepare a one- or two-sentence pitch about what you believe you can offer the firm. This statement will represent the things that you want the firm to remember about you. Prepare and practice this statement so that you are able to deliver it smoothly, even when you are nervous.

For example, you might say, "I am finishing my paralegal certificate and I enjoy the process of doing research. I've found that I work well both independently and with a team. I believe I will be able to easily jump in and contribute with the type of work you described earlier." (Be as specific as possible.)

Your pitch might focus on why you are changing careers: "I've spent seven years working as a first-grade teacher. This experience taught me to be extremely organized and to make good decisions on my feet. I can do a great job managing workflow and keeping things organized."

Your statement needs to be simple, memorable, and repeatable. You want those who interview you to remember specific strengths. Most of all, you want them to remember *you*.

Employer Analysis

Do some research before your interview so you know the following:

- How long will it take you to get to the employer's office?
- Does the route have traffic patterns that could affect travel time?
- Will you be able to park easily? Some offices have easy-access parking lots; others do not. Will you have to pay for parking? If so, be sure you have your parking money ready.
- What is the procedure for accessing the employer? Will you have to check in at a lower lobby? When interviewing in some offices, you have to obtain a visitor's pass first. If possible, try to identify these time-consuming tasks.

IN PRACTICE

Notes about Body Art and Body Bling

The legal profession in general, and law firms specifically, are very conservative. Because you are choosing to apply for work in this profession, you are agreeing to adhere to some of the standards that have been set. In other words, you should dress the part if you want a job in this profession.

If you have a tattoo, it needs to be covered during your interview and while at work. If you have a body piercing that shows (other than your ears—and these piercings should be kept to a minimum), you need to remove the hardware for your job interview and usually for work as well.

Some organizations have adopted much more casual policies, but you will want to take the lead from the employees who are there *once you get the job and start working*. Even if employees dress casually during your interview and even if you know the organization has a casual dress policy, you *still want to dress very conservatively for your interview*.

Your first impression may be your only chance to get a job with this organization.

- Will you need to remove your snow boots or check your hair?
- Work backward and set up a time to leave for your interview. A word of caution, though: do not arrive more than five minutes early. If you do, you may disrupt work-flow, which is never good. (If you *are* early, take a few minutes to relax by walking around the block or reading in the car.)

■ INTERVIEW: FROM BEGINNING TO END

Arrive on time or a few minutes before your scheduled interview.

Tell the receptionist that you are there for an interview with the name of the person you are supposed to meet. Be sure to have name of the person you are seeing readily available so you do not have to fumble to find it.

If you need to use the restroom, ask politely if the receptionist will wait until you are back before letting the person know you are there.

Next, expect to sit in the lobby for a few minutes. The receptionist may give you an application to fill out. Do not play with your cell phone or listen to your mp3 player while you are waiting. It may be tough to do nothing, but try to use this time to gather your thoughts and relax.

Your interviewer or your interviewer's assistant will meet you in the lobby. Stand up as soon as a person enters the lobby and you realize that person is there to meet you. Look the person directly in the eye and shake hands, using a nice firm handshake. Do not use jelly hands, a little half-handshake, or a death-grip shake. Practice with a friend if you are unsure of the firmness of your handshake.

You will be directed either into a private office or conference room. Your interview may be one on one or it may be with two or more people.

Chitchat: The Beginning of the Interview

Expect the interview to begin with some chitchat about the weather or a baseball game played the night before. If everyone in the room is talking about the Dallas Cowboys game, do not say, "I don't follow sports." Especially do not say this in a city where the sports team is revered. Instead, say, "I didn't catch the score. Who won?" You will not get the job during this small talk, but you could lose the job if you do not participate. People tend to bond over small things like baseball, barbecue, and hit TV shows. If you are the person who does not keep up with *American Idol*, it is perfectly okay. We just suggest that during this chitchat portion of the interview, you make neutral comments like, "I haven't been watching this season because I've been busy with school."

Tough Questions: The Actual Interview

As the actual interview begins, you will sense a shift from friendly chitchat to a very focused and serious business discussion. Interviews invariably begin the same way: "Tell me (or us) a little bit about yourself." Prepare for this question. Prepare your answer in terms of the job you have applied for. Memorize your answer and practice delivering it.

As the interview continues, the interviewer will tell you a little bit about the organization and ask if you have any questions about what the organization does. Do your homework. If you have questions, make them specific. For example, do not go to an interview at a pharmaceutical company and ask which drugs they developed. Find out before you get there.

The interviewer may give you some details about the job that were not in the job advertisement. Listen intently, but this is not the point of the interview where you need to hammer out the finer details of the position. Right now, you want to get a sense of the job and whether the people interviewing you would be okay to work with. Be sure to make eye contact and respond to everyone in the room. Expect some of these tricky questions:

- What is your biggest weakness?
- What is your best quality?
- What is your worst quality?
- How well do you work in groups?
- Describe a problem you have had on the job and how you solved it.
- This is the legal profession. Sometimes, people get a little stressed out. How well do you handle stressful working environments?
- In your last job, how often did you miss work?
- What is your favorite area of law? Why?
- Which paralegal class did you like the least? Why?
- Which paralegal class did you like the most? Why?

Some questions are off limits because they are illegal. These questions include the following:

- Are you married? Do you have a significant other? Do you have a boy/girlfriend? Are you gay?
- Do you have children? Do you plan to have children?
- Are you a Republican? A Democrat? What is your political view about _____? (If you are going to work for a political action committee, these questions might be relevant and permitted.)
- What is your religion? Do you go to church regularly? (These questions might be relevant at a private religious organization or affiliated business.)

Some questions are fair game and tell employers quite a bit about you:

- Are your work hours flexible?
- Can you work overtime?
- Are you available to travel?
- Can you lift more than 10 pounds? (This question is permitted if the job requires lifting, and some paralegal positions do.)

Some organizations may ask you to submit to a background search, credit check, or other investigative examination. Read the fine print on anything you are asked to sign. If you apply for work at a governmental agency, such as the Department of Justice, the FBI, or the CIA, you may have to submit to a polygraph and a very detailed security clearance check. Some organizations that work with these organizations also require such checks.

Squelch Your Curiosity: The Middle of the Interview

During the first interview, you may think of many things you would like to ask: Will I have an office? A secretary? A parking spot near the building? My own phone extension? A business card with my name on it? How much money can I make each year with the overtime you keep mentioning? **Do not ask these questions**. Stay focused on the job itself and how you can contribute to the organization. The focus of this portion of the interview should be about the office and how you can contribute. The focus on you comes later in the process.

Never ask any questions about benefits or salary during this first interview. These questions are inappropriate because they suggest that you are more curious about your paycheck than you are about doing good work for them. Many company websites include information about benefits, so you might want to search there for more information.

You may be asked about *your* salary requirements. You can be honest and give a figure or provide a range. Be aware that you could price yourself out of this position if the lowest number you give them is more than they are willing to pay. Sometimes, you can

It is okay to take notes at the interview, but if this disrupts the flow of discussion, stop writing. Do not use your telephone to take notes because that looks like you are texting rather than paying attention. In fact, your phone should be off and tucked away.

respond to this question by providing a vague answer, such as, "It depends on the entire benefits package." More and more, however, human resources personnel are reporting that they want a specific answer to this question.

Your goal during this interview is to really understand why the organization needs to fill this position, what the position is, and to begin to identify how you might be an asset to the company in this role. You need to find a natural way to specifically explain what you can offer.

Find a Spotlight: The End of the Interview

As the interview winds down, find a natural place to insert the pitch you prepared. If possible, try to tailor your pitch to the job: "I would enjoy working on investigating fraudulent products. I studied forensics in college before I got my paralegal certificate."

At the end of the interview, it is perfectly acceptable to ask for business cards so that you have contact information for each person who has interviewed you. You will need these to send thank you notes. Do not provide your own business card. If you need to leave a name and address you can hand them a resume, which should have your updated contact information.

Do not ask when you will know whether you got the job.

Shake hands after each interview with an individual or shake hands with each person during a group interview. Say, "It's been nice meeting you," or "Thank you for meeting with me today."

Smile. Leave. Do not try to toss out a funny remark. These often fail.

Food and Beverages During an Interview

Although rare for paralegals searching for entry-level jobs, you might be asked to drink a beverage or to dine with a potential employer. If you are asked during an interview whether you would like a cup of coffee, it is best to just say, "No, thank you." You do not want to take your attention away from the interview so that you can fuss with your coffee. No one wants to spend time watching you stir in cream and sugar. They want to know about your skills. (Plus, having no coffee guarantees you will not spill it.)

Should your interview take place in a coffee shop, drinking a beverage is appropriate.

If you do accept a beverage, place it on the table in a safe place where your arm will not accidentally swipe past it when you reach for a pen or if you are talking with your hands. In preschools, this area of the table is called the "safety zone." *Always* use the safety zone when interviewing.

If you travel out of town for an interview, drinking and dining will be expected. During these times, follow these guidelines:

- If others in your party are drinking alcohol and you are over 21, it is acceptable for you to join them for one drink. Your limit is one drink even if theirs is six.
- Choose foods you can eat with a fork. Even if they are ordering the very greasy, drippy chicken wings or ribs, order something that you can eat with a fork. Your manners are being evaluated. Their manners are not as important.
- When ordering, follow their example for a price range. You do not want to order the most expensive dish on the menu. If you are unsure what you should order, ask for a recommendation.

■ SAY THANK YOU

Employers report that receiving thank you notes from interviewees still matters. After the interview, send thank you notes. If you know the employer is making a quick decision, send a thank you e-mail, followed up with a handwritten or typed thank you. Refer to Chapter 7 for examples.

PRACTICE TIP

Beverages   Whenever you are in an interview or any business meeting, place your beverage out of the way of your hands, toward the middle of the table so you reduce your chance of spilling it. Be especially careful if you tend to talk with your hands.

■ THE WAITING PERIOD

After an interview, the waiting period begins. One student recently reported that she had to wait more than five weeks to hear back from an interviewer who suggested during the interview that she most likely would be their top choice. At the end of the interview, the interviewer told her that they needed to conduct one more interview the next day. The student waited. And waited. She waited three weeks before she got in touch with her key contact for an update. She finally received a job offer almost six weeks after the initial interview.

The good news is that when you interview, you *already* are one of the top contenders for the position. You have been *chosen*; yet, you still may not receive the position. Staying positive during the waiting time is difficult, and it is perfectly fine to pursue other job opportunities while you wait.

If you received a timeline for the hiring process during your interview, wait until *after* that time to ask for an update. If you did not receive a timeline, wait at least two weeks.

In the Meantime...

While you are waiting, you may continue to apply for other jobs. You may receive a job offer better than the one you are waiting for. If that happens, congratulations!

If you interview with two or more employers and receive a job offer from one of them, you have these options:

- You could take the job and send a courtesy e-mail to let the other organization or organizations know that you have accepted a position with another company. Be polite and explain that it was wonderful to meet the people who interviewed you. You never know, you may find yourself interviewing at a company again.
- You could let the other company or companies know that you have an offer on the table and ask where they are in the hiring process. They may speed up their process if you are high enough on their list. Again, be very polite.

■ THE JOB OFFER

Ultimately, job offers come when you least expect them—just as you are getting a haircut, during the loud soccer game, while you are in class. Try, whenever possible, to answer these calls in a quiet place, and be prepared to jot down the details: title of the position, salary being offered, any special benefits like paid parking, whether the job is salaried or whether you will receive overtime compensation.

As hard as this may be to do, say you would like to think about the position overnight and call back the next day. You should give yourself time to make a good decision. Below is an overview of things to think about during this phase of the job search, including the benefits you might be offered.

Considering and Negotiating a Job Offer

Most job offers come with two parts: salary and benefits. Together, these create your "compensation package."

Some positions in small offices offer salary only.

During the salary negotiation, consider the benefits you might receive. Benefits are important because they are part of the compensation package. You want to consider all of the benefits you will be offered, not just the salary, because choosing well can make a difference in your monthly expenses in the short term and, in the long term, may prepare you for retirement. Some employers provide an overview of the benefits they offer employees on their websites. Once a job offer has been made, it is time to discuss salary and benefits.

Salary

It would be so nice if we could give you a target salary to negotiate for your first job. The truth is that salaries vary from city to city from company to company, firm to firm, and organization to organization. Your salary depends on so many factors that it is impossible to give you a range.

You can draw on several statistics from different organizations. The Bureau of Labor Statistics reports the average annual salary for paralegals to be approximately $46,680. The National Association of Legal Assistant/Paralegal's (NALA) most recent National Utilization/Compensation Survey reports the average annual salary as $52,188. NALA's survey reports salary and compensation based on multiple factors, including years of experience and geographic region. Keep in mind that these averages include salaries of paralegals with one year of experience and salaries of paralegals with 25 years or more of experience. Salaries vary based on geographic location, size of employer, years of experience, and other factors. Entry level salaries in some areas could be as low as $29,000.

You can determine what the range is where you plan to work by using these surveys and by doing your own investigation. Your instructor may be able to help. You might get your classmates to all agree to do an informal salary survey before the next class and see if you can come up with different ranges from employers in your area.

Ultimately, your salary is a personal agreement between you and the employer that really serves to support you in the lifestyle that you need to sustain yourself. Without having a firm salary range, you still can determine an amount to serve as your base figure. To determine this figure, take the amount you pay for food, shelter, clothing, transportation, and school loans every month—your basics—and make sure that your salary will cover those.

You may have to reconsider some of your plans. For example, you may have to live in a modest apartment instead of a luxury condominium your first year out of school. All of your plans should be adjusted with a salary range in mind. Know what the lowest salary you can take is. This will give you an idea whether, with the salary offered, you will be able to afford to eat and get to work every day.

A caveat: In today's economy, it is not unusual for new graduates to get an entry-level full-time job *and* work a second job on the weekends. Not every legal employer likes this; some firms may prefer that you are available for overtime. Really consider your needs when deciding whether you can take a job.

When you are an entry-level paralegal, you will be making the lower end of the salary range, but you can look for opportunities to increase that amount. For example, some large law firms offer paralegals a lot of overtime. If you need to make more money or you are in a position where you can work a lot of hours, you might take a job at a law firm that offers a large number of overtime hours to increase your salary, pay off some of your school debt faster, save money for a vehicle or whatever it is that you need. Be aware, though, that not every firm offers this opportunity. Once you begin negotiating salary, you can ask that question: Does the employer offer a lot of paid overtime?

A Note about Negotiating: Negotiating a salary in any economy is tricky. You do not want to negotiate yourself out of a job, and at the same time you want to make sure that you are treated fairly. When you are offered a job, it is perfectly fine for you to ask for more money or to negotiate better benefits.

Keep in mind that the employer may return with a counter offer. For example, if you are offered a starting salary of $30,000 annually, you might ask for $33,000. The employer will probably come back with $31,000. You might continue to negotiate for $31,500, but in the end, you will feel like you got a little bit. You will go into the job feeling fairly compensated.

Also, in some areas, benefits may be determined by union contract or another method that makes these areas non-negotiable. Be aware of any rules like these in your state.

Medical and Dental Benefits

Medical benefits provide payment or partial payment for medical care and are an important part of your salary. You need to ask two questions related to your medical benefits:

- **What is the monthly premium?** The monthly premium is the amount you will pay each month. If you have a spouse or dependents that also need coverage, be aware that the premium could be much higher.
- **How is the policy structured?** The structure of the policy determines how much you will pay in addition to the monthly premium. For example, you might have a policy that requires a small co-pay of $5–$20 for each doctor's visit. Or you might have a policy where you have to pay a percentage of the health insurance every month, you have a large deductible of $5,000 every year, and then after you pay your deductible, the firm and the insurance will pay 80 percent of your medical bills while you pay 20 percent. Knowing that you will have the $5,000 deductible is a big deal because it really does mean that you will be out-of-pocket $5,000 before the insurance will cover any costs.

Ask the same questions about dental insurance coverage for your teeth.

Life Insurance

Life insurance is money that is paid to a beneficiary if you die. Some firms will pay for an initial amount of life insurance, often double your annual salary, and then allow you to purchase additional insurance if you want. The purpose of life insurance is to take care of those who depend on you. If you are single and have no dependents, you may find the amount that the employer offers is sufficient. You should consult a good financial planning book to determine how much life insurance you need and whether you should purchase it through your employer or through another source.

Disability Insurance

Disability insurance covers a percentage of your salary, should you become unable to work due to a non-work injury or illness. Some employers offer long-term and short-term disability insurance. Disability insurance usually covers 60–70 percent of your salary if you become unable to work after a waiting period.

Vacation Time

It seems rude to ask about vacation time before you start a job. After all, you have not even punched in yet. This is, however, something you should ask during salary negotiations.

Some smaller employers offer very little or no vacation time. Ask how much vacation time you get each year and how it accrues.

Note: Occasionally, someone starts a job but has a planned event that will occur before vacation time is permitted. Ask permission *now* to take this time off. Volunteer to take this time *unpaid* if necessary. Your goal is to be able to attend the event, so be sure this event is on your future employer's radar before you start your job because most employers do not expect new employees to request vacation time soon after starting. Understand that the employer may deny your request because of the current business cycle.

Sick Time

Sick time is a tricky concept. Some companies offer you a certain amount of sick time. For example, a firm may offer you two weeks of sick time per year. That does not necessarily mean they *want* you to take two weeks of sick time every year.

Some companies will let you roll the time over into an account for later. Some companies will pay you for remaining sick time at the end of the year. A few employers offer *unlimited* sick time. These employers expect that you *will not abuse* this privilege. In this situation, you get as much or as little time as you need, but you do not lose any or accrue any. This is a great benefit because if you have major surgery the firm will allow you to take time to heal, but this also means that they do not expect you to misuse it.

Personal Time Off

Some firms may offer a certain amount of "personal time off" to do things like attend funerals, go to dental appointments, etc. In some cases, there is no "sick time" but only "personal time off" that may be used in any way you wish, not necessarily only when you are ill.

Your Birthday

If you are allowed to take your birthday off, this is a real bonus!

Adoption Benefits

Some companies offer adoption benefits. This means that if you adopt a child, they will pay a certain amount toward adoption fees, offer you paid or unpaid leave, or some combination.

Family Leave

Some employers are required under the Family Medical Leave Act (FMLA) to offer up to 12 work-weeks of unpaid leave during any 12-month period. According to the U.S. Department of Labor, reasons for this leave include:

- the birth and care of the newborn child of the employee;
- placement with the employee of a son or daughter for adoption or foster care;
- care for an immediate family member (spouse, child, or parent) with a serious health condition; **or**
- medical leave when the employee is unable to work because of a serious health condition.

Not all employers are required to provide this leave.

Retirement Savings Plans

Many employers offer retirement savings plans. These plans help you reap tax benefits and save for retirement. Consult a financial planning book, or even a financial planner, for information about how to structure your retirement planning.

Some corporations may offer stock options, and many larger employers offer 401(k) retirement savings plans.

Sometimes a firm or company will deposit a set amount of money into your retirement account for you every month. You may or may not be required to put aside a certain amount of your salary. Some employers will put a percentage of your salary away, over and above your actual salary.

For example, if you make $30,000 a year, and the employer contributes 5 percent of your salary over and above that $30,000 for your retirement account, your salary increases by $1,500 a year.

Be familiar with the company's **vesting** period. This is the time before the shares of stock or deposits made by the employer on your behalf are yours to control. Some employers have a five-year vesting period, in which any deposits they make on your behalf can be kept by the employer if you leave before the vesting period ends. Other employers allow you to immediately control 100 percent of the deposits.

Emergency Child Care

Some employers offer on-site or near-site emergency child care that can be used when your own child-care provisions are unavailable—school closings, snow days, ill child care provider, and so on.

Flexible Spending Account

A flexible spending account is one that enables you to deposit some of your salary into an account that can be used for certain medical and childcare expenses. This money is deposited pre-tax, so you do not have to pay tax on this portion of your salary. You must spend this money by a certain date, usually the end of the year, or lose it, so you do not want to "over-deposit" money into this account. Consult a financial planning book or financial planner to help you decide whether this benefit is good for you.

PARALEGAL **PROFILE**

Tammy Brooks

Current position: Executive Assistant to the Mayor, City Administrator and City Attorney
Employer: City of Saint Robert, Missouri
Years in this position: 3
Years of paralegal experience: 8
Education:
A.A.S, Paralegal Studies, Tulsa Community College

Tammy Brooks networked her way to a new job. She explains how she did it.

In today's tough job market, it is more important than ever to use every available resource to obtain the best possible job. Working in a small town, with its limited options, can make that search extremely difficult. However, using networking contacts, a paralegal can open doors to job opportunities in unexpected places. This is Tammy's story, in her own words:

I began my paralegal career working at a medical clinic as a worker's compensation representative.

When I relocated to a different state, I got my foot in the door of a law firm by working as a runner and worked my way up to senior paralegal responsible for the hiring and supervision of three paralegals and other office staff.

While at the general litigation firm, a co-worker obtained a position in a newly created legal department at a bank the firm represented. I took note of that and when the city of Saint Robert hired a lawyer from the firm as an in-house attorney, I was able to use my previous contact with the City Administrator to obtain a legal assistant position in their newly formed legal department.

I have been employed by the city of Saint Robert, Missouri for three years now. I assist the city attorney in the preparation of municipal ordinances and codes, civil and criminal litigation, contracts, real estate, and employment-related issues involving the municipality. In my capacity as legal assistant to the city attorney and working closely with the mayor and city administrator, I continue to network with community leaders, business professionals, and other branches of government because you never know when or where the next professional opportunity will present itself.

I recommend that paralegals who are looking for a job use the people they know as a source for job leads. Do not be shy about making your contacts aware of your experience and qualifications. Treat every contact as a potential source for job leads and make sure that you always put your best foot forward. You never know when that contact might become your new boss.

■ INTERVIEWS, BUT NO JOB OFFERS

Sometimes, you know at the first handshake that no job offer will be forthcoming. Sometimes, you think you rocked the interview, but no job offer is forthcoming. The reality is that you may have many interviews and receive no job offer. If you are interviewing (which means your resume and application letter are working) and not being hired, do these things:

- Meet with someone who will be honest with you and go over the answers you have been giving. Figure out if you are saying something that could be misinterpreted. *Listen* to the feedback you receive.
- Maintain your physical health.
- Maintain your mental health by reading trade journals and staying on top of your game.
- Work as a temporary paralegal.
- Volunteer at a legal aid organization.
- Do not whine to anyone in the legal profession—not even a best friend.

Do not ask for feedback from an employer who has rejected you. Sometimes, the choice came down to *fantastic* vs. *fantastic*. If you want to check your interview style, set up a mock interview with your school's career center or with a trusted professor. Dress as you would for a real interview so the person can tell you if something about your clothing is not exactly right.

You may be saying something that you did not know was a problem. For example, a paralegal told us she kept mentioning the gap in her resume was there because she had taken time off work to take care of her dying mother, who passed a few months before. This statement had such a negative impact on the energy of the interview that the paralegal never got offers. Someone finally told her to stop talking about her mother during interviews. She then changed her answer to say she took time to take care of family business. Her luck turned around.

Finding a job can be both frustrating and exciting. Be persistent. Network. Keep your goals in mind. If things truly are not working, figure out a temporary path but keep your feet moving forward and never give up.

CONCLUSION

When your search for a job begins, interviewing and negotiating the terms of employment are tasks you hope to do but may put off thinking about until you get a call for an interview or an offer for a job. When calls for interviews come or when a job is offered, however, time speeds up. The employer wants you to interview soon or to respond to its offer of employment right away. Be as prepared as you can for both of these areas of the job search.

For interviews, have your "interview clothes" ready to go. Know what you will wear, which materials you will take with you, and quickly learn the route to the employer's office. For example, do not trust the free GPS application on your smart phone unless you are also familiar with the area.

For job offers, make your personal decisions before the offer comes. How much salary do you need? What is the lowest salary you can accept? What if the market in your area does not pay much? If this position offers medical insurance but a low salary, do you have a plan for making ends meet until you gain some experience that can lead to a better opportunity or higher salary?

Last, take care of yourself and remain hopeful. If you are not getting calls, brainstorm with someone you trust about the reasons. Take charge of the process by volunteering, networking, and making your health and well-being a priority.

Checklist for Success

☐ Decide what you will wear *before* you get an interview. Plan to wear a suit.

☐ Cover body art and remove body hardware.

☐ Decide which business accessories (calendar, resumes, portfolio, etc.) to take to the job interview. Make sure these are conservative in style and color.

☐ Print materials you need for the interview: resume, reference list, portfolio samples. Consider printing extra copies.

☐ Understand the general direction an interview can take.

☐ Practice your answers to potential questions.

☐ Practice shaking hands.

☐ Research an employer who offers you an interview.

☐ Decide the best route for driving to the interview and practice driving the route if needed. Figure out where you will park.

☐ Send thank you notes after the interview.

☐ Learn about benefits and negotiating before a job offer comes.

☐ Maintain your physical and mental well-being while you are waiting for a job offer.

☐ Consider working as a temporary paralegal.

☐ If you do not get a job offer, go over your interview questions and answers with someone who will give you feedback. *Listen* to the feedback.

ASSIGNMENTS: PREPARING FOR YOUR PARALEGAL CAREER

Career Management

Before class, prepare answers to the following questions. During class, practice your best answers by "interviewing" with a partner:

- What are your strengths?
- What do you consider your biggest weakness?
- What did you learn at school that has prepared you for this job?

Report

Interview paralegals working in different environments. Ask about the benefits they receive. How are the benefits the same/different? Are you surprised? (Do not ask about their salary because that is a private matter.)

Prepare

Plan how a successful candidate might dress for a job interview by using an online catalog for a store that sells professional clothing. Copy and paste the images from the website to a word processing document (Right click on the image and select "copy." Go to the word processing document and click "paste.") Explain why these choices would be good. Discuss in class how you might create the look on a tight budget.

INTERNET RESOURCES

Bureau of Labor Statistics. Occupational Outlook Handbook: *http://www.bls.gov/oco/*

National Association of Legal Assistants/Paralegals. 2010 National Utilization/Compensation Survey: *http://www.nala.org/survey.aspx*

Letter Opinion from the U.S. Department of Labor Related to Paralegal Salaries: *http://www.nala.org/New2/Upload/file/PDF-Files/News-Articles/06_Jan_letter-nonexept-states-several-examples.pdf*

REFERENCES

Bureau of Labor Statistics. (2010). Occupational Employment Statistics for 23-2011 Paralegals and Legal Assistants. Retrieved from: *http://www.bls.gov/oes/current/oes232011.htm*

National Association of Legal Assistants/Paralegals. 2010 National Utilization Survey Report. Retrieved from: *http://www.nala.org/Upload/file/PDF-Files/10SEC4.pdf*

CHAPTER **9**

STARTING YOUR FIRST PARALEGAL JOB

S tarting your first paralegal job marks the separation of you as paralegal student to you as a full-fledged paralegal. You may use some of the same strategies to settle into your first job as you used during your internship, but there are many differences.

Your internship is considered an extension of learning and preparation for your work. In your first job, you are expected to leave the role of "student" behind and transition into the role of "professional."

During this time, you may feel like you must constantly be "on," and in reality, you are. Each time you meet someone new, you are making a first impression. Employers are watching you to see if you connect well with clients and other employees and if you settle into the ebb and flow of the office. Your co-workers are watching you to see if you are going to be a good collaborator and contributor.

Because people will be watching (and judging) you, you want to do things that demonstrate to your employer and other employees that you are committed to a successful start.

By the end of this chapter, you should be able to:

- Get organized for your first paralegal job
- Know how to update your wardrobe to fit your current situation
- Know what to do on the first day
- Learn how to settle into an office environment
- Understand time and billing practices
- Be prepared to develop a good reputation at work

■ ORGANIZING YOURSELF

Regardless of your current professional status—still a student, still searching for a job, or ready for your first day on the job—you need to organize yourself with your number one goal in mind: obtain and successfully begin your paralegal job.

You do not want to be like Lydia. Lydia, a paralegal specializing in real estate and working for a solo practitioner, recalls how she sat in her professor's office to discuss her progress in her paralegal classes. She was mortified that the professor used words like "unprofessional" and "disorganized" to describe her. The professor explained that if she really wanted to be a paralegal, Lydia had to pull herself together because the professor would not be willing to recommend her for an internship if she did not.

Lydia, who could not bring herself to talk about this conversation until years later, said she felt horrified after the meeting, but that her professor had been right: she was often late to class, did not do her best work on all her assignments, and sometimes did not take time to do the work at all. What the professor did not do was provide any guidance as to how Lydia could get organized. What would you do if you were Lydia? Do you need help figuring out how to get a grip on yourself and your time?

Organizing yourself should be your first priority. Begin to adopt organizational strategies that reflect where you are in your paralegal career. If you are a student, start with getting organized for class. If you are job searching, you must be able to talk about your own organizational and time management strengths during an interview. If you are working as a paralegal, you want to understand how to manage yourself and your workload. Because you may be asked about time management and organizational strategies during a job interview, learning techniques now is very important.

When You Are a Student

Paralegal students are sometimes hired right out of the classroom by an attorney teaching the class or by recommendation from a colleague. Your performance in class is like a semester-long interview, or at least, that is how you should treat it. You want to appear to be the professional paralegal you will be once you graduate. Never be the late/disorganized/folded-up-homework kind of student.

Even if the attorney teaching the class is not planning to hire, consider that the attorney and every one of your classmates are potential leads for a job in the future. If your future employer asks if you know of a good paralegal to hire, you are going to think of the paralegals you know—your classmates. Which classmates would you recommend? Why? What traits do they display during class that suggest to you that they will be good workers?

As a student, you should dress as if you have your personal life together—regardless of how much of a time crunch you experience during your busy day. Here are some tips for dressing and personal organization:

Dressing

- Dress yourself a step above student casual.
  - **Men:** Do not wear ripped jeans. Instead, wear nice jeans or khakis. T-shirts are okay, but should not advertise alcohol, should not have rude sayings, and should not brag about a weekend party. Golf shirts or button downs are even better.
  - **Women:** Wear nice jeans (again, no ripped jeans), pants, or a skirt. T-shirts are okay, but no spaghetti straps, revealing tank tops, and the T-shirt rules for men apply to women as well. Never wear tops with your bra straps showing. To really set yourself apart, wear a nice blouse or shirt.
- Groom your hair. Wash it, style it, comb it. The idea is to appear well groomed. No baseball caps (men or women) and no unwashed hair. Showing up in "finals wear"—sweats, baseball cap, and yesterday's shirt—screams poor organizational skills. When you appear as if you slept 8 hours and had time to groom, you make an impressive statement.
- File or trim your fingernails and remove chipped nail polish.

- Wear shoes. Flip flops are not shoes.
- Shorts should be worn rarely; always think carefully about the image you portray when you wear shorts.

Organization

- Organize your papers: use notebooks, folders, and a backpack.
- Use a calendar to keep up with important course dates. You do not want to be the student who turns work in late.
- Organize your backpack or book bag so you do not have to dig for things. Make sure you have the right supplies for class: pens, paper, calendar, textbooks.

Time Management

- Understand what you need to do for the next class before you leave the room.
- Set aside time in your calendar to finish your work.
- Turn your work in on time.
- If you must have an extension—yes, sometimes you will need one—ask as early as possible and give a good reason. Traveling for a school-sponsored event is a good reason while going to a concert is not.
- Arrive on time. Turn off your cell phone. Look and act interested, even if you are rearranging your sock drawer in your mind.

Remember that you are going to school to achieve a specific goal: to become a paralegal or to complete the education that goes with the work you are doing in the legal profession. Consider class a professional networking event. The moment you step into the classroom, you begin networking with future colleagues, potential employers, and others who can help you find work in the legal profession.

In classrooms geared for professions, like paralegal studies, professional rules apply. For example, if you already have a professional job or if you are a parent, you occasionally may need to keep your phone on or may need to miss class. Introduce yourself to the professor on the first day and explain your situation. Explain: "I work for a solo practitioner and we have a trial coming up. I am going to keep my phone on vibrate." Dealing with the situation professional-to-professional shows that you take charge of your responsibilities.

The most impressive students treat class importantly and protect the time needed to complete the work.

When You Are a Graduate Looking for a Job

If you have graduated, but have not found a job, you need to treat finding employment as your full-time job and work all day at it. The ironic thing about job searching is that you cannot always afford to look as professional as you would like, but you still need to shine.

Go to workshops on campus for resume building. Attend professional organization meetings for paralegals and legal professionals. Shake hands with, and introduce yourself to, people who work in the legal profession. Look for and attend job fairs on your own campus and at other schools or locations.

All of the student organizational strategies apply, and now a few new strategies come into play:

Dressing

- Start building your professional wardrobe. Give up your jeans and your t-shirts.
- Improve your footwear. No sneakers or flip flops.
- Wash those blue or pink stripes right out of your hair.
- Get a professional haircut and style and maintain it.
- Learn how to cover visible tattoos.
- Determine which body piercing hardware you will remove for job interviews, internships, and professional work.

Organization

- Organize your job search papers.
- Gather the important documents you will need for starting work such as Social Security card or work papers. Be sure your passport or driver's license is up to date.
- Use your calendar to track interviews, job fairs, and career-oriented workshops.
- Always have a pen with you.
- Carry multiple copies of your resume at all times. Your resume is the least expensive marketing tool you can have.

Time Management

- Dedicate a portion of every day to job searching.
- Follow up on leads and networking tips.

Working Students

In today's economy, most students work either part- or full-time. Some paralegal students already work in law offices in a support staff role. Once you are working (even if you are not yet working as a paralegal), your ability to organize yourself and your time (as well as your work space, as we will cover in the next chapter) is paramount to building a good reputation at work. The cliché "fake it until you make it" does not really apply: paralegals must be organized because simply faking it means you might miss something important.

Use this list to be sure you are projecting a professional image at your current job:

Dressing

- Build and use your professional wardrobe. Give up jeans and t-shirts, even for casual Fridays, until you have earned the reputation you want.
- Choose professional footwear. If you can wear your shoes with shorts, do not wear them to the office.

Organization

- Do not look disheveled when you walk through the office door. Use a briefcase-type bag (ditch the backpack).
- If you bring your lunch to work, store it in a reusable lunch bag in a conservative color. Be sure that everyone in the office cannot smell whatever you have packed for lunch.
- Establish and follow a morning routine at work: Hang up your coat, put away your lunch, turn on your computer, check your calendar, and begin your day.
- Carry a notepad and a pen with you as you move from meeting to meeting or task to task.
- Instead of carrying extra resumes with you, carry business cards so that you can provide them to vendors, clients, counsel and paralegals from other firms, as well as other professionals you meet on behalf of the firm. NOTE: Some small law firms do not provide paralegals with business cards. If you can, suggest that you also have cards to give to contacts you meet on behalf of the firm. There are three good reasons for this: you will appear more professional, you will save time writing down your address and phone number, and every card serves as a marketing tool for the firm.

Time Management

- Put your calendar on your nightstand or dresser and scan it quickly before you pick out clothes for the day. You want to be sure you are dressed appropriately, especially if you work where you dress one way for a normal day in the office and another way for court or meeting with clients. Check your calendar again when you arrive at

IN PRACTICE

Some First Week "Don'ts"

- Do not assume your new employer is closed on a day that is considered a holiday for some employers. For example, some companies close for Memorial Day, while others do not. If you are supposed to start work on Memorial Day, confirm with human resources whether the business will be open or closed.
- Do not ask to leave early.
- Do not complain about colleagues. You do not know where the allegiances lie, and you might be complaining to someone's significant other or best friend without knowing it.
- Do not assume what the previous paralegal did was "good enough." Create your own rapport with supervising attorneys and ask for their preferences on key tasks.
- Do not appear unhappy.
- Do not chew gum or make personal calls.
- Do not badmouth your former employers or professors.

work and then again before you leave for the day so you can be ready for the next day's schedule.

- Keep a running to-do list. Know what needs to be done and have a sense of the priorities, even if they keep changing day-to-day or moment-to-moment.
- Acquire a flexible arsenal of time management strategies to help you stay organized when working with colleagues who have different organizational and communication strategies.

The most important point to remember is that you are no longer a student, and your working style needs to reflect this career-building period in your life. Even if you are switching careers, you must build your reputation and prove that you can be responsible. Behavior that you may have engaged in while a student is often not acceptable in the law office environment. Attorneys are on the hook legally and ethically for your work product. Attorneys need to be able to trust you to do a good job. Even if you have a Ph.D. in physics and your job is to help with patents only, you must still earn a good reputation at work.

■ START RIGHT

When you start your first paralegal job, you are going to spend the first month making many first impressions. You will be meeting new people, working with attorneys and other paralegals for the first time, interacting with other colleagues, and getting to know outside vendors who serve your office. You will most likely be getting acquainted with court personnel, as well as others who work in various county and state capacities. The impression you make with these people is very important to your future success. Start with these practices in mind:

Know your workday hours and be on time for everything. Always arrive at work on time. Go to meetings on time. Respond promptly when summoned to a supervisor's or supervising attorney's office. Showing up on time is so basic that if you do it consistently, no one will notice, but if you run late, everyone will notice (and not in a good way).

Arrive ready to work. Being ready to work means arriving a few minutes before you are supposed to "clock in" in order to put your things away and get ready for your morning routine. Drink your coffee before you get to work, especially in the early days. No one wants to see you hauling around a coffee cup.

Meet people graciously. Get to know as many people as you can. Smile, hold your head up, and make eye contact. Shake hands with people. Remember their names. (Make notes later at your desk if you need to.) It is important to get to know people and understand their roles, as well as help them understand your role, as best you know it. Do not snub or ignore anyone because you will need help from almost

IN PRACTICE

Business Cards for Paralegals

Not every organization provides business cards to paralegals. If the organization that hires you does not provide them, the reasons provided below may help you convince your firm that you need your own cards:

- Every business card is a marketing piece for the organization. The organization's name, address, phone number, and website can be printed on the card. Business cards are relatively inexpensive and are much more impressive than having a paralegal jot down office information for others.
- Paralegals tend to deal with vendors, court reporters, clients, and others often. Having a card to provide saves time.
- A paralegal who does not have business cards often uses the attorney's card and writes his or her name/information on it. This kind of communication may be confusing and appear unprofessional.
- Paralegals attend continuing legal education, meetings of paralegal organizations, conferences, and so on. At national events, especially, you will trade business cards or meet paralegals from other states. Some paralegals refer to the cards they collect to help attorneys at their own firms find outside counsel in different cities or states when needed.
- Business cards are a standard communication piece in the United States, and providing paralegals with business cards sends a clear message that the office runs itself professionally.

You should never use your business cards to network your way into a new job, but carrying them with you to meetings and events allows you to network with others.

A word of caution: most states (check your own State Bar rules) allow business cards for paralegals and other members of the legal support staff. The primary caveat is that your card must clearly state your status and never imply that you are an attorney.

everyone at some point and you never know who might be helpful when you are working on a project. A good rule is simply to be nice to everyone.

Do your assignments quickly and to the best of your ability. Everyone will watch to see if you can do the work. When you are given work, start it right away. Deliver the work on time as promised and take any feedback graciously. You are expected to be absorbing information and adjusting your knowledge and working style according to the atmosphere of your new job.

Following these practices will help you get off to a good start and put you on the road to success in your job.

■ WHAT TO TAKE THE FIRST DAY

Do not arrive the first day loaded down with bags and boxes as if you are moving in. Instead, limit the possessions you take to the office. You may spend a week or two training with the person who currently occupies your future desk. The things you definitely need on the first day include:

- Directions to the office. You do not want to be late because you cannot find the office.
- Name of the person you need to see when you arrive.
- Your driver's license and Social Security card or your passport. You will need forms of identification to complete the required tax documents.
- Lunch. You may be asked to go out for lunch, but have a back-up plan in case you need to eat at the office. If you are asked to go out for lunch, go. Use the opportunity to get to know your new boss(es) and colleagues. That peanut butter sandwich will wait.

Once the job is yours, that is, after the person who has the position currently moves on and you have the desk/office/cubicle to yourself, it is okay to bring in reference materials you own that you would like to have available, as well as a plant and a photo or two. Do not fill your space with clutter.

■ SETTLE IN

Settling into a new job happens differently from office to office. Your goal is to determine the employer's preferred way of doing things, as well as how things flow in the office. If the office has an employee handbook or a standard procedures manual you should obtain one and become familiar with its contents. You can acclimate gracefully with the efforts described below.

Find Out How-To

No matter how much experience or education you have, one thing others in the office know better than you is how things work: the copy machine, the postage meter, the lock on the supply cabinet. Listen closely when someone tells you how to do a mundane task. Most likely they are not being condescending, but trying to save you grief because in that office the thing they are showing you may not work as you would expect.

For example, you may know how to use a copy machine: You walk up, put down the paper, and push the big green button. But in an office environment, copy machines become tricky. First, they may be the size of a small Toyota. Second, some of the machines can make photocopies, staple, sort, hole-punch, and bake a pizza, so you need to pay attention to how to use the functionality. Then, even if you master the art of staple-sort, you may not have heard the person who said, "First, you must enter a code." Offices tend to be obsessive about tracking everything from photocopies to paperclips, so listen when people describe how to use office equipment.

Carry a small notebook with you at all times so that you can write these things down. You will not look silly taking notes during the copy machine lesson; you will look savvy and committed to learning. Take our word for it that many paralegals before you did *not* take notes at the copy machine and later regretted it.

Do Not Whine about the Technology

Not every law firm or company stays up to date with its technology. Small law firms often are a round or two behind the latest software updates. Understand what the office has and learn to use it, even if you are taking a step back from what you learned in school. Do not whine. You may have an opportunity later to suggest or recommend upgrades as things become too outdated, but during your first weeks, accept what you are given and move on.

Follow the Dress Code or Elevate It

Unless you are issued a uniform (unlikely in the legal profession), wear your interview-best on your first day and then follow the lead of other paralegals after that. Sometimes,

IN PRACTICE

Take Notes

You need to take notes about everything the first few days. People will give you a lot of information about how to use equipment, how to unlock doors and cabinets, how to send packages overnight, where the mail arrives or goes out, and how to do many other tasks. Use paper and pen to take these notes, *not* your telephone, unless your employer pre-approves using it.

Using your telephone to record office information shifts your phone from personal use to professional use, crossing a line. If your office assigns you a smartphone or tablet PC, certainly asking if you can take notes into it makes sense, but in the beginning separate personal devices from professional devices. Law firms must adhere to specific ethical guidelines regarding technology, so before you use personal technology to do your professional work, know the rules that your employer wants you to follow.

organizations allow you to wear business casual unless you are going to court or have specific meetings. Other organizations expect professional attire all the time. One of the largest firms in Boston has casual Friday, and the usually buttoned-up staff pushes the limits, including wearing worn-out sneakers and ripped jeans. Monday through Thursday, however, everyone is dressed in suits—even the receptionists.

Focus on the Work

Your boss(es) and colleagues want to see that you are focused on the work. You may bond over a playoff game or a department store sale, but for the most part—and especially during the first few weeks—people are watching your *work*, not your ability to snag a digital camera for half off during your lunch hour.

Ask What Else You Need to Know

Every office has quirky things that are important to know: how to unlock the office on weekends, where to park, what time the mail comes, the latest time for a Federal Express pick-up. You will learn most of these things as you go, but be aware of things that people may not think to tell you until you really need to know. As they are giving you instructions, always ask what else you need to know. You will be surprised what you will learn.

You may feel unsettled in the legal profession when you start a new job, especially when you do not receive much feedback from busy attorneys. You are settling in positively when you feel confident in these areas:

- You feel confident speaking to the attorneys who supervise your work.
- You *know* your work product is good without having to be told (although it is always nice to hear).
- You begin to anticipate what attorneys or others need and plan accordingly.
- You begin to gain the trust and confidence of lawyers and supervisors.

■ UNDERSTAND TIME AND BILLING PRACTICES

Every law firm, regardless of size, has time and billing practices that it follows. On the first day of your job, one of the first things you need to find out is what the firm's practices and policies are. You must follow the established practices. This section provides an overview of time and billing procedures to give you a general idea of how firms record and bill time.

Law firms make money by providing services to clients. Law firms get paid in the following ways:

- **Per-hour charge for time spent:** Lawyers and paralegals bill clients for the time they spend working on a case.
- **Transactional:** A law firm earns a set fee regardless of time spent. Some examples of work that might be billed per transaction include real estate closings, estate planning, and annual corporate recordkeeping.
- **Contingency:** A law firm is paid a percentage of the money collected on behalf of a client. Personal injury and collections are two examples of work sometimes billed on a contingency basis. This is called a "contingent fee."

Law firms that bill clients per hour require attorneys and paralegals to record descriptions of how they spend time on behalf of a client. Law firms that bill in other ways require time recordkeeping as well. You will hear law firm employees ask, "Have you entered your time yet?" They are asking whether you have typed descriptions of how you spent your time into the firm's time-and-billing system. The rest of this section describes how to record the time you spend working on a task for a client for billing purposes.

You will have two rates at your firm: the dollar amount you earn per hour and the dollar amount, or rate, at which your time is billed to clients. Your firm may pay you

$17 per hour, but your billing rate may be $85 per hour. This means that clients will pay $85 per hour for your time. Your time is expensive, and you need to record what you do for clients so that they understand why they are being charged.

In order to enter your time accurately and ethically, you must keep good records as you go through your day. Some people choose to enter their time directly into the firm's time-and-billing system as they complete each task. Others prefer to keep handwritten notes and transfer the notes later. New applications for hand-held devices make keeping up with descriptions of billable time easier.

To report your time accurately, you need a portable notepad, organizer, book, or hand-held device to record descriptions of each task you complete. Once you figure out which recordkeeping organizer works best for you, make a habit of recording your time descriptions throughout the day. Do not wait until the end of the day and try to "remember."

Time entries need to include the client's name, account number, and matter number. Refer to Appendix D for timekeeping forms you can use. For example, if your client is Lincoln Builders, the information you need may look like this:

Client	Matter	Client Number	Matter Number
Lincoln Builders	General Matters	9902	0001
	Commercial Real Estate Closing – Broad Street	9902	0002
	Commercial Real Estate Closing – Main Street	9902	0003
	Due Diligence for Rogers Street purchase	9902	0004

If you work on the Broad Street closing, you will record your time under Client Number 9902 and Matter Number 0002.

To record your time accurately, you must describe what you do concisely and completely. At times, the work you do may not be billable; however, you should record it anyway. The attorney will decide whether to "write off" or "write down" your time. For example, you may spend time doing work that is secretarial in nature because you work for a small law firm and you are both paralegal and legal secretary. Unless you have a clear understanding from the attorney about what to bill and what to omit, record all your time and the attorney will decide which tasks are not billable.

Photocopying, for example, falls into a category that can be billable or secretarial. Straight photocopying is not billable; however, if you are photocopying, labeling, and preparing documents in response to discovery requests, the work may be billable because it requires decision-making and 100 percent accuracy.

Your time entry needs to reflect the substance of the task. The following description is not good enough if you are working on discovery and want to bill the time:

Client	Matter	Client Number	Matter Number	Time Entry
Abby Corporation	Litigation	1202	0002	Photocopying (2.0)

No client wants to pay $85 per hour for photocopying. Instead, explain what you did with more detail:

Client	Matter	Client Number	Matter Number	Time Entry
Abby Corporation	Litigation	1202	0002	Prepare documents in response to discovery requests; identify relevant documents, label, photocopy, and check accuracy of documents (2.0).

The (2.0) indicates the amount of time spent on the task. Some law firms charge in increments of six minutes. So, if you make one telephone call that takes three minutes, you would charge one increment of time, or six minutes. The following chart shows the increments of time to use if your firm bills in six-minute increments. Until you memorize these increments, keep this list in the notebook where you record your time.

Minutes	Time Increment
0–6	.1
7–12	.2
13–18	.3
19–24	.4
25–30	.5
31–36	.6
37–42	.7
42–48	.8
49–54	.9
55–60	1.0

Examine the following entry:

Client Number	Matter Number	Time Entry
1202	0002	Schedule court reporter for deposition of Jason Lee (.2); draft subpoena and request check for witness fee (.6); find and contact process server in Montana (.3).

This entry breaks down for the client how much time you spent on each task. Your firm may prefer a bundled entry:

Client Number	Matter Number	Time Entry
1202	0002	Schedule court reporter for deposition of Jason Lee; draft subpoena; request check for witness fee; locate and contact process server in Montana (1.1).

The pattern for each entry should be as follows:

[ACTION] re [REASON FOR ACTION]

or

[ACTION] with [PERSON] re [REASON FOR ACTION]

A time log for recording your time can be found in Appendix D. Recording time so that you describe a task accurately without giving too much information requires practice. Ask for some examples to use so that you can see how much detail your firm likes to record. Asking for examples or modeling someone who is successful at the firm is always a good practice.

■ SECRET SUCCESS STRATEGY

Some paralegals find that they can settle in more quickly by closely observing someone in the office who is respected by everyone. This person will have earned this respect with hard work, knowledge in the field, and a willingness to communicate well with colleagues.

PRACTICE TIP

If you start working and no one can answer your time and billing questions right away, keep up with your time in increments of six minutes and keep notes detailed enough so that you can enter time into the time-and-billing system after you learn what the firm requires.

IN PRACTICE

Advice to First-Career Paralegals

Lauren Thomas, a paralegal at Blakeley & Blakeley LLP, has learned during her first three years working as a paralegal that she needs to be challenged on a daily basis to feel satisfied at work. When Lauren accepted her current position at Blakeley & Blakeley, she wanted more responsibility and an opportunity to use the analytical and reasoning skills learned during her education.

In this position, Lauren is responsible for management of all bankruptcy cases, mainly large Chapter 11 reorganization proceedings, and works directly with the partner and an associate who handle them. Her duties include facilitating all court filings and service, research tasks, preparation of analyses, and calendaring.

She feels valued and appreciated by Blakeley & Blakeley because she is able to learn and grow professionally.

With three years experience, Lauren offers these tips for the first-career paralegal:

1. Strive for perfection, but do not be frustrated with small mistakes.
2. Do not be afraid to ask a lot of questions, and make sure you write down the answers. Sometimes, especially when I am not familiar with a type of law that I am working in, it really helps to have the attorney explain why I am doing something (e.g. the law behind it, the process, etc).
3. Always, ALWAYS strive to learn. Keep yourself up to date with the area of law that you are working in.

Lauren earned an A.S. in Paralegal Studies from Fullerton College in 2008.

This is not a person who *demands respect* by giving orders. You will be able to see the difference. The paralegal who commands respect receives compliments behind her back. The paralegal who demands respect will seem rude in comparison, *telling* people to do things rather than requesting. This paralegal will be argumentative with colleagues rather than collaborative and will create a wake of uneasiness within the office.

When you find people who command respect in the office (they could be attorneys, paralegals, secretaries or other staff), watch closely how these people organize their time and go about their work. In other words, choose good role models. Look for answers to these questions to help you decide how to create your own professional image:

- How do they dress? Casually? Professionally?
- What time do they arrive? Leave?
- Do they work as independently as possible or do they collaborate and work around conference tables?

Ask these people questions and show that you are genuinely interested in being successful in this job. These people usually respond openly and will help you. As you work collaboratively with people, your own reputation will begin to emerge.

■ ESTABLISH YOUR REPUTATION

The following story is true but the paralegal asked to remain anonymous:

A partner of a large law firm sent an associate and a seasoned paralegal to a law firm in another city to help with an emergency privilege review. The team—almost all attorneys—met and began working. The paralegal, who wore suits similar to the lawyers', worked steadily, and contributed ideas to the project, became an accepted member of the team, so much so that on the last day of the project, an attorney from the host firm asked, "Where did you go to law school?"

"I didn't," the paralegal replied.

"But you know so much about discovery rules," the lawyer went on.

On that day, the paralegal felt like her reputation was complete. She was good at her job and others knew it.

PARALEGAL PROFILE

Andrea Schultz, CP

Current position: Senior Paralegal

Employer: Rice, Amundsen & Caperton, PLLC

Years in this position: 4

Certification: Certified Paralegal – National Association of Legal Assistants/Paralegals

Years of paralegal experience: 5

Education: A.A.S., Paralegal Studies, Southwest Tennessee Community College, Memphis, Tennessee

Andrea Schultz, CP, found more than a job to support two teenagers. She found a career she loves.

After 17 years of marriage and after being a stay-at-home mom for most of those years, Andrea Schultz, CP, found herself facing a future with two children to support without a husband. She was working at a large church as an administrative assistant, but knew she needed a job that paid a higher salary.

She volleyed between administrative assistant positions in an effort to increase her salary a bit each time.

Without a degree or certification in administration, she found she would soon "top out" in salary. Andrea said, "The thought of going back to school while working full-time and raising two teenagers was overwhelming. I put it out of my mind. I believed going back to school was not a practical option for me."

After her divorce, with the guidance of a self-help book, she began a practice she continues even now. She spent time alone reflecting on the previous year, asking herself these questions: *What good things happened? What did I accomplish? What do I wish I had done, but did not do?* Then, she spent time setting goals for the next year, asking herself these questions: *Where do I want to be financially in the next year or what major purchases will I want/need to make? How can I achieve this? What relationships do I need to nurture? What must I do to make this happen?*

She realized how quickly the two-plus years since the filing of her divorce had passed and thought, "Where do I want to be two years from now?" She felt that as quickly as the previous two years had passed, the next two years would pass even quicker. She explained that, "It was then, during this quiet moment, that I remembered my research into associate degrees at the local community college."

At age 39, Andrea entered a paralegal program. True to her assumptions, two years passed very quickly, and she graduated *Summa Cum Laude* from an ABA-approved paralegal program at Southwest Tennessee Community College.

The paralegal never told her firm the rest of the story. On the last day of the project, she received a job offer from one of the host firm's partners. No resume. No interview. Just an offer to negotiate terms.

The paralegal declined because her own firm treated her well. She had earned respect there, was challenged, compensated fairly, and felt valued.

This paralegal attained enough knowledge to work at a high level and presented a personal work ethic and skill set that garnered respect from others. You will not be this paralegal the first day, but you can strive for this kind of reputation.

Adjust Your Attitude (To Be a Colleague, Act Like a Colleague)

Being a colleague means acting like one. Three rules for earning respect at work include:

- Do not complain about your employer, your salary, or the management structure. No matter what.
- Do not engage in office gossip.
- Arrive 30 minutes early to plan your day, respond to e-mail, and drink your coffee. Be ready to go when the work-day starts. (By the way, walking around half the

morning with a cup of coffee in hand really screams, "I am taking my time getting started." Until you feel like you have truly settled in, you need to drink your coffee before you get to work.)

Complaining about company policies gives off negative energy. When someone around you starts to complain, say something like, "Oops, forgot to do something," and slip away from the group. *Not* complaining may lead to improved relationships with management and will be a definite move toward earning respect.

Arriving 30 minutes early gives you time to spend preparing to work. Sit in your office, a war room, or the coffee shop around the corner, but drink your coffee and plan your day. Identify the top three priorities on your to-do list. Think of this as time for strategic planning. What can you successfully delegate? Which task should you do immediately?

Your planning may seem to spontaneously combust after a conference call 20 minutes into the morning, but because you planned well, you can say, "By taking on this emergency, I cannot finish the documents for the Jones real estate closing." Knowing the exact task that will suffer will allow the supervising attorney to decide how to juggle projects.

Because you spent 30 minutes preparing yourself for work, your first official 20 minutes can be spent on the most important project, giving you 20 minutes of progress that you would not have made if you were still drinking coffee and hanging up your jacket.

During this time, use your personal laptop at the coffee shop to check your favorite news website, respond to your personal e-mail, and take care of personal tasks that you should not do at work.

Ask Questions and Communicate Well

Delivering excellent work is one of the best ways to establish a good reputation. In the beginning, get feedback early if you are not sure you are headed in the right direction with a project.

Ask questions to confirm details about an assignment, including when completion is expected. Asking questions says to others that you are thinking through a project and processing how you will do it. This quality is important to develop, and by asking questions, you are allowing the person assigning the project or a person who has done a similar project in the past, to give you some insight and tips that will help you do your best work. Asking questions is almost never a bad thing.

Sometimes, however, you may have what you feel is a "stupid" question. Maybe it is a question someone answered for you last week and you are embarrassed to ask again. The worst thing you can do is to *not ask*. If you have to ask, try these strategies:

- "I know you explained this to me last week, but can you show me again, please?" By acknowledging that you have been shown before, you are at least demonstrating some effort at remembering.
- Call a friend from paralegal school to ask the really ridiculous questions: "Where's the court?!" Be her ridiculous question person, too.
- Confirm details by saying, "I have done this kind of project before, but can I confirm with you the steps I am going to take so that I do it right the first time?" Then, outline what you are going to do and you will be able to work in the questions you need to ask.

Take it upon yourself to ensure that you understand what you have been asked to do.

No office has perfect communication. In the legal profession, where stress can rise quickly, always seek an understanding of what you are being asked to do. Ask questions until you understand. If you are still unclear—and sometimes you will be very unclear—find someone who has done a similar task before (or is familiar with projects of this type) and ask for help. Never do your work just "hoping" you are doing things properly.

Do Not Sweat Your Specialty—Yet

During your paralegal training, you may find that you are drawn to a particular specialization and really want to work in that area. Sometimes, though, you may not find your first job in the specialty you want. Try to feel okay about that.

You do not need to specialize right out of school. Some paralegals never specialize because the lawyers they work for have clients in several areas of law. Both generalists and specialists are needed in the paralegal profession. Usually, the larger the city and/or law firm, the more you are able to specialize. Smaller firms and firms in smaller cities tend to provide a wide range of services to clients, and being a paralegal with a wide range of skills is important.

Typically, specialties *choose you* based on the work you are doing and the pieces of that work that interest you the most. For example, you might think you never want to work in personal injury because some of the clients' stories are so sad, but then discover that you are good at accident reconstruction, collecting medical records, and reading police reports.

If your first job offer does not seem like it will be your "dream job," do not worry. Approach the work with a good attitude and an eye toward the types of work in that job that you do really well. You may be surprised to find that you are in the perfect job after all, but even if you are not, you have established some credible work history.

Participate in Your Profession

Join a professional organization and become involved. Attend CLE events. Attend a convention. Network whenever possible. You will be able to find your own place and voice within the profession.

■ RECEIVE ASSIGNMENTS WELL

Attorneys learn a lot in their three years of law school, but they rarely learn how to delegate work or how to work collaboratively in a professional environment. New attorneys often are so focused on the pressure of doing a good job themselves that they do not notice if they are failing to be excellent communicators when they delegate work. As a paralegal, your job is to make sure they delegate successfully. When they delegate successfully, you are able to contribute to a project successfully.

The worst feeling is to get a delegated project back and to discover that the work is totally and completely wrong. To ensure that you understand the assignment and that the attorney knows you understand, try repeating the assignment back to the person who gives it to you and check in during the task to confirm you are headed in the right direction.

First, **repeat the assignment** back to the person delegating it. Say, "Okay, you want me to. . . ." Repeat this step until everyone seems clear on the parameters of the work.

Second, **check in** with the person making the assignment as you go along, especially the first time you work with someone. If the project is very small or not time sensitive, complete a draft and check in to be sure you are headed in the right direction. If the project is large, start the project or create a project plan, do a little bit of it, and check in to see if you are producing the expected outcome. Create your own guidelines for how much to do and when to check in. The idea is that you gain confidence by knowing you are headed in the right direction. Also, check in early enough so that you have time to make adjustments, if necessary.

■ OFFER WHAT OTHERS NEED

Make information useful by purposefully watching for opportunities to offer suggestions that will improve service to the firm's clients or to the lawyers whose practices you support. Your paralegal practice can grow through meaningful information exchanges. In addition, such suggestions show that you are thinking independently and are concerned about the success of the enterprise.

CONCLUSION

Being a paralegal is like being a service provider to others. You may work for one attorney or several; you may have a paralegal supervisor or an office manager or a department head. These are your "clients." When you see an opportunity to contribute special skills to a project, offer.

For example, if you have special skills, such as a foreign language, excellent medical research skills, knowledge of the patenting process and U.S. Patent & Trademark Office databases, be sure to tell the attorneys you work with most.

Your job is to provide the best support you can. Think of ways to improve the services you offer and the efficiency with which you offer them.

Checklist for Success

- ☐ Dress for your career. As a student, start thinking like a professional. As a professional, wave good-bye to your student wardrobe.

- ☐ Organize your personal belongings, including your backpack (students only) or briefcase and other belongings you carry with you during the day.

- ☐ Pay attention to basic office etiquette and focus on your work.

- ☐ Arrive on time (preferably early).

- ☐ Plan your day and work hard to finish tasks.

- ☐ Learn to use office equipment.

- ☐ Learn the quirks that *this* office has.

- ☐ Accept the technology available.

- ☐ Watch others who are respected in the office and follow their lead.

- ☐ Hold yourself to high standards.

- ☐ Ask questions.

- ☐ Communicate and confirm details about assignments. Check in as needed.

- ☐ Pitch in and help others whenever you can.

- ☐ Participate in the profession by joining a professional organization and attending CLE events.

- ☐ Do not worry about specializing in one area yet.

- ☐ Improve your service offerings by looking for opportunities to contribute.

ASSIGNMENTS: PREPARING FOR YOUR PARALEGAL CAREER

Report

Interview one or two working paralegals and one working lawyer. Find out their best tips for starting work successfully. Did the attorney and paralegals have different suggestions? In addition, ask what surprised them when they started their first jobs. Write a memorandum to your instructor and report these tips. Explain which you might use yourself.

Report

Keep up with your time while you complete one assignment for this class or for another class. Record all of the smaller tasks and the time these tasks took. Prepare a time entry log using the guidelines in this chapter and the time log in Appendix D.

CHAPTER **10**

TECHNOLOGY TIPS AND TRAPS

Many colleges and universities have the newest computers and access to the most recent software, so you may have become accustomed to working with the best during your paralegal studies.

Remember there are MANY software packages. Some may be introduced while you are in school but others may be learned in the law firm setting.

Law firms tend to be what experts call "late adopters" of new technology. Law firms often take a "wait and see" approach to determine what the social and legal implications are going to be before they implement the equipment, software or systems. When you get your first job, you may wonder if you have traveled into the past when you find the office technology to be, well, old.

Paralegals need to understand the history between technology and the practice of law and what to expect on the job.

By the end of this chapter, you should be able to:

* Understand the history of technology in the legal profession
* Know how to ask for new software or hardware
* Recognize that your employer has specific rules related to technology
* Understand the implications of using personal technologies for work and work technologies for personal matters
* Identify the possibilities for inadvertent disclosure when using technologies

IN PRACTICE

Client Confidentiality and E-mail

Attorneys and law firms need some level of comfort when using new technologies. The Electronic Communications Privacy Act (ECPA) of 1986 extended the scope of the Federal Wiretap Act of 1968 to include electronic communications.

In 1999, the ABA issued Ethics Opinion 413, which held that confidential communications by means of unencrypted e-mail is **NOT** a breach of the duty of confidentiality because the method of transmission affords a reasonable expectation of privacy. These rules, along with the social acceptance and use of technology, eased some worries about confidentiality.

In 2011, the ABA Standing Committee on Ethics and Professional Responsibility then published an ethics opinion, Formal Opinion 11-459 "Duty to Protect the Confidentiality of E-mail Communications with One's Client."

According to this opinion, a lawyer sending or receiving substantive communications with a client via e-mail or other electronic means ordinarily must warn the client about the risk of sending or receiving electronic communications using a computer or other device, or e-mail account, to which a third party may gain access. When a lawyer communicates with a client by e-mail, the lawyer must first consider whether, given the client's situation, there is a significant risk that third parties will have access to the communications. If so, the lawyer must take reasonable care to protect the confidentiality of the communications by giving appropriately tailored advice to the client.

■ LAW FIRMS AND TECHNOLOGY

When e-mail first arrived in corporations across the United States, law firms held off using it until the corporate clients demanded the option of e-mailing documents back and forth to their attorneys. Seasoned paralegals remember when Internet access was available only to the law librarian and the entire firm shared one e-mail address, monitored closely by one person.

Some law firms were concerned about waiving attorney-client privilege or releasing confidential information when sending e-mail over unsecure connections. Others worried that the transmissions could be intercepted. They had the same fears about the use of cellular telephones.

With the adoption of the Electronic Communications Privacy Act (ECPA) of 1986, as well as ABA Ethics Opinion 99-413, the legal community became more comfortable with the use of e-mail and cell phones, so much so that they are now common means of communicating about confidential and privileged matters. However, they continue to pose a real risk for inadvertent disclosure.

Additional Reasons Law Firms May Not Adopt New Technology Quickly

Some law firms simply become comfortable with the technology they are using and do not want to upgrade because of the costs associated with buying software and purchasing new computers. Hardware and software must be installed, printers connected, accounts re-established. Staff need to be trained, and few people embrace taking time to learn how to navigate new electronic environments when what they are accustomed to works for them. The old adage "If it's not broken, why fix it?" seems to apply.

In addition to the productivity loss during upgrades and training, new hardware and software are expensive. Upgrading to the latest technology may not be economically feasible for some law offices. If you work in an office that watches its technology budget closely, you will need to figure out how to make the most of what you have. Instead of software geared for making case timelines, you can make them in a word processing program. You can create databases using Excel. Ask your colleagues how tasks are completed using existing equipment and programs before you ask for new hardware or software.

If you truly need an upgrade or a special software program to do your job, ask for it, but be prepared to demonstrate how the new technology will benefit the firm.

IN PRACTICE

How to Ask for New Technology

Before you ask for new hardware or software, think through your reasons for the request. Write out your needs and how the hardware or software will help you accomplish tasks. You might write a memo to organize your thoughts regarding the reasons you need it.

Use these tips to help you formulate your strategy for requesting new technology:

- Know why you need the new technology. Are you planning to use it for a special case?
- How will the new technology benefit the firm? Is it more efficient? More accurate?

- Include the potential costs and compare cost to benefit.
- Provide names and addresses of potential vendors.
- Provide reviews of the product.
- Identify how others might benefit from the software. Will it be easier to share information?
- What is the learning curve? How long will it take to learn the new software? Is it intuitive? Can you use it without a lot of training?

■ FOLLOW THE FIRM'S RULES AND LEAD FOR TECHNO-ETIQUETTE

One of the first things you should do when you begin your new job is find out your firm's policy with regard to technology and its use. You need to know your firm's expectations. If the firm has a policy handbook that addresses such matters, you should obtain a copy and become familiar with its contents. Find out the expectations in relation to:

- your computer/printer
- a firm-issued laptop, cell phone, tablet PC, or other equipment
- the Internet
- your desk telephone
- fax machines and other electronic devices

For example, are you allowed to borrow the firm's video camera for personal use? Can you use your firm-issued cell phone to make personal calls? Is your Internet usage tracked or monitored? Do you need approval to download programs or applications onto your personal computing device?

Your Personal Technology

Social media provide excellent networking opportunities, and should be used off the clock. Traditional-aged college students use social media to provide instant access to updates about friends' location, relationship status, and general well-being.

This generational practice shifts somewhat when professional work begins. For example, status updates should be made at lunch via your personal phone. Some employers mandate that employees not mention work at all on social media status updates. These employers do not want their employees to report that they are going to work or how the day is going. Find out what your employer's rules are before you post.

The same goes for calls and text messages on your personal cell phone. Keep your cell phone turned off during work hours or on "silent" or "vibrate only." Your boss and other associate attorneys may use their cell phones all the time. This practice does not give you permission to use yours.

As always, some "gray areas" exist because you may be allowed (even expected) to use the Internet at work. Paralegals often need to read professional publications, check websites, and perform online research.

PRACTICE TIP

Personal and work e-mail should never cross. Discovery rules make mixing home and work technology tricky. Before you use your home computer or personal e-mail for any work-related activities—sending an e-mail, finalizing a brief, etc.—ask your supervising attorney to explain the rules.

There is the possibility that using your home computer to finalize a brief might make the files on your computer discoverable. The Federal Rules of Civil Procedure are directive about what is discoverable, but do not interpret these rules yourself. Find out from your supervising attorney how the rules are applied in your jurisdiction.

IN PRACTICE

Relay Information to Clients Ethically

Your state provides ethics rules about the kinds of information you can give clients. This information applies to talking to people on the phone as well. For example, paralegals are typically not permitted to quote fees to clients, but you could relay a message from the attorney: "I spoke to your attorney, and she said preparation of your documents will be $500."

Knowing the rules about what you can and cannot tell a client or potential client is important and a good reason for having a paralegal answer the phone instead of an untrained receptionist. In larger firms, receptionists typically transfer calls only; they never give any information over the phone. Consider answering the phone or screening calls for attorneys as important and do it well.

Again, if the firm has a policy concerning such matters it should be obtained, consulted and followed. The instances of employees suffering adverse employment consequences from unauthorized/inappropriate use of such technology are more common.

Your Desk Telephone

Your firm will most likely have a policy regarding calls made from, and received at, your desk telephone. In fact, answering the phone may be one of your primary duties, especially in a smaller law office. Your job may be to screen calls for the attorney or attorneys, take down information about potential new clients, and answer questions for clients.

Usually a code is provided for each client so that the charges can be billed to clients when making phone calls on their behalf. Employees may be provided with a code for their personal calls and expected to reimburse the firm for those calls. Regardless of the policy, keep personal calls to a minimum.

Another issue with a desk telephone is whether or not you are allowed to put the telephone on "Do Not Disturb" or let calls roll to voice mail for a certain amount of time. While you should not leave the "Do Not Disturb" service on all day, it can be very helpful when you have work to do and need to minimize distractions. Some firms absolutely do not allow you to have your calls held because of the needs in the office, so you should be sure to ask before doing this.

Your Cell Phone

Many large law firms allow you to use your office telephone to make personal long-distance phone calls, as long as you pay the bill yourself. What about your office-issued cell phone? Are you allowed to use minutes for personal calls? Are you allowed to access the Internet or send text messages? How is your Internet access monitored? Are you expected to be available to your employer by cell phone 24/7? Know the rules that apply to your cell phone when it is issued.

When carrying a cell phone, confidential conversations should not take place in public locations or in the presence of others. Case law has held that conversations taking place over cell phones have an expectation of privacy as long as the parties take care to isolate themselves and talk only when they are out of earshot of others. Always excuse yourself and find a private location for your call.

The expectation of privacy would be nonexistent if those same conversations took place in a crowded restaurant. On the other hand, even if you are very cautious and avoid anything but a hard-wired telephone to communicate with clients, or always take care to be sure no one else can hear the conversation, you cannot guarantee that clients will be as cautious, nor do they always understand that when privileged information is disclosed to a third party, even accidentally, the privilege may be waived.

The Internet

The Internet can be helpful when you are doing research or vetting an expert witness. The Internet also can be a huge distraction and interrupt your work. Limit Internet usage to only work-related tasks. Firms often monitor your web usage, and more than one firm has fired staff that spent time on inappropriate websites or spent work time on personal online activities.

Checking Facebook, finding LinkedIn connections, or posting on Twitter can be addictive. You think you will take just a quick break to read status updates, and before you know it, a half-hour (that should have been billed) has gone by or your boss is looking over your shoulder. Social networking should be saved for your personal time. Playing games on the Internet during work hours is also unprofessional and may result in your being reprimanded or fired.

E-mail

Ask about your employer's policies regarding e-mail:

- Are you expected to answer all e-mail immediately? Or, only from your boss? How is e-mail filed and billed?
- Can you use your e-mail account for business related to professional organizations or to receive professional e-zines or other information?
- What kind of information needs to be included in your e-mail "signature"? Usually law firms attach a confidentiality notice and contact information.

E-mail is now a common means of communicating about confidential and privileged matters, but you must use e-mail carefully so that you do not disclose confidential and privileged information.

IN PRACTICE

E-mail Signature

Your e-mail settings can be programmed to automatically generate a signature at the bottom of every e-mail message. Use a signature that includes a statement of confidentiality, like the one shown below.

This disclaimer can help you make the case that any accidental disclosure was inadvertent and that the communication should retain its confidential and privileged status. Most signatures look like this:

Jackie Wellington
Paralegal
Smith, Howard, and Jones, LLC
123 Main Street
Little City, AZ 02222
Phone: 123.444.5566
Fax: 123.444.5588
E-mail: jackie.wellington@email.com

Notice: This e-mail transmission, including any attachments, may contain confidential information protected by the attorney-client or other legal privilege. Unauthorized use, distribution or copying is prohibited. If you received this e-mail in error, please notify the sender by replying to this e-mail or by calling Smith, Howard, and Jones, LLC at 123.222.3333 and deleting the erroneous transmission from your system without copying it. Thank You.

Keep Professional and Personal E-mail Accounts Separate

The line between professional and private e-mail accounts can become blurred the minute you use one for the other. Rule 34 of the Federal Rules of Civil Procedure allows the discovery of any matter relevant to the claims of a party as long as the request appears to lead to the discovery of admissible evidence. It is best that employees do not use their personal e-mail accounts to send business communications, and vice versa. You do not want your personal e-mail subject to discovery.

Statement of Confidentiality

All e-mail messages, whether they are routine or contain privileged information, should include a statement of confidentiality. The statement should identify the message as privileged and if received in error, the recipient should be asked to inform the sender and to delete the e-mail. This disclaimer cannot prevent someone else from reading the message, but it can help you make the case that the disclosure was inadvertent and that the communication should retain its confidential and privileged status.

Learn and Respect Preferences

The use of e-mail to communicate with clients will be limited by the client's preferences and issues of confidentiality. You will work with people who have different comfort levels when it comes to e-mail and other technology. Some people will want everything sent by e-mail. Some are not able to download attachments or do not have access to a printer. Some people check their e-mail so rarely that sending the communication by U.S. mail would be faster.

For others, confidentiality is an issue. Consider the client whose assistant receives all e-mail. It is possible that the assistant will view confidential or privileged information or, at the very least, see information that only the client should have. You should get the client's permission to communicate by e-mail and be sure the client is available to receive electronic documents. You should take this precaution so that the documents do not fall into someone else's hands. Remember, if they go to a third party, it is very likely the privilege will be waived.

Keep E-mail Professional

All e-mail prepared on your work account, regardless of your profession, should stay focused on work and should not include any statement or sentence you would not want read out loud in court or read by your colleagues or supervisors. This principle is especially important in the legal profession.

The tone of your e-mail should be professional at all times. Ignore chain e-mail, "pass it on" messages, and jokes that are forwarded to you from others. Do not pass these messages on.

Be wary of using "reply all" to respond to a message. Always review the list of e-mail recipients to make sure you are writing to the correct person. Even though e-mail is fast, treat it as carefully as you would a letter printed on paper, especially when corresponding with people outside the firm.

Inside the firm, consider that what you say in e-mail can be intercepted by anyone monitoring the office server and might be read by others. Do not say anything in e-mail you would not want your colleagues to hear you say aloud.

The Fax Machine

When you send documents by fax to clients and other law firms, the risk of sending confidential and privileged information to the wrong party is almost as high as by e-mail. Be sure you enter the correct fax numbers and only the numbers of the intended recipients. Some fax machines will have speed dial set up, and you should be sure you choose the correct key for your document.

Use a Statement of Confidentiality

As with e-mail, a statement of confidentiality is important to include on a fax cover sheet. As you learned earlier, this statement warns the recipient that the document may be privileged or confidential and if received in error, the recipient should be asked to inform the sender and to delete the e-mail. While this disclaimer cannot prevent someone else from reading the document, it may help you make the case that the disclosure was inadvertent and the communication should retain its confidential and privileged status.

Practice Tip: As an aside, some IT professionals are suggesting that law firms prepend the Statement of Confidentiality so that it appears at the top of an e-mail or fax cover sheet where it is more likely to be noticed by the reader.

The Photocopy Machine

Most paralegals develop strong feelings toward the photocopy machine. Some dislike making photocopies very much. Others find the work to be a change of pace from desk work. However, accurate photocopying is important to the practice of law. You must be copying the correct document, and the document must be copied correctly. Can you imagine submitting a document with a missing page as an exhibit at a trial?

PARALEGAL **PROFILE**

Erica Nantais

Current position: Paralegal and IT Support for Carr Maloney P.C.

Years in this position: 5 years as a paralegal, started in IT Support in early 2011

Exact title: Paralegal

Years of paralegal experience: 7 years

Years of legal experience: 12. I previously worked as an administrative assistant and a legal secretary.

Education: B.A., Theater Management and Directing with Minor in Arts Administration

Erica Nantais explains why paralegals need to keep up with technology.

Erica Nantais works as a paralegal and in IT Support for Carr Maloney P.C. in Washington, DC. Erica advises that, "You can't help your company choose the best tools unless you know what's out there." Erica answered some important questions about technology.

How should a paralegal learn and stay ahead of the curve, especially when an employer does not have the latest and greatest software?

Make friends with legal service providers who work with the kind of technology in which you are interested–court reporting, e-discovery, legal research, trial presentation, etc. They can provide a wealth of information about industry trends, best practices, and the differences between offerings. In addition, seek out training on the Internet; there are free and low-cost continuing legal education courses, product tutorials, webinars, and even user manuals that can teach you what you need to know.

What if you are not the one making the technology decisions?

Think ahead. Just because you are not currently a decision maker does not mean that you never will be. You might switch jobs, or you might even show off some of your new knowledge to your colleagues and become a resource for them when questions arise. In turn, your recommendations might have more weight once you demonstrate your understanding of the various products on the market.

What if you cannot use what you believe is best?

There is no good excuse for working inefficiently, so use what you have to the best of your ability and learn everything you can about it. As paralegals, our job is to be proactive and informed, and there will always be new technology we can conquer.

Data Security and Photocopy Machines

We have been using the copy machine for more than 50 years. There have been many technological advances in the copy machine, though, and now these machines do just about everything but wash windows. They also have opened a dangerous hole in data security.

The office copy machine may digitally store thousands of documents that may be passed on at resale. Nearly every digital copier built since 2002 contains a hard-drive that stores an image of every document copied, scanned or e-mailed by the machine.

In this process, an office staple has been turned into a digital archive packed with highly confidential or sensitive data. These machines have all types of information stored on them: social security numbers, birth certificates, bank records, income tax returns and other valuable information. The information would create opportunities for identity theft.

When trading in a copy machine, special steps need to be taken to manage or delete the data on a copy machine storage device. Since attorneys must preserve the confidences and secrets of their clients, they have to take some basic responsibility and understand that copiers are actually computers that must be cleaned up before they are sold.

■ TECHNOLOGY AND YOUR REPUTATION

Even if you do all your Facebook status updates, tweets, and blog posts on your personal time, you are not relieved from your ethical responsibilities. There is always a danger of disclosure of confidential and privileged information, even inadvertently.

Never Give Away Your Firm's Strategy

The following posts look innocent enough and none identify a client, but think of the way the other side in a lawsuit might interpret them, especially on a case where they *know* you are the paralegal:

- Spent all day in document production hell and still can't find any good docs.
- Love Google translator! It's making reviewing German case law a snap!
- Like the color choices in TimeMap. Used it to prepare exhibits for tomorrow's court date.

While none of these updates seem particularly informative, they do give clues to what might be happening in an office at a given time. This information could prove helpful to opposing counsel.

Do Not Damage Your Own Reputation

Remember, too, that the people you work with might be offended by the things you post on Facebook or Twitter, even if you are "just" venting. In any law firm, a post like this one can cause hard feelings:

> Talk about a BAD Monday!! Is it over yet? I've got discovery due on one case in five days, and for some !@#m reason the secretary in the office didn't get an order signed like she was told over a month ago!!!

Never mind that it is not the secretary's responsibility to get an order signed (whatever "getting an order signed" means), it is certainly going to cause some hard feelings in this three-person office if the secretary reads this post, and in all law offices, the secretary is a vital part of the legal team. If this secretary reads the post, the paralegal will not be granted any favors, and in the legal profession, helping each other out in a pinch is very important.

PRACTICE NOTE

Sometimes, you may find a paralegal on Twitter who seems to be posting all day long. You will see links to news items, referrals to blogs, and sometimes tiny updates that seem timeless in nature. Most likely, the paralegal is using software that "feeds" the tweets to Twitter at intervals that are set the previous day or night. The paralegal appears to be using Twitter all day, when in reality, most or all updates are written off the clock. At least that is what Charlsye and Vicki hope the paralegal is doing.

Another mistake is posting your whereabouts after calling in sick. Here is an exchange posted to Facebook:

>I called in sick today so I can get some things done. Hee hee.

>>What kind of things?

>Just stuff around the house.

>>Better be careful that your boss doesn't see this.

>Why?

Perhaps it is not illegal to take a personal day when you need to take care of personal things, but calling in at the last minute is bad citizenship and, at the very least, not something you want to become known for doing.

The rule to follow so that you never have trouble with your posts on social networks is the following: **Never post anything you would not want your mother, your boss, or the opposing party to see.**

Paralegals typically hold themselves to high standards as required by ethics rules. Being responsible with office and personal technology is one way to maintain these high standards. After you learn the firm's policies on technology use, develop your own safeguards so that you do not inadvertently disclose information, or overstep the boundaries between the office technology and personal use.

CONCLUSION

When you begin your work as a paralegal, you will have to deal with the technology systems that are in place, though they may be antiquated in comparison to the technology you used in the classroom. Once you have been on the job a while, you will be able to recommend changes in equipment and software but you should be prepared to explain how your suggestions will benefit the firm as a whole. It is also important to know and follow the firm's technology policies and to remember that your reputation and your job demand that you use the Internet and social media with professionalism.

Checklist for Success

☐ Law firms tend to be "late adopters" of technology, so when you begin working at a law firm, accept the technology that you are given.

☐ When you want the firm to purchase new software or hardware, be prepared to explain why you need it.

☐ Use your personal phone and social media off the clock.

☐ Follow the firm's rules and lead for using firm-issued and personal technology:

    ○ Using work-issued cell phone for personal calls

    ○ Photocopying for personal use

    ○ Using desk phone to make personal long distance calls

☐ Your Internet usage may be tracked or monitored.

☐ E-mail that goes through a central server can be read by others.

☐ Technology creates ways to inadvertently disclose too much information: using a cell phone in public; updating your status with clues about your workday; and accidentally keeping too many names on an e-mail message reply.

ASSIGNMENTS: PREPARING FOR YOUR PARALEGAL CAREER

Career Management

Set up a LinkedIn profile. Then create a PDF of your profile using the tool on LinkedIn and print it for class. Discuss your profile with others to determine how LinkedIn works as a mini-resume.

Report

Use Google to search for "paralegal ethics technology" without quotation marks. Find one ethical dilemma involving paralegals and technology. Write a memorandum to your instructor that summarizes the dilemma and explains how it should be resolved in your jurisdiction. You will need to locate the rules in your jurisdiction related to technology.

Network

Find a paralegal who actively uses Twitter and review her last 25 "tweets." Write a memorandum to your instructor that summarizes or analyzes how the paralegal uses Twitter. Identify posts that could be damaging ethically and explain how those posts could lead to problems in your jurisdiction based on the rules in place. Look for posts that could cause problems in the office or among colleagues. Most importantly, identify how this paralegal uses Twitter to network with others. How does the paralegal reach out to others and how do others respond?

INTERNET RESOURCES

TweetDeck, a status-update feeder for Twitter that allows you to manage your social networks more effectively off the clock: *http://www.tweetdeck.com*

Federal Rules of Civil Procedure: IT Obligations for E-mail: *http://www.inboxer.com/downloads/Whitepaper_FRCP.pdf*

Paralegal Gateway offers legal news for paralegals and links to social networking sites geared for paralegals. *http://www.paralegalgateway.com*

The Paralegal Mentor website offers training and tips about the ethical use of technology: *http://www.paralegalmentor.com*

CHAPTER **11**

ORGANIZING YOUR TIME

n law, time is money. Even if you do not bill your time, a value is placed on your productivity. Consider these situations:

- Paralegals at a large law firm share a secretary with two attorneys, except for one: Melody. As one of the most productive paralegals in the trial department, she shares a secretary with only one attorney so that she can remain highly productive.
- Jolene cleans off her desk when an out-of-town attorney arrives because he thinks a messy desk means she is overwhelmed and things are not going well. She keeps the usual contents of her desktop in a box in a storage closet until the attorney leaves.
- Daniel never answers the phone when a certain attorney calls (he has caller ID on his phone). Their communication styles are so different that to stay organized, he lets the call roll to voice mail so that he can listen to the message several times. He wants to understand the request and make a few notes before calling the attorney back, which he does promptly. He is able to ask better questions and the communication is clearer.
- Aaron travels with two cell phones: an office smart phone and a phone for his personal calls. Separating his personal and professional lives helps manage the flow of work, and he can keep the personal phone turned off during working hours.
- What seasoned paralegals know: What seems important when you arrive at work might become the least important after one mid-morning phone call. Staying organized on the job is a task that requires attention every day. Paralegals must prioritize, change gears, find space or time to concentrate, and be able to locate information and documents instantly.

Many paralegals enter the profession with a natural affinity for organization. Some paralegals contend that typical time management strategies do not work. No matter how many times you try to barricade your office door or how much you want to let calls roll to voice mail, the requests from supervising attorneys manage to arrive, sometimes in a magical Harry Potter-ish way, regardless of self-promises to "get things done."

Paralegals also deal with a variety of personalities, dueling deadlines, and different management styles. All can impact time management. This is the way the legal profession works. Paralegals must learn techniques to stay organized, to work efficiently, and to deal with interruptions.

The best approach to using your time wisely is to develop multiple strategies. When one tactic does not work, you can reach into your skill set and find another approach. Even if you are very organized, you need to develop an arsenal of time management strategies because you will be working with supervising attorneys and paralegals whose communication and organizational skills differ from yours. Having a variety of strategies to choose from will help you keep things moving.

Keep in mind that, depending on the flow of your work, the method that works one day may not work the next day. Because we do not recommend one particular time management system (paralegals need multiple systems and strategies), we provide strategies structured by categories. At the end of this chapter, you will find a list of our favorite organizing gurus and their books.

This chapter prepares you to:

- Use multiple organizational and time management strategies to be efficient at work
- Prioritize your day to allow for flexibility when priorities change
- Use technology for organization and time management
- Delegate tasks to the most efficient resource

■ GETTING STARTED: THE TRUTH ABOUT TIME MANAGEMENT

Many people believe you can manage time, but time manages itself: there are 24 hours in every day, no more and no less. No matter where you live, how much money you have, or how old you are, the amount of time you have in a minute, an hour and a day is exactly the same. The challenge is to manage how you spend your time. In a sense, time management is really life management.

Experts say that the trick to managing how you spend your time is to decide what is really important and then eliminate the unimportant. It sounds so easy, but paralegals are in a unique situation in that once you get your to-do list prioritized, an attorney will call with the news that the case that has been your number one priority has been settled, and the twelfth thing on your list is actually now your top priority.

For paralegals, deciding what is important has to occur on three levels: the **immediate workload**; your **personal life**; and **where the personal-professional lines cross**.

Your immediate workload should be prioritized according to criteria set by your colleagues and yourself. Only the supervising attorneys and your own colleagues can help with that. This does not mean you ask someone to organize your to-do list, but it means that you evaluate your workload in terms of what you have been asked to do, the deadlines that must be met, and the time each task takes. (See our tip about the Hope-It-Goes-Away Tray.)

Personally—and this is where paralegals have to look hard at finding the unimportant things to eliminate—you must decide what your real priorities are. One of our reviewers pointed out (and rightly so) that you cannot bring the personal to work. And one way to make sure you really separate the two is to *really* separate the two. Turn off your personal cell phone. Do not respond to personal e-mail or check Facebook. As you are ramping up your career, you cannot do everything you did during your student days. Your goal now is to make time for the most important things.

IN PRACTICE

The Hope-It-Goes-Away Tray

Everyone has one of these. (If you do not, get one right away.) This tray is for things you hope will go away. Do not put your unpaid parking tickets here; those will not go away. Instead, fill this try with those little things that could possibly go away.

For example, this tray might include a telephone message from a client who says she might need you to pull some information together for her, but she is not sure. She simply wants you to have a "heads up." Or, you might put an assignment for a case that may settle in the tray, especially if you are not supposed to bill any time on the case until you hear more about the settlement outcome.

Once a week, quickly go through this tray to see if anything "goes away" and decide whether something needs to be moved to your task list.

Do not put things here that need to be done; put things here that are on hold. Then, hope they go away.

Personal-Professional crossover occurs when your personal goals are your professional goals. As your career progresses, these goals will merge. For instance, if you hope to take a certification exam, you have a personal goal that is also a professional goal. Or, if you want to become a paralegal manager someday you might take some master's classes in management. These are terrific goals, and how you manage these goals will determine the trajectory of your career.

How you manage the **personal-professional crossover** requires deciding what is really important to you. You must determine what fits with your values and goals, as well as what absolutely has to be done. Learning to determine the important and let go of the unimportant is a skill that may take some practice.

If you are the person who shows up for every single professional development event in your area, then you might ask yourself if attending all those events is moving you forward toward your annual billable hour goals. Your professional goals? Your basic goal of being excellent at your work?

If you prioritize, the important things will get finished and you may even have time to spare.

■ HOW TO TAKE CHARGE OF YOUR WORKLOAD

As a paralegal, **you must take charge of your work** if you want to manage your time. It is rare that your work will come to you at a leisurely pace. Often, it comes in waves, one assignment after another. If you are not careful, you will be working in layers, one file on top of the other with a sea of paper on top of your desk. When this occurs, it is easy to misunderstand instructions, miss deadlines, lose documents, and become confused. Three practice tips will keep your workflow in check:

Assess

Manage the work as it enters your workspace by doing an immediate assessment: What are the deadlines? How long will the job take? How can the work be done to meet the deadlines? Does the work have any restrictions?

Take Notes

Be sure to take careful notes when you are given an assignment. Never trust your memory. The atmosphere in the legal setting is usually very fast paced and it is easy to forget details. Keep a spiral bound notebook on your desk for all your notes. Be sure you choose a notebook that is large enough that you will not lose it but small enough not to be in your way. Carry it with you to meetings.

IN PRACTICE

The Notebook

A shorthand notebook works well for keeping a running diary of notes.

Some people choose to organize their notes by case: each case gets its own notebook. Others use one notebook, date the top of each page, and write to-do lists, notes and assignments from attorneys and colleagues, and any other information that needs jotting down.

As the work on a page is "finished" (you do not need the notes anymore or you have transferred them to the proper file; you have completed the assigned tasks; etc.), you can put a small check in the corner of the page. The check represents that the page is "complete" and you can ignore it.

In its entirety, the notebook provides a running journal of working notes and, if managed correctly, you also could note your time for transferring to the billing system later.

Understand

Each paralegal/attorney relationship is different. To maximize productivity, become familiar with the work habits, work styles, and expectations of the attorney or attorneys with whom you work. Understand the expectations an attorney has for you. Once you do, you will be able to agree on how work should be finished.

■ PLAN AND PRIORITIZE

To decide how your work will be done and how the deadlines will be met, make a list of all the work that you have to do to meet the deadline and break that work into pieces.

For instance, if a trial is three months away, think of all the steps that must be completed to prepare for trial and when each one should be completed, as well as who will perform each step. If you are working on the probating of a decedent's estate, you will need to plan for the deadline to file the inventory of decedent's assets with the court. What has to be done to accomplish that?

For tasks that you will do many times, the firm may have a master checklist or you could create one for yourself. When you use a checklist, you do not have to re-think everything you need to consider for a particular task. For example, paralegals working in personal injury use checklists for obtaining medical records to ensure records have been obtained from all sources. This systemization of the law office through the use of checklists, etc. makes for greater productivity and allows the paralegal to function more independently with less need for attorney supervision.

Using a checklist helps maintain accurate records, too. You will not have to rely on your memory to know whether you requested a record in one case but not in another. You can consult the checklist. If you create or revise a checklist, meet with your supervising attorney to be sure that everything is included.

Once you understand what has to be completed, prioritize each step. Some tasks will be highly urgent and must be done immediately. Some tasks can be completed when you have time. Some tasks may require setting deadlines for other people in the firm. Schedule each step in your planner or in your firm's calendaring system. Microsoft Outlook works very well for this.

All of this sounds insanely organized, but you must learn to accomplish these tasks "on your feet." For example, as you develop your career, you will be asked questions like, "How long will it take for you to catalog the contents of the Bennett estate?" You will know exactly what questions to ask and based on the answers you receive, be able to give a time estimate right then.

PRACTICE TIP

It may be helpful to place a status sheet or checklist at the front of each file.

Plan Your Daily Work

Unless you know where you are going, you will never reach your destination. The same goes for each day at work. If you do not have some sort of "road map" for each day's work, you will reach the end of the day and find you have not accomplished nearly enough, and perhaps nothing at all.

Before you leave the office in the evening, or first thing when you arrive in the morning, check your planner or calendar for deadlines that must be met for the day and their order of importance. Make a list and note the task that either must be done first or requires the most energy.

Time management experts agree that you should first work on the most important task, or the one that will take the most energy, to get it out of the way. Your own body clock may come into play here. Some people are most energetic in the morning. Others find that peak energy comes later in the day. You must decide what works best for you. If possible, use your peak energy time to work on your most difficult projects, but make sure you meet your daily deadlines.

Your goal is to manage your flow of work as efficiently as possible. When priorities suddenly shift, you must be open to the shift. You can handle shifts, which are common in the legal profession, by making sure you pad larger tasks with a bit of extra time. Extra time means you will be able to handle interruptions or new work that must be completed quickly. Padding a project does not mean telling someone it will take two days when it should really take only one. Instead, pad the projects that have a longer deadline by starting them earlier. These are longer-term projects that are not due in a few hours or the next day. If you have some work that you know will take three days of two-hour blocks, start four or five days out. Chances are, your two-hour block will be interrupted with another assignment more than once, but because you started a couple of days earlier than the deadline requires, the interruption can be handled while you still meet the deadline.

A Note about Interruptions

Interruptions are viewed negatively in many organizational manuals, and while we provide some advice for minimizing interruptions, they are a standard part of the ebb and flow of a paralegal's work. Try not to view them negatively; instead, think of managing interruptions as important to your job as responding to e-mail or answering your phone. Just like a shop owner who could unpack a lot of inventory if it were not for customers who keep "interrupting" (and therefore keep the business going) the paralegal's ability to fold interruptions gracefully into the workday is what separates a good paralegal from a great one.

IN PRACTICE

Take Advantage of Small Chunks of Time

Once you are organized and managing how you spend your time, you may have some periods of empty time that are too short to begin a long project, but long enough to need filling.

Learn to take advantage of these small bits of time. It is amazing what you can accomplish in 5, 10, or even 15 minutes.

Instead of wasting those small pockets of time, use them to make a phone call, write a memo, straighten your desk, plan for the next day, put away some materials from another project, etc.

You can also approach this from a different angle by starting a project you dread. If you have a large project you need to work on but just do not feel you have time to tackle the whole thing, start working on it for just a few minutes.

Fifteen-minute increments seem to work well for a lot of people. If you work for 15 minutes again and again, your project will be done before you know it.

Multitasking vs. Single-Tasking

Multitasking became popular in the 1990s as hand-held gadgets emerged, but studies are showing that multitasking is not effective. At least one study suggests that multitasking costs more.

Still, we know that to get things finished efficiently, we must be the best users of time. The following situations work for multitasking:

- Send out documents to be photocopied while you work on something else.
- Pull the materials together for several phone calls and make them in one session.
- Eat lunch and catch up on professional publications.

Notice that in these scenarios, you really are not working on two things at once, but more than one thing is being completed. That exemplifies efficient multitasking. Unless urgent, group tasks together: photocopying, faxing, mailing, filing, etc.

The best way to work is to single-task: work on one thing at a time. Starting a task—even to write a letter—requires some ramp up time: you have to get the file, sit at your computer, open the document, think about what you want to say, and write the letter. If you are interrupted, you will have to save your letter, make a note to come back to the letter, and ramp up to take care of the interruption.

Sometimes, you may feel that you have "started" the same letter all day because you keep getting interrupted or distracted. You cannot stop legitimate interruptions. They are part of your job; you can, however, work to rid your day of distractions and costly time leaks.

The next section describes the difference between an interruption and a distraction and how both can affect the flow of work.

IN PRACTICE

Take the Initiative During Slow Times

When you have down time, which will be rare, look for work to do:

- Ask your primary supervising attorney, associates or other paralegals for some of their overflow work.
- Use this time to learn a new skill in your own or another practice area by offering up your services.
- Look at deadlines on the firm's calendaring system and pick a project that may not yet be scheduled but will be necessary and start on it, with permission.

- Skim through the pile of professional publications or newsletters you have collected and identify articles to share with others or to read later. Be sure to look for any judicial changes that affect your work.
- Create databases of cases, opinions and orders that you use often.
- Organize/file/collate.
- Do some pro bono work.

■ DISTRACTIONS AND TIME LEAKS

Distractions and time leaks are exactly the type of interruption that organizing books write about so negatively. Distractions take away from your work unnecessarily. These are not the interruptions that are standard in the paralegal's work life. Learn to identify the interruptions (expected in the legal profession) from distractions (unappreciated in every profession).

If you are extroverted and enjoy distractions and personal interaction within your day, you will have to work hard to stay focused on your work.

Identify Distractions

Distractions can sneak in and gobble up time that should be spent on those things you have decided are important. Examples include unnecessary meetings, telephone calls, cruising the Internet, checking Facebook, texting, the co-worker who stops by your office to ask a question that will take "just a minute," and then rambles about last night's game.

Every time you are distracted, you are taken off task. It takes precious minutes (perhaps as much as 15 minutes) to get back on task. These distractions, paired with interruptions, can eat a lot of time.

Try these tricks to stop distractions:

- **Reorganize your workspace so visitors are not as welcome.** If your desk faces the door, move it so you do not look right into the hallway at everyone passing by. Once a person makes eye contact with you, they tend to stop to chat. Stack some files on your guest chair so the office pest (i.e., time waster) cannot take root for a half hour of chatting. Never keep a bowl of candy on your desk. Few can resist a handful of M&Ms and a little conversation to go along with it.
- **Never ask "How are you?" when someone stops by your office or reaches you on the telephone.** This is an open invitation to chat. Instead, ask "What can I do for you?" This will get right to the point of the interruption.
- If possible—and with your supervisor's permission—**put your phone on "Do Not Disturb"** or let it roll to voice mail for a designated length of time so you can finish a project. Change your message during that time to indicate how you are handling calls. Simply say, "You have reached Jill Craft. I am in the office today, and will be returning calls at 2 P.M. If this is urgent . . ." Obtain permission to use voice mail this way.
- **Do not let your e-mail control your day.** Paralegals must respond to their e-mail; however, you do not need to check it every time you hear the "ping." Instead, you could turn off the inbox "ping," and check e-mail the last five minutes of every hour. Create a plan that works for you in your office.
- **When someone wants "just a minute" of your time**, and it is not your boss or a legitimate interruption, tell them frankly that you are working on something important but you will get back with them later in the day. If possible, set a time for the follow up. Of course, if they just want to chat, plan to catch up with them during the lunch hour.
- **Stand up when someone enters your workspace** or when you are ready for a person to leave. When you stand, you send a message that the meeting will either be brief or that it has ended. This works every time. You start moving, they start moving, end of distraction.

Make Sure You Are Not a Distraction

Remember to check your own habits. You do not want to sabotage yourself. Make sure that you do not become the person who does a loop around the office every hour or so looking for conversation.

If you find you are interrupting yourself by checking e-mail, calling your friend to set up a lunch date, or making a third trip to the supply closet, you could be sabotaging your own day. You can stop interrupting yourself by following these tips (try these as a student to figure out which techniques work best for you):

- **Turn off anything that might be noisy or distracting,** including music, television, instant messenger, e-mail alerts, and your cell phone.
- **Do not stop to read every e-mail as it comes in,** and definitely do not check status updates on Facebook every few minutes. Instead, schedule a time that works

with your office's expectations for checking e-mail and stick with it. When you start an internship or a job, never check Facebook on work time. Save it for after hours.

- **Your telephone time should be scheduled.** When possible, plan to return calls just before lunch (people will be ready to leave and will not talk long) or later in the afternoon. Prepare ahead for the calls so that you get right to the point and take care of the business. Many calls must be returned immediately, and you will know the difference between these types of calls and those that can wait.
- **Keep your desk stocked with all the supplies you need** so you do not have to replenish them during the day. It is easy to have legal pads, file folders, stationery, pens, staples, and other supplies on hand within easy reach. As a student, needing to make a trip to the office supply store is an excellent procrastination technique.
- **Let questions accumulate.** This is a tricky tip, but if you can swing it you will find you have achieved efficiency nirvana. When working with other paralegals and support staff, create some agreements about when you will get together to go over work in progress. As you create better working relationships, you will know whether you can save a question for your scheduled time or whether you need to ask immediately.

Try keeping an "important person log" where you maintain a separate page for each person with whom you routinely share work or other responsibilities. When a question comes to your mind that you need to ask that person decide if it is something that can wait for a while. If it can, then put the question down under that person's name in your important person log. When the items listed begin to develop a critical mass, make arrangements to meet with that person or cover the items during an upcoming regularly scheduled meeting.

This is not a tip to practice during the beginning of your career, but one to work toward as the years pass. You can model this type of communication for colleagues by asking, "Can I have a few minutes before lunch to discuss Cases X and Y?"

At the beginning of your career, you will be the one asking the most questions, so think about how to ask them without being a distraction. Certainly, do not let an assignment go unfinished or do it incorrectly because you have a question, but if you have a project with tiny questions that crop up as you go, let them accumulate and quickly go over them with the appropriate person at one time.

IN PRACTICE

What Is Your Status?

At work, you will limit or eliminate your use of Facebook and personal e-mail. As a student, though, clicking over to check Twitter updates may be such a habit that you do not realize exactly how many times you are checking in. Consider evaluating your use of social media to determine if it distracts you from your work:

Day 1: Shut down your e-mail and log out of Facebook after you check each one. You will begin to see how reflexive it has become to click over to these screens while you are working.

Day 2: Try checking your social media—e-mail, Facebook, Twitter, etc.—only three or four times a day (morning, mid-day, toward the end of the day, late-night working session).

Day 3: When you open your e-mail and click on a message, reply to it and then file away the message. The idea is to become adept at handling e-mail during your e-mail sessions. Otherwise, you are using e-mail to look for something more interesting to do than homework.

Day 4: Take stock of the situation. Do you have habits to break? Did you learn some new techniques for managing your social media so that it does not manage you?

■ USE VOICE MAIL AS A TIME MANAGEMENT TOOL

Most law offices have specific guidelines about answering phones. While you want to be sure to comply with those expectations, you can use voice mail to help manage your time.

Using voice mail to manage time does not mean letting all calls roll to voice mail and returning them later. Instead, it means (1) learning how to phrase your outgoing message so that you get vital information from callers and (2) learning how to leave a good message so that you do not get caught up in time-eating phone tag.

If your office insists that all phones be answered within three rings or if you are the one who fields all phone calls, you can still use voice mail to maximize your efficiency.

Use these strategies to use voice mail to manage your time:

Respect vital phone times: If you are working on a case or an event that requires immediate help by phone, be accessible. Sit at your desk. No one should have to look for you. Be responsive. That is your job.

If you leave your desk, ask someone else to sit by your phone during that time or this might happen: The attorney may be at court, mediation, a closing, a meeting, in an airport, on a runway, or some other place that requires quick reactions from those back at the office. When the attorney calls, the attorney may tell you to find three documents as fast as possible and fax them immediately. You run off to find the documents. Six minutes later (and while you are away from your phone), the attorney may discover that another document is just as vital. If no one is at your desk, you may miss the call or miss the opportunity to answer an important question.

It is possible that, in this situation, you may be able to forward calls to another person or perhaps to your cell phone. As always, do whatever works for you but be sure you have the situation covered.

If you are responsive during critical times, no one will panic if they occasionally get your voice mail during the not-so-important times. They will learn to trust that you will respond as soon as possible.

Use the office voice mail system to find time to concentrate. Paralegals, too, need time to concentrate. If possible, when you are working on projects that require quiet time, let your phone roll to voice mail and work on a project for 45 minutes, using the last 15 minutes to return phone calls and respond to e-mail. If you are able to do this once or twice a day—or even all day on occasion—you will find some chunks of time that you can use for projects.

You will need to get permission to let calls roll to voice mail. If you set a limit on how long you need to work quietly, and provide breaks to check your voice mail, your supervisor might be apt to agree to this chunk of time.

Your outgoing message should give your callers lots of information. Some paralegals change their message daily to let callers know if they are in the office that day, when to expect calls to be returned, and what to do if the call is urgent.

Plan your outgoing message carefully so you solicit precise information from the caller when you retrieve their message. In fact, you may not have to return the call at all if

IN PRACTICE

What Does Your Voice Mail Say?

Be certain your outgoing messages are good enough.

Your Office Phone: Carefully consider the message your callers hear. Does it include enough information so that your expectations are clear? Prepare scripts for different situations (you are at a meeting or a seminar or on vacation, etc.) and update your voice mail message as needed.

Your Personal Phone: If you are a student or searching for a job, your voice mail message needs to sound just as professional as if you were in an office. No music, no cute rhymes, no "Yo, Dude, wha's up?" and no, "You know what to do," types of messages.

you manage to get enough information from your caller. If you just say, "Hi! This is Alex. Leave your number and I'll call you back," you have not helped yourself at all. Be clear and concise and give your callers as many details as possible. Let them know when they can expect to hear from you, how to bypass your message or speak with someone else, and if there are alternative ways to reach you. Then ask them for a detailed message.

Voice mail is a two-way street so the message you leave must be effective. Always plan your phone calls and be concise. No one wants to listen to a message that rambles on and on. If you have to, make notes so you do not stammer or forget an important detail. Identify the best time to reach you and then state precisely what you need. If you do a good enough job, you may even avoid exchanging phone calls.

For instance, "This is Miranda Lincoln from Attorney Julie Jenson's office calling. Please fax a copy of Dr. Smith's IME report for John Jones to me at 231-555-5555," should get the results you want without spending any more time on the phone. Remember, too, that you are not in a race to talk as fast as you can. Say your name and telephone number slowly, and then repeat both before you end the call.

Remember that your voice mail message reflects your image. Whether it is the message your callers hear or the message you leave for someone else, this is your opportunity to project a professional image. These messages may be for people you will never meet face-to-face. Act accordingly.

■ DELEGATE RESPONSIBLY

Delegating means making sure the most effective person is doing a job. You do not have to have your own assistant or secretarial support to learn to delegate responsibly.

Delegating means seeking help with tasks when qualified people are available to help. Delegating does not mean telling someone else what to do. Delegating is the careful use of human resources within and outside your employer's company. When you delegate, you are asking someone else to do something for you:

- Ask, do not command.
- Always say "please," and "thank you."
- Do not overburden. (A secretary working for three people may not have time to do even a small job for you right now.)
- Look for hidden talents and not-so-obvious resources.

The easiest way to delegate is to use the resources provided by your employer to finish work efficiently. Ask your assistant (if you are fortunate enough to have one) to manage the tasks he or she is capable of. You should teach your assistant to do tasks that will help you be even more efficient. You might, for example, teach an assistant how to conduct computer searches.

Opportunities to do new things are often a welcome change of pace. Do not overburden anyone, though. Some secretaries work for as many as three people at one time. They generally have very little time to spare, so observe the workload before you add to it.

Even if you have an assistant, you most likely will not be the top priority. Often paralegals share assistants with attorneys, and the attorneys get top priority. In these cases, look around for "secret" resources for delegating tasks. Is a receptionist willing to stuff envelopes? Is the law librarian willing to find an obscure fact or legal precedent? Does a night secretary have so much down time that your work staves off the boredom? It is important to find your secret weapons. They will help you be most productive.

It is also possible that you may delegate tasks to outside vendors when possible and when more efficient. Caution: be sure you have permission from your supervising attorney prior to calling the outside vendor because there will be a charge for their services.

Never hang onto a job just because you think you are the only one who can do it or that you will do it better. When possible, always encourage and allow people to work to their strengths.

PARALEGAL **PROFILE**

Jennifer Karns, M.A.Ed.,

Current position: Legal Professional Training Manager

Employer: Snell & Wilmer L.L.P.

Years in this position: 6

Years of paralegal experience: 19

Education:

Graduate of University of Phoenix (M.A.Ed., with honors), Arizona State University West (B.A.S., Business, with honors), and Phoenix College (A.A.S., Legal Assisting, with honors); Received the Who's Who Among Students in American Junior Colleges for academic achievement while attending Phoenix College and elected to the Golden Key International Honour Society for academic achievement while attending Arizona State University West

Trainer Jennifer Karns, M.A.Ed., recommends paralegals never stop learning.

Jennifer Karns, M.A.Ed. advises legal professionals to never stop learning. She believes legal professionals should take advantage of every opportunity to learn new information, enhance a skill set, or assist in other legal practice areas.

Jennifer demonstrated this in her own life after she began working at Snell & Wilmer as a paralegal in February 2003. In 2006, she was promoted to Legal Professional Training Manager, and drew on her 13 years' experience in litigation to teach other paraprofessionals how to manage cases from inception through trial. She also used her knowledge to write a training manual and designed curriculum to teach other paraprofessionals litigation case management from case inception through trial.

Looking back on nearly two decades of experience, Jennifer recommends that you diversify your knowledge, whether on your own, through your local or national association or networking with paralegals in your community. She believes that to succeed as a paralegal, you need to stay current regarding new technology, changes in rules, and working efficiently. By continuing to learn, you will be more valuable to your firm and increase your self-confidence along the way.

Jennifer believes taking time to maintain and update skills brings added confidence. This will show in every aspect of your professional career, from feeling qualified to work on challenging assignments to having a can-do attitude when you are overwhelmed with deadlines. Attorneys will appreciate the ambition you show for your professional growth and will reward you with new opportunities or view you as the "go to person" when the need arises.

The benefits far outweigh the time you spend growing and learning in your career. Jennifer wants every paralegal to remember: "You can't stay competitive if you don't continue to learn!"

■ PLAY GAMES

If, at the end of the day, the pile of work on your desk is not dwindling, and you know you could work more efficiently, develop some game strategies to get the workflow moving again. Here are some possible strategies:

Do It Now

For one hour, immediately handle whatever you touch. Start with your desktop. If you pick up a letter that needs a response, write it. If you next pick up a file that needs to be returned to a drawer down the hall, return it. For 60 minutes, you are handling things that you have been picking up and putting down for a while instead of taking care of them. This might include listing incrementally the steps that would lead to the completion of the dreaded task.

By using the "do-it-now" principle, you stop procrastinating. When you pick up a task you have been dreading, look at it closely. What about it are you dreading? Make a list. You might find that once you have made a list, the project is actually not so daunting. Or that you really do not understand what you are supposed to do. Get the answers you need and get the project going.

Break Up the Project

When projects are really daunting, the best way to start is to make a list of the first three tiniest things you need to do and do them. Doing something will help you figure out what else you need to ask in order to complete the job.

Set a Timer

This is a great anti-procrastination method. Set a timer and work full blast on a project for 15 minutes. When the timer goes off, you can choose to do something else or to continue working on your project. Most of the time, you will have momentum going and want to reset the timer and keep on working. It is easy to work for hours this way but it does not feel that long because you always know that a break is just 15 minutes away.

You may find that things you thought would take forever to do really take only five or ten minutes. For instance, you may dread or put off entering your billable time when this would probably only take you 15 minutes.

Draw Straws

If your to-do list for the day looks ultra-boring or overwhelming or both, try this tactic: Write each task on a separate slip of paper. Fold the slips and put them into a bowl. Draw out one slip at a time and do the task on it.

You cannot put the paper back and draw again. Fate decides which task you complete first. Make sure that the tasks in the bowl have the same level of importance and that they can be completed in any order. (You cannot make photocopies of a memo you need to write, so writing the memo goes in the first round of tasks.) Once you have finished those tasks, go to the next level of importance and write new tasks.

Write a Terrible Draft

You may delay starting a project because you do not have time to finish the whole thing at one time. This all-or-nothing thinking is not good because you will rarely have large chunks of time to work on a project. Instead, vow to write a really quick, terrible draft. When you come back to the project, you will feel like you are in the middle of it rather than at the beginning.

Unpleasant tasks do not get any easier if you put them off; in fact, they get worse. And the worry over not working on a project takes as much energy as just biting the bullet and getting started. Think about taking a swim in very cold water. Some people prefer to dive in quickly and get the shock over with. Others stretch out the agony by stepping in inch by shivering inch. It is really easiest to plunge in and get the agony over with as soon as possible.

CONCLUSION

Time management for paralegals requires learning multiple strategies so that when your day is not going as you planned, you can shift strategies and still get your work done. By developing your own arsenal of strategies, you will be flexible enough to work with supervising attorneys and law office staff whose communication and organizational skills differ from yours. Having a variety of strategies to choose from will help you keep things moving.

Checklist for Success

☐ Use a calendar.

☐ Use a notebook to record information throughout the day.

☐ Make a plan, but be prepared to shift your priorities as new information or assignments come in.

☐ Doing one thing at a time may be more productive than multitasking.

☐ As a student, stop checking your personal e-mail, Facebook, and other social media every few minutes. Never check these at work.

☐ Use your voice mail as a time management tool.

☐ Treat your cell phone like an office tool, even while you are a student. Turn your personal cell phone off while working.

☐ Learn to delegate tasks to the most efficient resource.

☐ If you are stalled, use some of the strategies in this chapter to get your work started. (Do it now. Break it into chunks.) You do not have the luxury of wasting time.

ASSIGNMENTS: PREPARING FOR YOUR PARALEGAL CAREER

Report

Practice noticing how you spend your day by keeping a record of your time for three days. As a paralegal, you may have to record your time in increments as small as six minutes, so become aware of how you spend your time. After you record your time for three days, create a chart to show where the time went and discuss your findings in class.

Schedule

Julie Morgenstern, a time management and organizational guru, uses two questions to ask clients about their organizational system: What works about the system? What doesn't work about the system? Consider your own organizational system. What works for you right now, either at work or at school? What does not work? What are some strategies to change what does not work? Write a memorandum to your instructor reporting your assessment. What changes will you make?

Report

Why is time management so important to the legal profession? Interview a working paralegal about the importance of time management in the legal profession. Write a memorandum to your instructor that reports your findings. In the memorandum, also discuss concerns about your ability to be efficient on the job.

INTERNET RESOURCES

The Empowered Paralegal, A Blog for and about Professional Paralegals and the Paralegal Profession: *http://theempowered paralegal.com/*

SUGGESTED READINGS

The 7 Habits of Highly Effective People by Stephen R. Covey (Free Press, 2004).

Time Management from the Inside Out: The Foolproof System for Taking Control of Your Schedule and Your Life by Julie Morgenstern (Holt Paperbacks, 2004).

Organize Yourself! by Ronni Eisenberg with Kate Kelly (Wiley, 2005).

Getting Things Done: The Art of Stress-Free Productivity by David Allen (Penguin, 2002).

Time Management Secrets for Working Women by Ruth Klein (Sourcebooks, 2005).

CHAPTER **12**

ORGANIZING YOUR OFFICE

aralegals rarely have a say in how to organize an entire law firm or legal department. Unless you work for a solo practitioner from the day the firm begins, you probably will not get to set up a filing system there, either. When you begin a job, you must adapt to, and use, the systems already in place. You also have to organize your own workspace.

When you land your first paralegal job, you may not have an actual office with walls and a door; many paralegals work in an open office area or other kind of space, but you generally have a desk or table that is your own. You want to be prepared to get organized from the start.

One trait that every legal employer wants paralegals to have is the ability to find things quickly. This chapter provides some advice for getting organized even before you get your first job. You want to understand how to be organized at work before you are overwhelmed with disorder and disarray that will be difficult to sort out.

This entire chapter can be applied to your study space as well. Try to find your organizational strengths and, perhaps, form some new organizational habits by using the ideas in this chapter.

This chapter shows you how to:

- Identify your organizing style
- Use typical approaches to workspace organization
- Understand how your workspace is a reflection on *you*
- Explain how to manage paper coming into your workspace
- Recognize the importance of remaining organized while out of the office

■ WHAT IS YOUR ORGANIZING STYLE?

Study the following traits to determine which list describes you best (Lehmkuhl and Lamping):

Is this you? You...

- Are very aware of time
- Like to keep things where they belong, file things away, are comfortable with systems like color-coding
- Stick to the point when speaking or writing
- Plan what will happen next
- Impose limits on behaviors
- Throw things out when they are not needed
- Get irritated when others leave a mess

Or, is this you? You...

- Often lose track of time
- Like to keep things where you can find them, in piles so that they can be seen or organized by subject
- First write with free-flowing ideas and then revise as needed; may "think out loud"
- Act spontaneously (jump into a project without planning all the details)
- Do not limit behaviors (will work overtime every night despite needing time off for rest, exercise, or to recharge)
- Like to save things
- Are not bothered by another person's mess

Or, are you a combination of both?

The first list describes people who take a logical approach to organization. The second list describes people who take a creative approach to organization. It is entirely possible you have traits from both.

Law offices tend to take a logical approach. If your organizing style falls into the creative realm or somewhere in between, you will have to adapt to the organizational approach most offices use.

A note about law offices of all sizes: Almost everyone wishes they had more space. Sometimes, desks are too close together, file cabinets are overflowing, the copy machine is next to the kitchen sink, and space issues continue. You must adapt to these situations.

When you are an intern, you almost never get your own desk/office/space, so apply these tips to your student study space, modify them during your internship, and be prepared to implement organizational strategies when you begin a paralegal job.

PRACTICE TIP

Do not place important documents on or near the garbage receptacle or you may spend hours with the building management personnel sifting through the dumpster looking for those critical documents. Building management will probably charge for their efforts, and this is a total waste of your time.

■ ENVISION YOUR WORKSPACE

Your workspace is the area that you control—the spot where your desk is, the cabinet where your work goes, and the filing cabinet that only you use. What does your space look like?

- If you are a student, your workspace might be a bookshelf and a backpack that you move from the kitchen table to the library. Where do you study? Where do you keep your school materials organized at home?
- If you are an intern, your workspace might be a bit haphazard. Sometimes, employers take on interns, but do not have good spaces for them to work. If you are an intern without an official desk, where are you assigned to sit and do your work?
- Freelance paralegals might have a workspace in a home office. Is this space a dedicated room? a coffee table? the kitchen counter?

- A paralegal working in a law firm or corporate legal department may have separate office space or be assigned to a cubicle, depending on the size of the employer and space available.
- A paralegal in a small law office or non-profit organization might sit in an open floor plan office where everyone can see each other.

Wherever you work, your workspace should be conducive to doing your work. You will have to take steps independently to be sure your space works for you.

Do you want to change anything about this space? If yes, is it possible to make the change? If the space cannot be reconfigured or the furniture cannot be moved, you need to stop *thinking* about how to rearrange everything and work with what you have using your own organizing style as a guide.

Typical Workspaces

Most workspaces are set up for a logical approach to organization. Individual workspaces usually include a desk, desk drawers, shelving for books, and filing cabinets. Firm-wide organization usually includes filing cabinets and a filing system that is indexed.

These spaces are like kryptonite for people who take a creative approach to work. (Do not despair, the authors of this book have creative working styles and still developed lucrative and gratifying paralegal careers.) If you take a creative approach to work, you must adapt to the logical style of organization.

Your goal in organizing your workspace is to make it function as efficiently as possible. If you use creative strategies, you will have to think harder about how to make the systems work for you.

For example, those who take a logical approach to organization view a drawer as useful for storing letterhead and envelopes; for a creative-style person, drawers are the equivalent of out-of-sight, out-of-mind.

Organizing Your Space

The following techniques, recommended by professional organizer, Julie Morgenstern, work well for everyone, and allow for adapting to suit your strengths:

Organize by activity. Keep supplies for talking on the phone—notepad, penholder, phone list, and other reference materials you use while on the phone near the phone. You can use Figure 12-1 to make a list of the activities you do in your office.

Organize books by subject. Separate reference materials that a colleague may need to borrow from your continuing legal education materials. Remember to purge old professional magazines and journals (especially anything you can retrieve electronically if you need it later).

ACTIVITY	SUPPLIES	STORAGE UNIT

FIGURE 12-1 Use this form to itemize the tasks that you do and the supplies you need to accomplish these tasks. If you have a related storage unit, make a note of it as well.

PRACTICE TIP

Binder Clip Tip   You can easily identify the contents held by a binder clip if you label the binder clip by writing on it with a silver-ink Sharpie pen.

If you have a filing cabinet, store files A-Z or store files by client matter. Always use a file index so that you do not feel like things are "gone." Tape a small index card to the front of the drawer to identify the contents or place an index to the file cabinet on top of it. Make the file cabinet work for you.

Assign uses for drawers. Assign specific items to each drawer. If drawers cause you to think out-of-sight, out-of-mind, use your drawers for temporary or daily storage: Put your empty briefcase, lunch bag, and umbrella in one drawer. Until you are accustomed to using your drawers, keep a "map" on your desk of what is in each drawer. Your goal is to become comfortable taking things out and returning them.

Use top-of-the-desk organizers and containers. An incline file sorter works well for keeping things organized and handy. For larger projects, use labeled expanding Redrope files.

Use labeled stackable letter trays to organize desktop papers. Rather than stacking books in a pile, keep the books standing, spines aligned, on a bookshelf. If you do find yourself accumulating piles of papers, label each pile clearly with a sticky note or control them with a large binder clip.

Designate a permanent place for work in progress. In the legal profession, you may move from matter to matter quickly, and, at times, have piles of documents that have no specific "home" yet. Provide a temporary place for work in progress on your desk or on a shelf (think of the shelf as a permanent holding spot for work in progress). Stack the files or papers neatly and place a sticky note on top that includes the client matter and a reminder of what you are doing with the pile and where you stopped. Having a permanent, planned space for these files keeps things organized.

Use your floor space wisely. If you can avoid it, do not use floor or chair space to pile files or boxes. If you need to use your floor space, know what you are putting there. Piles on the floor and the chair become part of the landscape of your office and may soon be forgotten. They also work toward labeling you as "disorganized" and "overwhelmed." Still, many legal professionals use floor space for work in progress. Be strategic and purge this space often.

Most attorneys and paralegals are naturally good organizers, regardless of organizational strategy. Unfortunately, all legal professionals are susceptible to having an overwhelmingly messy and cluttered office because work moves quickly. You can avoid creating a cluttered space by recognizing your own approach to organizing. By understanding your strengths, your system for maintaining organization will become stronger and your office will look impeccable.

Your Workspace Reflects You

While your home workspace can reflect your eclectic tastes, your office workspace should reflect your professional efficiency. You absolutely cannot maintain an office that looks so cluttered and unkempt that colleagues worry you (a) will lose something important;

IN PRACTICE

Save Your Desk

If you are already working in layers or have the messiest desk in the office, you need to kick out the clutter as soon as possible. You will be amazed at how differently people treat you once your workspace is clutter-free.

Lehmkuhl and Lamping recommend cleaning off your desk using the "Five Minutes Before the Hour" approach:

If you have a desk or other surface that is cluttered, set aside five minutes before each hour to clear off

one small part of it. At the end of your five-minute session, set a timer for fifty-five minutes so you'll remember the next five-minute period. (66)

This approach is perfect for legal professionals because your workspace will improve without your devoting a huge chunk of unbillable time to organizing it.

(b) might confuse matters and accidentally release confidential information; and/or (c) are not capable of handling a more complicated task because you are not on top of your current work. Truly, a cluttered workspace sends a message that you are overwhelmed—whether you are or not.

Three rules of organization apply to everyone:

1. **Eliminate clutter.** Clutter is anything that you do not need taking up space that you do need. That space is valuable real estate in your office. An organized, uncluttered workspace will allow you to think more clearly and to be more productive. Keep the use of sticky notes to a minimum so they do not end up wallpapering your office. Instead, write your notes in a spiral notebook that you take from meeting to meeting. Always clear your workspace before you leave at night.

2. **Stop the chaos.** Think twice before you accept another free thing from vendors or pick up another giveaway at conferences. Your office is not a holding area for things you "might" need in the future. Just because a colleague is getting rid of 10 binders does not mean your office needs to store them. How many pens do you really need?

3. **Have a place for everything.** Do not waste time looking for things; instead, make sure everything has a place and that you return things to their place when you are finished. This does not mean everything needs to be color coded or returned to its specific file. The assigned place might be a letter file or stacking bin that you can see. Not establishing a "home" for things when you bring them into your office creates opportunities for things to be misplaced. The time you spend searching for lost documents or files is non-billable, and in the practice of law, non-billable time costs money.

■ MANAGE YOUR WORKSPACE BY MANAGING THE INCOMING PAPER

In the legal profession, paper is **not** harmless. The piles grow, spill over the desk, and eventually you feel overwhelmed and your employer worries that things are out of control.

We cannot stress enough how quickly your workspace can become cluttered with paper when you work in the legal profession. You need to handle the paper as it comes into your office. This requires continual decision-making, as well as some simple supplies.

The supplies you probably need include:

- Your trash can and recycle bin
- Interoffice envelopes
- Pen
- Sticky notes

The decisions you need to make are rather simple. As you look at an incoming document, you should consider the following:

Decision No. 1: What Do You Do with the Item?

When your mail comes in, go over it by your trash can and recycle bin and take one of the following actions:

Toss it. If you do not need it, throw it in the trash. This step may include shredding or recycling. The more you throw away, the less you have to take care of. You win!

Delegate it. If someone else can do it, pass it on. Take time to write a note and place the document in an interoffice envelope, using your handy sticky notes and pen.

Do it now. If the request is something you can do in two minutes or less, do it NOW. For example, if you need to sign a form and return it by mail, do that right away.

Do it later. If you need to handle the item later, write a note on your to-do list and move on to Decision No. 2.

Keep it forever. If you need this item in the future, move on to Decision No. 3.

Decision No. 2: When Do You Need to See It Again?

When you will need to refer to the paper again (as in the case of an invitation or a map) or you need to remember to take action on a specific date, you need to "file" it for later. One way to keep up with time-sensitive paper and projects is to create a tickler file.

Some law offices use shared software to track dates to remember. Shared tickler files are useful because everyone can see at a glance what needs to be done.

You can also create a paper tickler file (or a paper version to accompany the electronic version):

To create a tickler file, this is what you do:

1. Gather supplies:
   - A drawer or a box that will accommodate hanging files
   - 43 hanging file folders
   - 43 hanging file folder tabs, 31 of one color and 12 of another color
   - Your favorite pen or Sharpie
2. Label the files:
   - Write the 12 months on 12 tabs of one color; insert them down the left side of 12 hanging folders.
   - Write the numbers 1–31 on the 31 tabs of the other color; insert them in the remaining 31 hanging folders, staggering them in positions other than the left so you will be able to see them at a glance.
3. Put the folders in your drawer or box:
   - Whatever month you are beginning with, put that month's tab in the front of the drawer with the numbered folders for the rest of the month. (Example: if you are setting up your file on March 5th, you will begin with the folder for the month of March and in that folder you will put numbers 5–31.)
   - Behind this folder, place the remaining monthly folders (April through February of the next year).
4. File your papers:
   - Place papers in the files according to when you will need them, allowing time to finish the project. (Example: if your deadline is March 30th and you think the job will take two days, put the paper in the March 28th folder.) If you only need to remember to do something in June, drop it in the June file.
5. Review your papers:
   - Begin every day by reviewing the folder for that day and take the appropriate action on the papers in the folder. When you are through with a day, move it to the back of the next month.
   - Near the end of each month, go through the papers that have been dropped in the next month's folder and put them in the folder with the appropriate date. Again, be sure to allow for time to finish each project.

Sometimes, paralegals choose to use a system like a tickler file because the employer requests that you do. Or you might know that organization is a weakness of yours, and by adapting a strategy like a tickler file, fewer things will go wrong.

Decision No. 3: Do You Need to Keep It Forever?

When you receive something that needs to be kept for future use, follow these tips:

- Ask yourself if you really need to keep it forever. Organizing experts say that you refer to only 20 percent of what you file. The remaining 80 percent is unnecessary and never looked at again. Do not fill your filing cabinets with that 80 percent. Especially watch for multiple copies of the same document. These just take up valuable space in your filing cabinet.

PARALEGAL **PROFILE**

Kelly A. LaGrave, ACP

Current position: Paralegal

Employer: Foster, Swift, Collins & Smith, P.C.

Years in this position: Approximately 19 years

Certifications: CP, ACP (Intellectual Property, Real Estate, and Contracts Administration/Contracts Management) – National Association of Legal Assistants/Paralegals

Years of paralegal experience: 27

Education: B.A., Michigan State University

Kelly LaGrave, ACP, shares her top strategies for keeping her desk organized.

Over the course of her career, Kelly A. LaGrave, ACP has developed strategies for keeping herself organized and her desk clear. These strategies help her maintain a successful career and achieve professional goals, like serving on the Board of Directors for NALA—The Association of Legal Assistants/Paralegals, as Kelly currently does.

Kelly's tips:

Have a Place for Everything

Keep items in their proper place—when you finish with an item, put it back where it goes. That way, you don't waste time looking for things and your desk doesn't become cluttered.

Limit Files in Office

Only keep those files you are working on in your office space. You do not need to keep a file in your office or at your desk area just because you are waiting for something to come back from a client or a third party.

Instead, calendar what you are waiting for and put the file back in the file room or cabinet where it belongs. Calendaring deadlines and things you may be waiting on to complete a project is crucial. Remember to check your calendar daily.

Work on One Item at a Time

Try to only work on one item at a time on your desk. Have a place to put the files you need to do your work so that everything you have to work on is sitting on your desk. (Clutter, I think, makes it hard to work. It causes me to become discouraged and I find it hard to focus.) I use a bookcase. The top row holds files in alphabetical order that I need to work on. In the front of a file I will have a note as to when I received the project, from whom, and a brief description of what I need to do. I find sticky notes work really well for this. If someone brings me a file, I take a moment and write everything down, put the file in the bookcase and then return to what I am doing. The second row holds pending files. I have to keep these files because I'm waiting for a return phone call or something to come back quickly.

Do Not Leave a Messy Desk

At the end of the day, clean off your desk and put everything away. You can see my desk in Figure 12-2. I do a quick note of things I need to work on first thing in the morning so I know where I have to start when I come in. I think it is depressing to arrive in the morning and find your desk a mess. I find it hard to get motivated as to where to start.

Watch Out for Your E-mail Inbox

Do not leave e-mail messages in your "inbox." I only leave those messages in my inbox that I still need to work on. Delete those you do not need (the junk stuff). Print the important items and put them in the proper files. If you have some kind of document management system at work, put the e-mail messages in the client folders. I also keep several favorite folders in Microsoft Outlook that I use to hold pending items for larger projects.

- Do not overstuff the file drawers. Keep at least two inches of empty space in each file drawer so that you can get files in and out.
- Use an incline desktop sorter. If you have stacks of files on your desk that cannot be put away because you are working on them, put them in an incline desktop sorter. (Logical- and creative-style workers love these.) The files remain visible and organized.

FIGURE 12-2 Kelly LaGrave, APC, prefers to keep her desktop clear and to take out one file at a time. She helps herself stay organized by clearing her desk each afternoon.

Of course, not every file fits into a desktop sorter. Many are too large. The truth is that many attorneys and paralegals meet clients in conference rooms because their actual workspace has files on the floor and on desktops. Keep things organized by placing files together and in Redrope folders that are labeled. Move out files you do not need or will not need for a while and keep only the work-in-progress close at hand.

Trust us when we say that maintaining a good filing system will result in your looking like a superhero. Filing accurately and regularly is crucial in the legal profession.

A filing system is really a *finding* system. This is your method for storing information and finding it quickly and easily tomorrow. There may be a filing system in place when you begin your job. If so, learn it as quickly as possible.

Searching for a misplaced document or file is not only a waste of time and energy, it is also a waste of money. Assuming you work 48 weeks in a year and spend just five minutes of each hour of an eight-hour workday looking for lost documents or files, you will waste 160 hours per year. Using a billing rate of $95 per hour (insert yours here), the annual loss is $15,200. Usually this search involves several people and it delays getting your work done, so the cost increases proportionately. You also lose credibility and appear unprepared when you do not have information at your fingertips.

■ USE THE OFFICE FILING SYSTEM

In addition to your personal workspace, the office itself has an organizational structure that you may or may not influence. You may be the person in charge of filing; you may be the person who orders office supplies; you may be the person who decides where things go. If you are this person, you can work with your attorney or attorneys and other support staff colleagues to create a space that everyone can use easily.

You cannot create an organizational structure that works just for you. This would be irresponsible and the result may be that you spend your days finding things for other people. In fact, an employee truly committed to the success of the firm will design a system that is easily understandable and usable by all.

If you are the person who files and maintains office organization, create a strategy for yourself to keep up with the filing and create a system that everyone can understand and use easily.

■ STAYING ORGANIZED WHILE ON VACATION

It is one thing when you walk out of your office at the end of the day, knowing that the unfinished work will be waiting for you in the morning and you are going to be available to finish a project in time to meet the scheduled deadline. It is entirely different when you are taking a vacation or going to a conference and you will be out of your office for an extended period of time. You must take time to be sure that deadlines are met while you are gone and that work continues to be finished without you. If you plan properly, you should be able to be away from the office without receiving any panicked phone calls.

Write a Memo

In the week prior to your departure, begin preparation of a memo regarding current projects you are working on and the status of each case for each person who will be covering for you during your absence.

Write your memo using a "worst case" mindset. If a client needs extra attention, provide backup information to tell the client so the client will feel assured that his or her case is receiving ongoing attention.

This memo should include case deadlines and any work that must be done to meet the deadline. Is there a brief due? Is there a hearing? What has to be done to be prepared for those deadlines? Be sure you prepare as much of the work ahead of time as possible and then leave clear instructions for any remaining work that must be done.

Your Contact Information

You should provide your contact information and your itinerary in case of an *office emergency*. This information should be given to someone who is reliable, who will not lose the information, and who will not treat the number as if it is a 24-Hour Question Hotline. The point of taking a vacation is to have a real break from your office so be sure the designated person understands these boundaries.

Meet with Colleagues

Set up a time to meet with attorneys and other colleagues with whom you are working. This meeting should occur a few days to a week before you leave. Make sure each knows the status of your work. While you will include this information in your "while I'm away" memo, you need to go over it verbally to be sure everyone is on the same page.

At this meeting someone should be designated to cover any emergency situations for you. This person will probably be your main contact person should you need to be reached while you are away.

Ask if you can do anything to make your absence easier: find a file, put a set of documents in a certain location, draft any documents, etc.

Ask if the attorneys want to meet again before you leave. If you work in a solo or small law firm, you will definitely want to meet again.

Make Important Information Available During Your Absence

A really good idea is to have an incline file holder in your office in plain sight so everyone has access to it. Place multicolored file folders with the name of each case you are handling in large lettering (use a Sharpie). Inside the folder, place everything your supervising attorney would need to know about the matter, just in case you decide you never want to leave the beach in Jamaica or some other catastrophe prohibits your return to the office.

This will be very helpful for both you and the attorney. The type of case would determine the information that you keep in these folders. Some suggestions are lists of contact information for opposing counsel and court personnel, schedules, special rules, filing fees, and whatever you think the attorney might need in your absence. You will find yourself using these folders, too, because the information you use the most is always right at hand.

Send Reminders

As soon as you know you will be out of the office, send an e-mail or a memo to everyone who might be affected by your absence. Be sure the dates are noted on all appropriate calendars.

Because you may make plans months in advance of your departure, send out a reminder memo one week before you are scheduled to leave, and then another two days before your departure. In this memo, ask if anyone wants to meet with you before you leave.

Your goal is to get your colleagues to prepare for your absence by getting up-to-speed on matters that will need attention while you are away and also to avoid being "surprised" with an avalanche of work just hours before you are taking off.

Getting the attention of a busy attorney may take more than one e-mail. Pay particular attention to early planning and communication with colleagues who will be providing support while you are gone.

Pack Early

The advantage of packing in advance for your trip is that you will be free to handle any last minute emergencies at the office, perhaps staying a little later at work the night before you leave to be sure your office and your work are in order.

If possible, leave for your vacation or conference from your home instead of your office. As one paralegal says, "If I try to leave for the airport from the office, I always seem to be rushing around trying to take care of last-minute things. It's much less stressful to leave from home on my schedule."

This paralegal also recommends packing early in case any professional obligations take longer than expected. "This way, I do not forget anything I want to take on vacation."

Remember Plants and Food

Give your plants one last drink before you leave so they will be healthy when you return. Then go through your desk to dispose any perishable food you have on hand. A rotten banana left in your desk drawer is not going to be pleasant when you get back.

Clear the Clutter

Approximately one week before your scheduled departure, take 15 or 20 minutes to go through the professional magazines, newsletters, and journals that may have accumulated on your desk. Recycle or throw away any you do not think you will read. There may be a couple you will want to read on the airplane, so put those in your briefcase.

Be sure your filing is up-to-date and that you have responded to any outstanding requests from attorneys or clients. Label any remaining stacks of papers or files that others may be searching for while you are gone. A simple sticky note that says "Jones Document Production" on a stack of documents may prevent some frustration in your absence.

Program Your E-mail and Your Voice Mail

Most e-mail systems allow you to program an automatic response to any e-mail you receive during your absence. This message should be very simple: "Thank you for your e-mail. I am out of the office until. . . . I will respond to your request as soon as I return. Should you need immediate assistance, please contact. . . ."

Change your voice mail message to indicate you are out of the office, when you will be returning telephone calls, and alternative contact person in the event of an emergency. If you are going to have limited access to telephone messages, be sure to say so. If you tell the caller that you will be returning calls while you are away, be sure to do that. Then be sure to check your messages as scheduled.

Craft your voice mail message in such a way that it elicits as much information as possible from the caller. Is their issue urgent or can it wait until you return? What exactly do they need? How and when can they be reached? If you get enough information, you may be able to delegate the return call to your backup person or know that you can take care of the matter upon your return to the office.

Stock Your Office

Once you have cleared the clutter, re-stock your office with stationery, pens, legal pads, and any other supplies that are getting low. If you do this chore before you leave, you will not interrupt your first day back searching for letterhead or a new roll of tape.

Policies for Handling the Paper While You Are Gone

Designate a bin or Redrope file for your mail so that it is not spread all over your desk when you return. If someone is going through your mail, you might ask that they create two files: one for "junk" mail and periodicals and one for regular mail.

Your First Day Back

Along with the hectic get-things-done pace you keep before your vacation, the day you return to the office is fairly hectic, too. With careful planning before you leave, you can avert a paper avalanche waiting for you when you get back. If you can, and if you are fortunate enough to have someone fill in for you while you are away, try to spend some time explaining the filing system and plan some simple organizational strategies to help you when you return. While the stacks of paper and files may be waiting for you, at least they will be sorted so you can handle the most important first.

CONCLUSION

Your challenge is to determine your organizing style and then create strategies that will work for you. The time you take to be organized will pay off in countless ways: reduced stress and overwhelm, reduced wasted time looking for lost items, increased ability to better focus on your work and increased self-esteem. Kicking the clutter habit should be at the top of your list. You will also need to learn how to work with the different organizing styles of your co-workers. Even taking a vacation requires organization so that your time away is relaxing for you while things run smoothly back at the office—and you will be able to "hit the ground running" when you return.

Checklist for Success

☐ Use an organizational strategy that fits your working style to manage your workspace.

☐ Create strategies that work with the office's organizational structure so that you function well within it, especially if your job includes maintaining the structure.

☐ Learn to be flexible with organization so that you can adapt to the preferences of others (especially your employer) when you need to.

☐ Decide how you will use your workspace furnishings—desk, drawers, filing cabinets, bookshelves, etc.

☐ Stock your workspace with the supplies you need.

☐ Maintain your workspace so that it reflects your professional image.

☐ Handle paper as it comes into your office.

☐ Create a tickler file.

☐ Become excellent at finding things.

☐ Prepare carefully when you are going to be out of the office.

ASSIGNMENTS: PREPARING FOR YOUR PARALEGAL CAREER

Career Management

Michael Melcher, "The Creative Lawyer," blogs about creating a fulfilling life. Review posts on his blog, or, if your instructor approves, a similar type of blog. Create a PowerPoint presentation about how paralegals might achieve work-life balance and stay organized on the job.

Report

Interview a working paralegal about the importance of organizational skills. Ask what the paralegal's favorite strategies are. Write a memorandum to your instructor that reports your findings. In the memorandum, discuss concerns about your ability to stay organized at work.

Report

Write a memorandum to your instructor identifying your pet peeves when working with others who organize differently than you do. How do you handle these pet peeves? What would others say their pet peeves are about your organizational abilities?

INTERNET RESOURCE

The Creative Lawyer: Michael Melcher blogs about creating a fulfilling life and career. *http://thecreativelawyer.typepad.com*

SUGGESTED READINGS

Organizing from the Inside Out, by Julie Morgenstern (Holt Paperbacks, 2nd ed., 2004).

Organizing for Your Brain Type: Finding Your Own Solution to Managing Time, Paper, and Stuff, by Lanna Nakone, M.A. (St. Martin's Griffin, 2005).

REFERENCES

Lehmkuhl, D. and Lamping, D.C. (1993). *Organizing for the Creative Person*. New York: Crown.

Morgenstern, J. (2004). *Organizing from the Inside Out*. (2nd ed.). New York: Holt Paperbacks.

CHAPTER **13**

PARALEGALS AND PERFECTIONISM

Attend a meeting of leaders in the paralegal profession and you will find a room full of educators, managers, employee supervisors and other extraordinary people—all confident, skilled, and valued paralegals.

Some of these professionals will eventually branch out into fields such as risk management, insurance investigation, government work, banking, contracts management, and other fields because of the skills they develop as paralegals.

Paralegals who become leaders in the profession begin their careers with an entrepreneurial mindset: they seize opportunities; accept new challenges; learn new skills at every opportunity; travel when needed. They enjoy the perks: extra income from working overtime; large year-end bonuses; and, invitations to work on the most interesting cases. And, possibly years later, if these paralegals do not learn to manage their lives well, they may teeter on the brink of burnout.

One of the reasons that these paralegals have opportunities to develop stellar careers is that they say "yes," as often as they can at the beginning of their careers.

By the end of this chapter, you should be able to:

- Understand the importance of saying "yes" to your career and to yourself
- Be able to say "yes" without becoming overwhelmed and overburdened
- Identify good reasons for saying "no"
- Describe how avoiding perfectionism can help you excel at your job
- Explain why working too much overtime may be a problem
- Manage your work when other people are disorganized

IN PRACTICE

Say "Yes" to Yourself. This "Yes" is the Most Important One.

During your career, you will be presented with opportunities and challenges that may seem scary or impossible because you will have to step outside your comfort zone.

Instead of accepting the challenge and embracing the journey, sometimes people hang on to the past and offer up excuses why they cannot take the challenge: not enough time, not enough ability, not interested (even if they are!).

To move forward, to evolve, to become all that you can be, you have to say YES to challenges.

You have the ability to reach the next level and you will rise to the occasion. But only if you say "yes" to *yourself*.

Of course, it is important to say "yes" as often as you can when you start your career so that you accumulate as much experience and as many skills as possible. In this quest, though, many paralegals tend to strive for perfection, to overachieve, and get too close to burning out before learning to balance their jobs, careers, and personal lives. These paralegals get in a habit of saying, "yes" so often that they forget that it is okay, at times, to say "no."

At work, saying "yes" is key to receiving a paycheck, so you want to say "yes" as often as possible. Looking at your career, though, you have more options to say "no." If you are a member of a professional organization and someone asks you to work at the registration desk for the next continuing legal education event, you can say "no," especially if you need that time to complete the work you are being paid to do. The same goes for your personal life and goals. You may find that you have to say "no" to some personal events to make room to develop your career. Or, you may have to put off career advancement (taking a certification exam, for example) to make space for personal life events.

■ HOW TO SAY YES

If you say "yes" to everything that comes along, you will find yourself overwhelmed and overburdened. There are ways to say "yes" that will keep that from occurring. When your desk is full of to-dos and someone asks you to do one more task, try the following strategy for saying yes.

Consider this situation: It is the end of the month and you have huge deadlines looming. One of the partners in the firm shows up at your door with a project that has to be done right away. This is a situation that needs a "yes" response, but you have other projects that will suffer. In this situation, try saying "yes" using one of these responses:

- Yes . . . **IF** you give me access to a secretary.
- Yes . . . **BUT** I cannot work on that until this afternoon.
- Yes . . . **AND** someone else will have to take care of this other project I am working on.
- Yes . . . **WHEN** you give me all the information I need to do the job.
- Yes . . . **WILL YOU** be able to help with some part of this?
- Yes . . . **AS LONG AS** you get the approval of Attorney X whose project I am currently working on. (This approach is particularly helpful in resolving the multiple boss dilemma.)

Try this technique in all sorts of situations. "Yes, I can work at the registration desk at the seminar IF a slot is available for me on Friday from 9 to 11 A.M." or "Yes, I will stay late to wait for the hand delivery so you can go to the gym, BUT only if you can drop off the packages at Federal Express."

The key is to be cooperative and, at the same, come up with a situation that will work for you. This is much easier than saying "no" and following that with an excuse. No one wants to hear you are too busy or you do not have time. They will be much more willing to work with you if you give them options.

■ GOOD REASONS TO SAY NO

As a paralegal, there is quite a lot of workplace pressure to say "yes," so it is important to learn when it is okay to say "no."

The first thing you must do is separate the negotiable items from the non-negotiable items. You cannot go to work and tell your supervising attorney "no" to the first request of the day, but you could say "no" to the colleague begging you to stay late to wait for a hand delivery so she can go to the gym.

Saying "no" is not always easy, particularly at the beginning of your career when you do not get a lot of opportunity to say "no." The beginning of your career is the time when you are learning, gaining experience, building your reputation. Still, paralegals are notorious for taking on too many projects, so we want to provide some tips on how to say "no."

Often a request catches you off guard or you just hate to turn someone down because you like and respect them. Other times you may be confronted by people you just cannot refuse, such as a boss or a co-worker.

What "No" Means

Saying "no" does not mean you are uncooperative or unwilling. Saying "no" to one thing allows you to say "yes" to something else. *Still, saying "no" is perhaps one of the most difficult things you will have to do.*

Consider "no" a positive response because **saying "no" helps you set boundaries**. You should say "yes" when the request is central to your work and your goals, and *consider* saying "no" when the request is outside your expertise. If you feel resentment when you say "yes," it usually means you should have said "no." Learn to listen to your heart because nothing good comes from this resentment.

It goes without saying that you should not be selfish and never help anyone. But feeling stressed and overwhelmed happens when you say "yes" to everyone but yourself.

Saying "no" says that you value your time. You must realize that when you say "no" to one thing, you are then allowed to say "yes" to something else. When this happens, you usually say "yes" to the more important projects or tasks on your desk. When you need to say "no," consider these factors:

- You do not have to have another appointment first to say "no." You may be saving space for an important project you know is coming.
- You should not instinctively say "yes"; instead, buy time to think about it first. Always take the time to check your planner or calendar before taking on a time-consuming project. Your supervising attorney or the person making the request may have forgotten that you have other events or projects lined up.
- The more you practice saying "no," the easier it becomes. At first when you have to say "no" to something or someone, you may feel guilty. However, it is incredibly empowering when saying "no" is the correct decision.
- You do not have to offer an explanation. When you need to say "no" to an activity that is not directly related to your work—a professional organization or other event—try to say no without apologizing. "No" is a complete sentence, and outside of work, you are not obligated to add anything to that.

Try these nice ways of saying "no" next time you need to bow out of an invitation:

- I cannot help you this time.
- I can only help you next month.
- That is not really something I do well. Is there something else I can do to help?
- I cannot do that but I can . . . and then offer to do something that works for you.
- Simply say, "No thanks."

Again, remember, every time you say "yes" to something, you are eliminating time you would use to work on something else, something that might be more important.

PRACTICE TIP

Use a Timer   So you like the timer idea but you are mortified to think of your office desk ringing every few minutes, signaling to your co-workers that you need some support to stay on task?

Try the virtual timer available through Google Sidebar. You can download the sidebar at *www.desktop.google.com.*

You can set the timer to beep when time is up or it will pop up on your screen without any sound, giving you a quiet—secret—weapon for getting through your day.

PARALEGAL **PROFILE**

Heather G. De La Torre, TBLS, CP, PHP

Current position: Paralegal

Employer: McFall Breitbeil and Smith

Years in this position: 2 months

Years of paralegal experience: 5

Certifications: Board Certified – Civil Trial Law by Texas Board of Legal Specialization; Certified Paralegal – National Association of Legal Assistants/Paralegals; Professional Houston Paralegal – Houston Metropolitan Paralegal Association

Education: A.A.S., Center for Advanced Legal Studies

Three years after offering to volunteer for a paralegal association, Heather De La Torre, TBLS, CP, PHP, is elected its president.

Heather G. De La Torre, TBLS, CP, PHP, felt lost when she first attended CLE sessions and Houston Metropolitan Paralegal Association events because she did not know anyone, so she decided to get involved. Heather e-mailed the HPMA president and offered to volunteer. She began working on a committee and serving as the organization's historian. Next she ran for parliamentarian and worked on the Career Symposium and CLE Committees.

At the end of the year, the president-elect made a career change, which left the presidency open. The current president called Heather to ask if she would be interested in becoming the next president. She agreed and became HMPA's president in April 2011, less than five years into her career as a paralegal.

For Heather, serving as the organization's president was out of her comfort zone, but after flying to Amarillo to talk to the Texas Alliance of Paralegal Associations, she felt that she could do anything.

Heather said, "In the past three years, I have gotten so much more out of HMPA than I have actually put in. I have made really good friends, I have gained immeasurable confidence, and I have pushed myself to go farther than I ever thought I could."

Heather pushes herself at work, too: "My present job has growth potential and I find that I am continually pushed out of my comfort zone as I learn and try new things."

■ EXCEL BY AVOIDING PERFECTIONISM (SOMETIMES)

When paralegals say "yes" to a request, they commit to doing a good job and have to fight off the desire to do every job perfectly. Clients want a legal team that is as near perfect as possible, and lawyers and paralegals try to deliver that quality. For these reasons, paralegals and attorneys tend to be perfectionists.

The truth is that for some tasks or certain phases of a project, perfectionism is a nasty time waster and can paralyze you. For example, you may be reluctant to start a project because you desperately want to do a perfect job. The time to be perfect is as the project nears completion, but trying to prepare a perfect first draft is a waste of time. Perfection emerges through editing, rewriting, and double-checking of facts and citations.

Or (and this is one of our favorites), a case has ended and files need to go to off-site storage, but you cannot send them until they are indexed and labeled. Some paralegals strive to do this task perfectly—indexing all the documents, preparing typed labels for each file folder, and double-checking that every document is in its correct file. Perfection for this job is a waste of time. The reality is that files often are kept in off-site storage for a certain number of years and then shredded. If a document from this case is needed from off-site storage, file labels that are descriptive enough will lead the paralegal looking for the document to it. Do a good-enough job and move on.

IN PRACTICE

Never Work Late on Fridays

Sometimes, work takes over and you may find yourself *wanting* to spend as much time as you can at the office. You might be making extra money or learning how to manage a document production or have other reasons for working more than 40 hours a week. As long as you are making the choice, you are in control of your schedule and time management plan.

Just remember that working too intensely without time for recovery leads to burnout.

One way to make sure that you take time for yourself is to set your own rules about working overtime or intensively on a project. You might need only one rule. Some examples are the following:

- Never work late on Friday. Go to work on Saturday or Sunday or both, but savor Friday nights.
- Hire a helper if you work more than X number of hours of overtime per week. A helper can do everything from picking up a wedding gift to cleaning your kitchen.
- Promise yourself healthy food by preparing a lunch and snacks to take with you to keep your energy up.

Letting go of perfectionism does not mean lowering your expectations. Letting go of perfectionism allows you to be more productive. You may find that when you stop trying to be perfect, you are able to write a draft more quickly and have more time to spend getting feedback, revising, and polishing.

Consider your projects and decide which need to be near-perfect and which can be good enough. The use of good judgment in this regard is particularly important in relation to client billing practices because it is a waste of client resources and arguably an ethical violation to bill excessively for the perfect completion of a task when perfection is unnecessary.

■ OVERTIME: DO NOT FALL INTO THE LATE-NIGHT TRAP

One of the annoying things that happens to students, to lawyers, and to paralegals is that we need to concentrate on a task but we cannot make ourselves sit in the chair long enough to get it done, so we work late. We wait until everyone else has gone home and then we write.

You will have occasions when you need to work overtime. Deadlines, rush jobs, special projects, and trials often require working beyond 5:00 P.M. These special circumstances are not a problem. They happen, they pass, and life returns to normal. When these "special circumstances" become habitual, when you are working overtime whether it is needed or not, or when your whole life revolves around being at the office or texting on your BlackBerry, you may need to examine whether you *need* to be connected to work that many hours.

The answer may be YES, because you have an intense project/case/job. Some paralegals at large firms take jobs as document analysts *anticipating* and *hoping for* lots of overtime.

Sometimes, though, working overtime can become a terrible habit and can be destructive to other aspects of your life. If you find yourself working a lot of overtime, examine your answers to these questions:

Is your ego tied to working overtime? Sometimes we feel better about ourselves if we are giving 150 percent to the team, whether anyone else notices or not. Check your ego at the door and do what is best for you.

Is working overtime causing you to procrastinate? You may find that you are not productive during regular working hours because you have the option of finishing the work later, after everyone is gone, when you can concentrate. Your inclination to put off work because the whole day and evening stretch before you leads to procrastination.

Is working too many hours causing you to make mistakes? You simply cannot be your best 24/7. If you are consistently working overtime, the quality of your work may suffer. In addition, if you are working late on your own time, you may feel you are being taken advantage of and, therefore, justified in turning in a second rate performance.

Without a definitive end to your day, you may allow too many interruptions. You will always find something to do to fill the time you have, whether it is churning out the work or drifting around the office to chat. When your workday has no definitive end time, you may also be more apt to tolerate unnecessary telephone calls and e-mail or distractions by your co-workers. These distractions waste your time and keep you from getting your work done. The result is that you work late and your personal life suffers.

Are you letting other people's procrastination rule your overtime? Some people simply cannot do their work unless they are up against a deadline. If your supervising attorney has this tendency, you are going to find yourself working late often. If at all possible, do what you can to head off a potential late-night crisis by completing some parts of the project ahead of time. Also, if you do not tolerate constantly being asked to work overtime, you may find that the last minute behavior changes.

■ OTHERS' DISORGANIZATION AND YOUR JOB

The good news is that in the legal profession, your colleagues' organizational habits are their own problem and rarely does their disorganization affect their final work product. If it did, they would lose their jobs.

Unfortunately, their disorganization can rule how you spend your day: finding things, working on projects that were "forgotten" until the last minute, rushing to make sure deadlines are met and clients are happy, etc. When paralegals try too hard to be perfectionists (and, yes, overachievers), they find the chaos created by disorganized colleagues to be . . . well . . . annoying.

Sometimes, a colleague's disorganization can lead to office bickering and discontent among the staff because in the process of getting to the good final product, the disorganized colleague may:

- Expect you or others to drop everything and help (Are you envisioning that little sign that reads, "DISORGANIZATION ON YOUR PART DOES NOT CREATE A CRISIS ON MY PART?" Well, in law, it does. You are forewarned.)
- Ask you for copies of documents you have already provided. Twice. (Tough love does not work. You will provide new copies. It is your job.)
- Need you to make a miracle happen: a late-night court filing, a late overnight delivery that requires driving to an airport. (You are not a magician, but you had better have a few tricks up your sleeve.)
- Want to work in this mode so often that if it is not due today, it is not important in their eyes. (You can adapt or find a new job, which is tough in this current market. Sometimes finding a new job is the only way to survive professionally, but the more realistic solution is to try to adapt.)

Pretend for a moment that you decide to adapt to your disorganized colleague because you like your work. You also need to thrive in this environment, and if you want to become a leader in the field, you need to learn to manage work, despite your disorganized colleague. After you have established your own reputation, you may be able to help your colleague. In this case, you would diagnose the problem, plan a solution, and enlist some allies.

Diagnose the Problem

You may not feel comfortable talking with your disorganized colleague about the problem, especially if the colleague is a supervising attorney. Instead, look at the problem as best you can privately. What, from your perspective, is causing your colleague's disorganization?

Some common causes include:

- **Not enough time in the office:** Too many meetings/too much travel/too many days in court
- **Poor inbox management:** Too many documents coming in without a sorting process in place; unpacking from one trip onto the floor or onto the credenza and repacking for the next
- **Not enough support staff:** Did the assistant quit recently? Is the temp terrible?
- **Too much fun until crunch time:** Too many long lunches, leaving a bit early nearly every day, working out a bit longer than time allotted for "lunch," shopping online

Your first step to working with this colleague is to understand the problem by looking at the situation from his or her perspective. Your colleague may be working as hard as possible and not want—or have time—to discuss that "they are disorganized." Frankly, the disorganization may be caused by some outside source that is driving them as crazy as it is you.

Plan a Solution

Most disorganization is a sign of being overwhelmed. The following ideas might offer you some control over the situation. In the next section, we discuss how to talk with your colleague about the solutions.

- **Too much time out of the office:** Develop a triage system and a communication plan. You could, for example, send one wrap-up e-mail at the end of the day with questions. Your colleague can respond that night and you will be productive the next day.
- **Poor inbox management:** Get permission to clear the inbox yourself. Using 15 minutes a day to sort might make a huge difference.
- **Not enough support staff:** Can you identify new procedures that would make things more efficient? Can you help the current assistant put some systems in place to make things run easier?
- **Too much fun until crunch time:** This problem may be the only one you cannot solve or discuss. Instead, move forward with work despite delays. Ask the colleague to approve small tasks you can do so that at crunch time, things are ready: envelopes addressed, documents drafted, and, if possible, process servers on stand-by.
- **Mail management:** Get permission to review the incoming mail and take control of the items that are headed for your desk anyway (i.e. discovery that needs to be completed).

Discuss the Problem

Once you have some ideas for resolving what you perceive as the problem, set up an appointment to talk with your colleague or mention it casually. The timing of this discussion is crucial. Do not raise it when stress is high and deadlines loom. Always discuss the problem with your colleague by saying, "I noticed that you've been in trial a lot this month and things are piling up. I have some ideas to help." You are focused on the problem, not what led to the problem.

Remember that legal professionals never want to be perceived as weak, and disorganization is a weakness, so always talk in terms of the result of the problem, not the person or their habits. Your message will be clear enough: This is not working for you or me. And if the colleague truly is overwhelmed, the result also will be clear: appreciation and relief.

Recognize You Cannot Always Help

One problem we have not discussed is the colleague with the trashed office. You enter and you cannot breathe because clutter and paper fill every surface. *This* colleague truly has issues with organization.

You may *not* be able to solve the problem, but you can help yourself by following these tips whenever possible:

- Stay focused on your work and ignore the mess as best you can.
- *Never* give this colleague original documents. Let us repeat that: No matter how much care they promise to take, do not give this colleague original documents. If you are ultimately responsible for the location of documents, then you are the one who should be controlling them.
- Minimize the problem, if possible, by offering to help clear paper clutter, but get permission from the colleague first.
- Maintain your breathing room by maintaining a clutter-free space for yourself.
- Once files are organized, you may want to be the gatekeeper for documents to be taken out and then replaced/refiled after use to ensure they are replaced in the appropriate file(s).

■ CONCLUSION

Your challenge is to be ready for a career with endless possibilities, but also to find your boundaries and limitations so that you do not burn out. When you can, choose greatness over mediocrity. Know that you have the ability and the capacity to take yourself to the next level, to do anything you want, to be anything you want, but only if you say, "yes," to the journey and, "no," to the obstacles that delay the trip.

Checklist for Success

☐ Say "yes" as often as possible.

☐ Learn to say "no" when it is the right decision and response.

☐ Let go of perfectionism in order to keep the workflow moving.

☐ Work overtime for the right reasons.

☐ If you can, diagnose the problem leading to a colleague's disorganization and help implement solutions.

☐ Maintain an organized work area.

ASSIGNMENTS: PREPARING FOR YOUR PARALEGAL CAREER

Career Management

What do perfectionism and burn out have in common? Why do paralegals need to worry about burn out at the beginning of their careers? How do you think perfectionism hinders or helps career growth? Consider and conduct research to better understand perfectionism. Prepare a presentation for your class that explains your findings. Lead a discussion about the issue of perfectionism in the paralegal profession.

Report

If you have worked in a law firm or are working in one now, describe some examples of disorganization that you have seen. What might have been the underlying problems? What solutions might be helpful? Write a memorandum to your instructor explaining what you observed and what your recommendations might be to resolve the underlying problems.

INTERNET RESOURCES

Laura Vanderkam: Time and financial management.
  http://www.my168hours.com

CHAPTER **14**

FOCUSING ON YOUR CAREER

You have reached the last chapter in this book, but your work is not done. This book is designed to travel with you on your career journey and to be a reference for years to come. This last chapter is devoted to helping you make the most of your paralegal career. This chapter is meant to help you:

- Recognize the value of planning for success
- Know the steps you can take to get involved with the profession
- Discuss the benefits of professional certification and identify sources for certification examinations
- Recognize the importance of focus and flexibility in your career

The first thing you must remember is that your job is not your career. Your job is what you do each day to earn a paycheck. Your career is the whole collection of activities you do related to your profession. These activities include working, belonging to a professional organization, volunteering, choosing to broaden your education, becoming certified, and the list goes on.

The key is to get started, not to wait for the perfect opportunity.

■ THINKING ABOUT TOMORROW (OR NOT)

At the beginning of your career, you may not be able to state with conviction where you want to be in five years (or even five minutes) because you simply do not know what options are available. This is fine because you are just getting started.

Your immediate goal of getting a job and doing good work at that job is important to establishing your career. When you start your first job—or any job—you should observe, make notes about procedures, and work hard to understand what is expected of you. Do not make suggestions for changes unless you are asked to do so, because you do not want to be perceived as a know-it-all or as someone who is not a team player.

In the beginning, it is important to work in the moment, and not try to lay out the future right away. Establish a good reputation by being dependable and by doing good work. Use the first year or so to explore options rather than to map out the next 5 or 20 years. In other words, use this time to get your feet wet; you can swim later.

Before you can map out your career, you need to:

- Find a job
- Become good at your job
- Understand the options available in your area of the country
- Decide whether you want to specialize and, if so, in which area
- Begin thinking about the next step in your career

You may not know what the next step is until you figure out the first and how it plays out in your part of the country. For example, you may *think* you want to work for a corporation, but if you live in an area that has primarily small law offices or solo practitioners, you may have to reconsider your goals.

Some law firms help you think about your career through paralegal career tracks. Others offer a coordinated paralegal career program. In most cases, you can find out whether such a program exists at a firm by doing an online search.

Most legal employers do not have a paralegal career track, so do not be surprised or disappointed if you do not find that. Instead, start watching and learning as soon as you begin a job. Paralegals who work for corporations, including insurance companies and banks, will find that their paralegal training and experience can lead to other opportunities within the company.

The point is that *you* are in charge of *your* career, and deciding how to shape your career takes time.

■ PLAN FOR SUCCESS

Even if you never plan to leave the job you have or the one you will soon get, you are responsible for building the kind of career you want.

From another perspective, you are responsible for the professional dilemmas you face as well and need to have your career in a position to handle those dilemmas.

Some dilemmas are good: Do you take on a new challenge at your current job? Did you read about a job opportunity that would fit your description of a "dream job"?

Some dilemmas are not so good: The solo practitioner you have been working for retires, moves, or changes professional directions. Your corporation decides to outsource its legal department. Your organization downsizes. Your family moves.

In both the good and not so good dilemmas, you may need a new job. Are you prepared? You can be if you prepare yourself for success by immersing yourself in lifelong learning and personal development. Why? Because it is essential that you work harder on yourself than you do on your job. If you do, success at your job will follow and you will be prepared to succeed in life regardless of the dilemmas that come your way.

■ GET INVOLVED

Getting involved in the profession is the best way to network, learn new things, and find colleagues that you admire and can share ideas with. Sometimes finding a place to begin getting involved is difficult, especially when you work in a small town or for a solo practitioner. There are several simple ways for you to begin.

PARALEGAL PROFILE

Kris L. Canaday

Current position: Freelance Paralegal/Legal Analyst

Employer: Owner/sole proprietor – legal support services for attorneys at ParalegalSvcs4Attys.com

Years in this position: 4 years

Years of paralegal experience: 9

Total years in the legal profession: 11

Education:

B.S., Legal Studies and Psychology, University of Maryland, University College

Paralegal Certificate, University of Maryland, University College

Legal Transcription Certificate

Kris Canaday did not think she liked attorneys, until she took a temporary assignment. Now she owns a business supporting them.

Kris Canaday never intended to become a paralegal. She had to be talked into taking a two-week temporary assignment as a legal secretary. She did not expect this assignment to change her life.

In fact, Kris believed the stereotypes from which lawyer jokes are made: they are dishonest and only interested in money. With that perception and lack of legal experience, taking a job at a law firm—even a temporary one—was the last thing she wanted to do.

Kris said, "When I was tapped for the assignment, I had not the slightest inkling of what to do in a law firm. I had tons of office experience – administrative, bookkeeping, and some management but that was it. I knew I couldn't do whatever it was they needed."

Kris said, "I fell in love with the legal field that very first day and the rest, as they say, is history." She enjoyed the fast pace, the necessity for detail and organization, analytical skills and what she then dubbed "organized chaos" – everything she enjoyed and thrived on. She quickly realized that public perception of the legal industry, and of attorneys in particular, was grossly incorrect, too. "I've learned in working in the legal field that attorneys care greatly about their clients and their situations and often go the extra mile for them."

After taking that temporary position, Kris said, "I knew I had found my calling. Working in the legal field provided a way for me to fulfill my need to analyze everything and desire to draft formal documentation. After I completed my temporary assignment, I immediately sought full-time employment at a law firm. I learned about the various legal positions and the duties each carried. I obtained a legal transcription position at a private firm and worked myself into a paralegal position within a couple of months. Later, after relocating, I obtained a position as a legal secretary in the public sector and worked my way into a legal analyst position.

"I found I loved every aspect of my work in the legal field and connected with the people I worked with. I knew that being a paralegal was what I wanted to do for the rest of my life. To support my work and advance my career, I went back to school to pursue a bachelor's degree in [para]legal studies and attained a paralegal certificate while working toward my degree. It's one of my proudest achievements."

It took many years of juggling school with work, young children, and a military lifestyle but now, with her education and experience, Kris says she is fortunate to have the opportunity to support attorneys from various locations around the country. "My experiences have taught me that it *is* possible for active duty—even career—military spouses to get a degree and have a career of their own regardless of where the military takes them. But if I had not accepted that two week assignment, way back when, I wouldn't be here to share that now."

First, as you read professional publications and listen to professional podcasts, send a note to the authors or producers when there is an article or program you enjoy. Your name will begin to appear on their radar, and the authors and producers of professional publications are usually heavily involved in professional activities.

Also, if your office does any kind of volunteer work, offer to help. Help with *pro bono* work or organize an annual fundraiser that your office supports. Participation helps you learn more about your colleagues and shows you are a team player. Even if you work in an office with one attorney, handing out water bottles at a marathon fundraising event together helps you bond, which in turn, prepares you to work better together.

When you are ready—or even if you are not—step out into the profession and join an organization, attend CLE events, and go to a conference. This will further demonstrate your commitment to the profession.

■ JOIN A PROFESSIONAL ASSOCIATION

Joining a professional association will play an important part in shaping your career. Paralegals can join professional associations at the local, state, and national level.

Depending on where you live and work, you might join a local association. For example, if you live in the Dallas, Texas area, you might join the North Texas Paralegal Association or the Dallas Area Paralegal Association. If you are in San Diego, you could attend events offered by the San Diego Paralegal Association. If you are in Jacksonville, you might join the Northeast Florida Paralegal Association or the First Coast Chapter of the Florida Association of Paralegals.

At the state level, a paralegal in Michigan might join the Paralegal/Legal Assistant Section of the State Bar of Michigan. Nationally, paralegals are able to join one (or more) of several organizations established specifically for paralegals, such as NALA… the Association of Legal Assistants/Paralegals, NALS – The Association for Legal Professionals, or the National Federation of Paralegal Associations.

You also might join an organization that focuses on a specialty area, such as the International Trademark Association for paralegals working in trademark law.

How to Get Started

Locating an association in your area is as simple as doing an Internet search, since most have their own websites or blogs. In addition, you can search the websites of the national associations and your state bar. Co-workers may also provide this information.

Once you have determined which association you wish to visit, attend a meeting and get acquainted with the members. Remember, if your area does not have a local organization, consider joining a state or national association, even if you cannot attend meetings very often.

Once you pay your fee and complete the required forms (which may include an attestation from your employer that you are, indeed, employed as a paralegal), you should receive membership information from the organization. You will be able to see when CLE and social events are scheduled.

Attend Live Events

The more often you attend live events, the more comfortable you will become with the organization. Local associations may meet as often as once a month, including some meetings during the lunch hour that may be called "lunch-n-learn" events. State and national organizations usually do not have as many events, and those they provide may be more expensive, although the educational offerings will be more extensive. Because of these differences, paralegals usually find it beneficial to join their local associations, as well as available state and national organizations.

Volunteer

A really good way to learn more about the association and to become acquainted with its members is to volunteer to help. You do not have to do this right away, but when you are ready, choose an area where you feel comfortable contributing and dive in. As a volunteer, you will be working closely with the other paralegal members and getting to know them better. This will also put you in touch with people in the community and, perhaps, members of other professional associations.

■ ATTEND CLE EVENTS WHENEVER POSSIBLE

CLE will allow you to keep your skills up to date, introduce you to new people, and provide tricks of the trade that you have not picked up on your own. It is also a great time to share experiences. You may find you are not alone in some of the more challenging aspects of your job.

These events may also protect you from "burn out" because CLE is meant to educate and refresh. While some employers encourage paralegals to attend CLE events, others are not sure the time and cost is worth the investment. Whatever the circumstances, you should make time to regularly attend these events, even if you have to go on your own time and your own dime.

Sometimes attending CLE events may not be just a choice for you, as continuing education is required by state law (such as in California where Section 6450 of the Business and Professions code was adopted in 2004) or by a state or national certification body. Your attendance at CLE events will help satisfy those requirements.

When you attend a CLE event, use some of the same strategies described in the next section for attending a convention.

■ ATTEND A CONVENTION

Attending a convention provides you with several days of intense CLE and networking opportunities.

Attending a convention may be expensive, so being there means you are making a financial investment as well as an investment of time and energy. You may have to use precious vacation days to attend an event or you may have to pay the registration fees yourself. You may be able to negotiate with your employer so that your registration fees and other expenses are a benefit of your employment.

Because these events are so worthwhile and very important to the overall advancement of your career, you should attend with a plan that will help you optimize the experience.

Settle the Details

As soon as you decide to attend an event, start a file for the registration materials, travel itineraries, notes, and a list of people you may want to contact before the event. Make any reservations you need early—air, hotel, car rental, etc.

Plan Your Attire

Be sure to ask how you are expected to dress. If you are going to a conference that will be held over several days, business casual is usually the expectation (which means no denim or anything that could be construed as beach wear, like shorts). Review the complete schedule to see if you will need dress clothes for a banquet. Sometimes banquets have a theme and you might have to finagle a costume. Plan early.

For daytime CLE, dress professionally. Even if you work in a dress-down office, dress up. We want to explain why you should do this: You are attending this event to learn and to network. If you show up in jeans while most others are wearing suits or dressy office attire, you will not make a good impression on anyone you meet. Attend these events with this mindset: *You might meet a future colleague, boss, or find an opportunity you never knew existed.*

Keep in mind that this kind of networking is not always about finding a future job. You may love your job and hope to keep it forever, but as you gain experience, you might be asked to serve on a committee, in a volunteer position, or to give a talk or workshop. If you are dressed down, you risk people questioning whether you are a good choice.

Note: Meeting rooms are notoriously cool. Be sure to take along a sweater or jacket.

Bring Business Cards

When you attend an event where other legal professionals and vendors that serve legal professionals are gathering, bring business cards. You will exchange them with people you meet, toss them into baskets to register for door prizes from vendors, or use them to request that vendors or other legal professionals send information to your office.

If your employer does not provide business cards, print your own using a service like Vistaprint (*www.vistaprint.com*). These are personal cards that you should not use in an official capacity for your employer, but that can be used for connecting with others on a personal/professional basis. For these cards, include your name (and certification designation if you have one), your telephone number, mailing address, and e-mail address. If you print your own cards, do not use your employer's name or logo.

Be careful when handing a personal business card to a potential employer, however. Business cards that are not professionally printed look amateurish and business cards that are professionally printed suggest you are "off the job market" and committed to working for yourself.

Bring a Notebook

You should bring one notebook. Buy a new one for the conference. Use this notebook to take notes and to write a "to-do" list for when you get back to the office. Do you want to send a networking note to someone? Do you need to thank anyone? Congratulate anyone? Having your notes in one place helps this process go faster.

Pick Up Your Registration as Soon as You Arrive

Pick up your registration as soon as you arrive so you can go through the meeting materials and familiarize yourself with the schedule. Put your nametag on. Scan the attendee list to see if you know anyone or to see if you can identify one or two people you would like to meet.

Meet as Many People as You Can

Plan to meet as many people as you can while you are at a conference. Start practicing right now: Put out your hand and say, "Hi, my name is Shellee, and I'm not sure we've met." Introduce yourself to as many people as you can. Others may have a difficult time doing the same and will be grateful if you take the first step.

Visit the Vendors

Vendors come with loads of interesting information regarding their programs and products. They also contribute to the cost of the event, helping to keep your own costs down. Be sure to visit their booths, give them your full attention, and then make every effort to use their services when you can.

Think about Getting Involved

Attending a conference may inspire you to become even more involved in paralegal association business. Becoming a leader in a paralegal organization at the local, state, or national level is rewarding, but takes a lot of work.

If you are interested in getting involved, start locally and work your way up. If you are involved locally and want to move on to the state or national level, do not ask for a position on a board. Instead, find the person in charge of a committee you think you would be able to contribute to and say, "I'm really interested in getting involved. If you ever have something you need help with, please let me know." Follow up this offer with an e-mail to the committee chair.

Usually, people who offer to help—without directly asking for a seat on a board—are asked to volunteer in small ways that lead to larger roles within the organization, including later becoming a member of the board of directors.

Paralegal associations really do need your help, so volunteering your time and energy is a great way to get involved.

Wrap Up

As soon as you can after you return from the conference, take time to wrap up loose ends: write notes; tally your expenses and submit them if you are being reimbursed or save them for your income tax preparation; create a file for the event and save attendees' names and other information.

■ UP YOUR GAME: SEEK CERTIFICATION

You may find that in your area, paralegals seek certification. Certification comes in three opportunities: state, national, and national advanced. Just like the job market, certification expectations are different in various areas of the country.

Some states have their own certification processes. The State Bar of Texas, for example, offers certification for paralegals in some specific practice areas.

Nationally, you have options through paralegal organizations such as the National Association of Legal Assistants (NALA); NALS . . . The Association for Legal Professionals; or the National Federation of Paralegal Associations (NFPA) to pursue certification and advanced certification.

Certification is usually attained through an exam process that includes multiple choice and writing components. Advanced certification can occur through examination and/or advanced training. In addition, some organizations offer certification processes that are not limited to paralegals. For example, the Professional Risk Managers Association offers the PRM Certification in Risk Management. Because risk management is a specialty area that paralegals sometimes transition into, being aware of these opportunities is important.

■ CHOOSING TO SPECIALIZE

The reality about the paralegal profession is that many paralegals take the job they are offered—regardless of specialty area. When you take a job, you may even promise yourself you will switch later to an area you really love. Sometimes, though, you may find you excel in the work you are doing in an area of law that you never thought you would like. In this case, your specialty may find you.

Be open to starting your career in any area of law and check in with yourself after six months. If you are still interested in something else, create a plan for a transition to that area. These guidelines may help you with your transition:

- Try to begin working on the type of work you would like to do while you are in your current position. For example, if you would like to do more real estate closings, is it possible to do some work in that area at your current job?
- Attend CLE events in the area you are interested in pursuing. Make contacts and brush up on the new strategies, technologies, and law in this area.
- Use certification processes to show you are qualified.

When you decide to specialize or to change specialties, learn as much as you can. Take on small assignments, if available in your current position, and show that you can do these jobs well.

Even though you are planning to leave your current practice area and perhaps even your employer, keep striving to do your best work. You will need references and a good reputation to change jobs. The legal profession is a surprisingly small community—even in large cities—so always do your best, even if you hope to change specialty areas as soon as possible. It is *always* easier to find a job if you have a job.

PRACTICE TIP

Never use the excuse that you are "too old" to pursue certification or additional education. The years fly by no matter how hard you try to slow them down. You might as well have that certification and education when you reach a "certain age" as not.

■ STAY FOCUSED BUT BE FLEXIBLE

Always focus on your work, but always be ready for new opportunities. Highly successful paralegals take advantage of any opportunities that come their way. In fact, most successful paralegals tend to believe that success is just "an opportunity waiting to happen." These paralegals expect wonderful opportunities to come to them and they are always on the lookout for possibilities. Usually they are not disappointed.

The best opportunities occur for those who are prepared and open to the opportunity. Preparation creates an optimum opportunity. Preparation creates advantage. Preparation minimizes fear of failure. It can often be said that success is the point at which preparation and opportunity meet.

Opportunities may be disguised as risk and hard work but risk and hard work lead to professional growth and ultimate success. How do you prepare for opportunities? Take the time to make a list of all the skills, resources, and opportunities you DO have. Try to see things in a new way so that you do not miss opportunities right in front of you.

As you develop your career, you will begin to realize you have things *you* want to say about the profession and things that *you* can teach others. When that happens, do it. Speak at local events. Write for local or national publications. Teach. Take on paralegal interns and mentor them. As your voice becomes more confident, so will you.

Dream and Set Goals

Whether you are embarking on your first job or you are firmly established in your career, you must keep an eye on your future. The goal setting, the networking, and the learning should never cease.

Your dreams are visions of the future you want: your desires, ambitions, and career goals. Your dreams should paint the target and lead you forward. You have the ability to reach your full potential if you embrace, pursue, and focus on your dreams with a determination to succeed. Never hesitate to dream big.

Your circumstances may determine the magnitude of your dreams and desires. This is called facing reality. Reality is what you know, what you can feel, smell, and touch. It is something you deal with everyday; something you can relate to.

Realism in large doses, though, can be fatal to your dreams. You must use reality to determine *where you are*, and dreams to determine *where you are going*.

Dreams are visions of your future; dreams are not necessarily a look at yourself in a different job or even a different city. You may love where you work and your dream may be to make this job something unique by tweaking it in a way that puts your own stamp or brand on the position.

For example, you may take a job previously held by someone who was not dreaming at all, who just came to work, did what was asked, and went home at 5 p.m. Your supervising attorney may believe that is all anyone in that position can do, and that paralegals cannot do anything more. When you take this job, you may be disappointed that it is so lackluster and, well, *boring*. But you like the attorney and you love the office, so instead of looking for another job, dream about how you can recreate the position, ideas you can offer that will both better serve the attorney and provide you with interesting work.

The more you dream, the more vivid your ideas become and as you make suggestions and do good work, you will be moving toward the dream job you want, working for an attorney you like, and in an office you love.

Beware of Someday

While dreams are important, do not lean on dreams so much that you fall into the "someday" trap. The "someday" trap brings your goals to a standstill. It plays havoc with your future. It kills productivity. It causes procrastination. You might think, "I'll get around to that in the future," or when the sticky notes and piles of papers and files accumulate in your office, you might think, "I will ignore this clutter for now." If you allow yourself to let "someday" be a part of your thinking you are going to find it very difficult to move your career forward and reach your life goals.

To avoid the "someday" trap, try these strategies:

- Put your goals in writing and refer to them periodically. Ask yourself, "What have I done this day/week/month to advance toward this goal?"
- Determine your top five short-term goals, perhaps what you want to accomplish in the next 90 days. Then examine those goals to determine the steps you will take to reach them. Once you have done this, schedule the steps as an appointment in your calendar so that they get done.
- Use the same process to determine and accomplish your long-term goals (goals you plan to achieve in the next three years), and then consider your really long-term goals. What do you want to accomplish in your lifetime? As you do this, dare to dream and to think big. Do not limit yourself.
- For all these goals, make an appointment in your calendar to complete each step and do not let the "someday trap" stop you.

You cannot do everything at once, of course, so you will have to make choices. You will have to choose to do the things that are important to you and your goals and let the other things go.

When you change your thinking to "today" instead of "someday" you are not only going to feel better about yourself, but you will move your career in the right direction: forward.

Imagine seizing opportunities when they come your way. Visualize your office without clutter and piles. Picture being able to find documents when you need them. Imagine the feeling of accomplishment as you reach your goals. When you imagine that, it feels wonderful, right?

CONCLUSION

Before you can create a career that will sustain you, take time to decide what your career needs to have. Your answers will differ from your colleagues' answers because you may not yet know what you want your career to look like.

As you gain experience, you will develop a clearer view of the career that you want. At each point of clarity, set goals that will help you achieve this career. Developing a career is much like running a business; in order for your career to evolve, you have to learn as much as you can, identify your selling points and, in turn, teach as much as you can.

Careers in the paralegal profession can be lucrative, enriching, tedious, interesting, exhausting, and limitless. Your attitude and approach to all aspects of your career will determine the words that ultimately describe *your career*.

Checklist for Success

☐ Do not worry about establishing a specialty area until you begin working and have time to explore possibilities.

☐ Attend CLE events.

☐ Get involved with one or more paralegal associations.

☐ Consider certification at the local, state, and/or national level.

☐ If you choose to switch specialty areas, try to gain the necessary experience or education for that area before you give up your current position.

ASSIGNMENTS: PREPARING FOR YOUR PARALEGAL CAREER

Career Management

Begin a new career management notebook. This can be a simple spiral notebook or a folder on your computer. Describe your career as you envision it now. Date this description and place it in your career management notebook. Be sure to note:

- How did you establish your specialty area?
- Are you certified?
- How did you know you were working in an area that you enjoy?
- How long did it take you to figure it out?

Report

Examine the legal industry where you live. Make a list of common areas of specialization and prepare a memorandum to your instructor about your findings. During class, discuss your conclusions.

Report

Find the following:

a. CLE opportunities in your area
b. Paralegal organizations
c. Other organizations that paralegals join

Decide which are beneficial to you and why. Determine the membership requirements and what steps you would have to take to join. Prepare a memorandum to your instructor to turn in. During class, discuss your findings.

INTERNET RESOURCES

The Paralegal Voice, a podcast co-hosted by Vicki Voisin, ACP, and Lynne DeVenny, NCCP, produced and provided as a free resource by Legal Talk Network: http://legaltalknetwork.com/podcasts/paralegal-voice/. Also available through iTunes®.

Download professional development audio books onto your favorive mp3 player using a membership to *www.audible.com*. iTunes® also has many podcasts and other programs available at little or no cost.

PARALEGAL EDUCATION OPTIONS

Post-Baccalaureate Program

Post-baccalaureate paralegal programs range from three months of all-day intensive study to two years of weekend study. At the end of these programs, you earn a certificate. You may or may not earn college credit through these kinds of programs. These programs require a bachelor's degree, which means the program assumes you enter with skills in the following areas:

- Critical thinking and reasoning
- College-level math
- Writing
- Self-discipline and motivation for intensive study

Your bachelor's degree does not need to be in "pre-law" or paralegal studies. It can be in any field. Most programs place students in an internship toward the end of their programs and have a job-placement center.

If you are considering this type of program, look for one with a high job placement rate, a job-placement center that you can use even after you are no longer a student, and one that offers an internship opportunity.

Bachelor's Degree Program

The bachelor's degree program wraps your paralegal education and college education into one package. The attractive part of this degree program is that you should be ready to begin an entry-level career upon completion of your bachelor's degree.

These programs sometimes offer longer-term internship assignments that last a full semester. They may depend on the college or university's career services to provide job placement.

If you are considering this type of program, look for one that has a strong internship program, an active student organization, and faculty members who are a mix of full-time university employees dedicated to paralegal education and part-time faculty who are actively practicing as attorneys or working as paralegals.

Associate Degree Program

The associate degree program combines general education college courses and paralegal education courses into one program. This program can take two years of full-time study or usually can be completed part-time.

Associate degree programs tend to be lower in cost than other programs because they are offered at community colleges. These programs usually offer a cooperative education or internship experience that lasts a full semester. Associate degree programs may not provide job placement services.

If you are considering this type of program, look for one that provides an internship opportunity and faculty members who are a mix of full-time university employees dedicated to paralegal education and part-time faculty who are actively practicing as attorneys or working as paralegals.

On-the-Job Training

Some paralegals still enter the profession through on-the-job training. These paralegals learn about substantive law and the practice of law during their day-to-day work at the firm. Some start as file clerks and others as legal secretaries.

The benefit of on-the-job training is that you are able to learn the preferences of your current employer as you learn about the legal system and you are gaining experience in the legal profession because you already have a job.

On-the-job training may limit the breadth of your training. For example, if you work in a personal injury firm, you may not get a chance to learn generally about other fields, like real estate or estate planning. Formal paralegal education provides a broad overview of many practice areas.

If on-the-job training is your route to a paralegal career, expand what you are learning by joining a professional organization, attending continuing legal education events, and reading paralegal publications. You'll develop a network of contacts and become immersed in the field.

Mix and Match

If you have a bachelor's degree or beyond already, but you want to move into a paralegal career, look around for options.

Some schools will let you complete only the paralegal courses and give you a certificate, which would be the equivalent of a post-baccalaureate certificate, except that you would be earning college credit.

Master's Program

Master's programs are usually called something besides "Masters in Paralegal Studies" programs. These programs focus intensely on specific areas of law. For instance, Montclair State University offers programs in conflict management and peace studies; governance, compliance and regulation; intellectual property; and legal management and technology.

If you are considering earning a master's degree, examine what students who earn the degree do upon completion. Master's degrees tend to be expensive, so you want to make sure earning a master's will help your career move forward. In some larger cities, having a master's degree and five or more years of experience working as a paralegal might help you become a manager of paralegals or technology.

NATIONAL PARALEGAL ORGANIZATIONS

For Paralegals

American Association for Justice: *http://www.justice.org*
American Bar Association Standing Committee on Paralegals: *http://apps.americanbar*
    .org/legalservices/paralegals/
Association of Litigation Support Professionals: *www.alsponline.org*
NALS... The Association for Legal Professionals: *http://www.nals.org*
National Association of Legal Assistants/Paralegals: *http://www.nala.org*
National Federation of Paralegal Associations: *http://www.paralegals.org*

For Paralegal Managers and Legal Administrators

Association of Legal Administrators: *http://www.alanet.org*
International Paralegal Management Association: *http://www.paralegalmanagement.org*

For Paralegal Educators

American Association for Paralegal Education: *http://www.aafpe.org*

APPENDIX C

NETWORKING LOG

To start your network, develop a list of people you know or people you would like to know. Also include professional organizations that would be beneficial to visit.

People

Name and Title or Connection	Email Address & Phone	Notes

Professional Organizations or Continuing Legal Education Opportunities

Name of Organization Key Contact Email Address	Website	Notes

Opportunities to Network

List three opportunities for networking with these people or organizations during the next three months.

1.

2.

3.

TIME LOGS

Incremental Time Log

Timekeeper: _____   Day/Date: _____

8:00		2:00	
8:15		2:15	
8:30		2:30	
8:45		2:45	
9:00		3:00	
9:15		3:15	
9:30		3:30	
9:45		3:45	
10:00		4:00	
10:15		4:15	
10:30		4:30	
10:45		4:45	
11:00		5:00	
11:15		5:15	
11:30		5:30	
11:45		5:45	
12:00		6:00	
12:15		6:15	
12:30		6:30	
12:45		6:45	
1:00		7:00	
1:15		7:15	
1:30		7:30	
1:45		7:45	

Time Log

Timekeeper: _____   Day/Date: _____

Time Start	Time End	Total Time	Entered?	Client/Matter No.	Description

MY WEEKLY PLAN

Time	Monday	Tuesday	Wednesday	Thursday	Friday
8:00					
9:00					
10:00					
11:00					
12:00	Lunch	Lunch	Lunch	Lunch	Lunch
1:00					
2:00					
3:00					
4:00	**Enter Time**	**Enter Time**	**Enter Time**	**Enter Time**	**Enter Time**
5:00					
6:00					

Productive Time? Meet w/Clients? Return Phone Calls? Check E-Mail? Meet w/Staff? Administrative Time? CLE?
RECORD TIME!

PHOTO CREDITS

Chapter 1
Page 1: © Luminis/Shutterstock.com
Page 5: Wil Antonides

Chapter 2
Page 15: © Jupiterimages/Thinkstock
Page 18: Caitlin O'Neill, Wilmer Cutler Pickering Hale & Door, LLP

Chapter 3
Page 29: © Michal Kowalski/Shutterstock
Page 35: Zachary W. Brewer

Chapter 4
Page 39: © Stephen Coburn/Shutterstock
Page 47: Photo by George Elanjian

Chapter 5
Page 55: © StockLite/Shutterstock
Page 60: Anne Hughes/Pictureme!

Chapter 6
Page 65: © Andresr/Shutterstock
Page 68: Helsell Fetterman LLP

Chapter 7
Page 87: © Tiplyashin Anatoly/Shutterstock
Page 97: Kisha Washington

Chapter 8
Page 103: © Alexander Raths/Fotolia.com
Page 114: Tammy Brooks

Chapter 9
Page 117: © Stephen Coburn/Shutterstock
Page 128: Andrea Schultz

Chapter 10
Page 133: © Guy Shapira/Shutterstock
Page 139: Photograph courtesy of David Lomison

Chapter 11
Page 143: © Yuri Arcurs/Shutterstock
Page 153: Eddie Gordon, Snell & Wilmer LLP

Chapter 12
Page 157: © Kurhan/Shutterstock
Page 163: Foster, Smith, Collins & Smith

Chapter 13
Page 169: © Kzenon/Shutterstock
Page 172: Heather De La Torre, CP, TBLS, PHP

Chapter 14
Page 177: © Brett Rabideau/Shutterstock
Page 179: Bill Darby Photography

INDEX